FAT MAN
IN FRANCE

SIX TOURS FOR THE CYCLIST

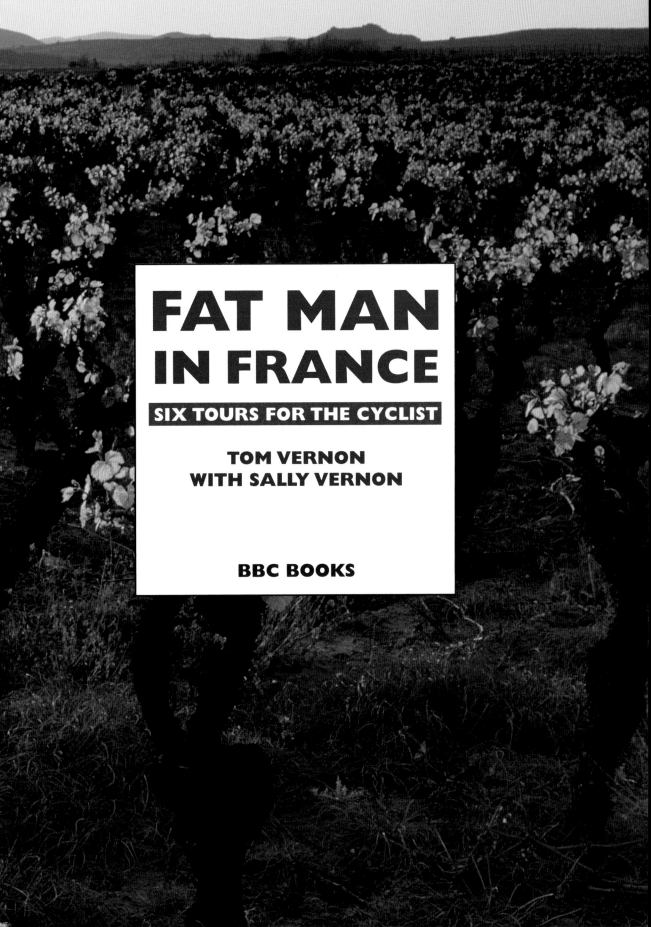

FAT MAN
IN FRANCE

SIX TOURS FOR THE CYCLIST

**TOM VERNON
WITH SALLY VERNON**

BBC BOOKS

For Michael Clarke

A recording of *Fat Man on a Bicycle* by Tom Vernon
is available from the BBC Radio Collection.

This book is published to accompany the
television series entitled *Fat Man in France*
which was first broadcast in September 1994
Published by BBC Books,
a division of BBC Enterprises Limited,
Woodlands, 80 Wood Lane
London W12 0TT

First published 1994
© Tom and Sally Vernon 1994
ISBN 0 563 37051 3
Designed by Andrew Shoolbred
Maps by Eugene Fleury
Set by Ace Filmsetting Ltd, Frome
Printed in Great Britain by Cambus Litho Ltd, East Kilbride
Bound in Great Britain by Hunter & Foulis Ltd, Edinburgh
Colour separation by Radstock Reproduction, Midsomer Norton
Jacket printed by Lawrence Allen Ltd, Weston-super-Mare

Preceding pages: Part of Languedoc's great wine lake – vineyards near Pézenas

Contents

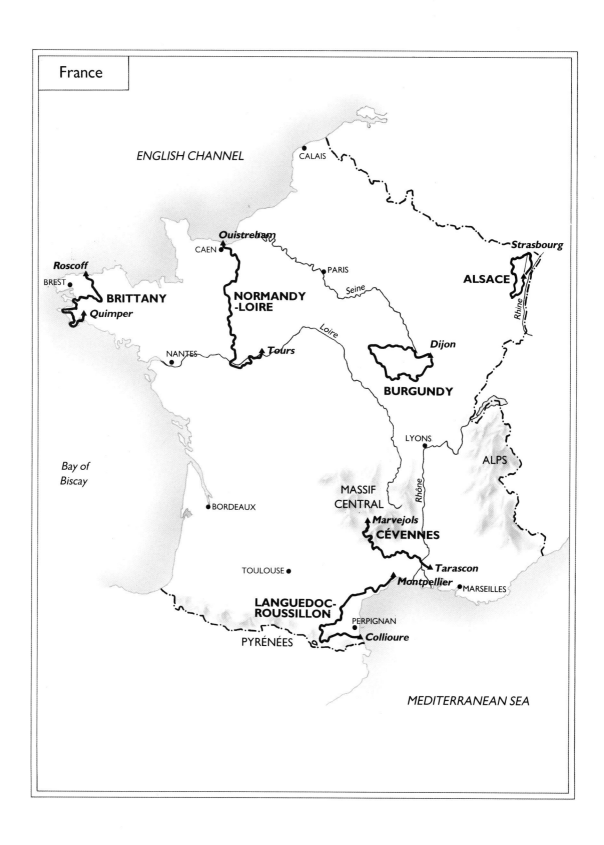

France

ENGLISH CHANNEL

CALAIS

Ouistreham

CAEN

PARIS

Roscoff

BREST

BRITTANY

Quimper

NORMANDY -LOIRE

Seine

Strasbourg

ALSACE

Rhine

NANTES

Loire

Tours

Dijon

BURGUNDY

Bay of Biscay

LYONS

ALPS

MASSIF CENTRAL

Rhône

BORDEAUX

Marvejols

CÉVENNES

Tarascon

TOULOUSE

Montpellier

MARSEILLES

LANGUEDOC-ROUSSILLON

PERPIGNAN

Collioure

PYRÉNÉES

MEDITERRANEAN SEA

Acknowledgements

This project has been very much a joint venture between Sally and myself. Except for the cycling, Sally has done at least as much work on the book as I have. Many other professional people have helped us with advice about the routes, including individual enthusiasts in local tourist offices and local cycling associations. Most important of all, we could not have managed without the help of our friend Elizabeth Guillosson who did much of the initial research for us.

We must also thank those we met on our travels, who generously gave us their time and talked to us freely about their places. For want of space only a few of them can be mentioned in our text, but their contribution has nonetheless been fundamental and we hope we have captured the spirit of their feelings and ideas.

We are also grateful to the friends who have worked with us in Fat Man Films and the hard-working editorial department at BBC Books. Most important of all, without the inspiration of the BBC we would never have had the opportunity to produce either the book or the television series.

Foreword

Apart from feet, the bicycle is the most personal and democratic means of transport that ever was. Horses beat it for crossing rough ground, but even in their day they were never as easy or cheap for ordinary people to own. That is why the early years of cycling generated a passionate sense of liberation, as people shut up in Victorian towns and confined by the habits of that era wheeled themselves out into the sunlight and began to take a new pleasure in the countryside. A century later, that tide of discovery still returns Christmas after Christmas, birthday upon birthday as a bicycle is still a special present for children looking to make their own way in life – even an adult may find themselves riding not a machine but a wave – a modest dream of air and openness.

One of the great qualities of cycling is that it is always memorable. Moving more slowly on a bike, you are in contact with what you see for longer, rather than being swamped by hundreds of miles' worth of images in one day. And you have all the time in a ride to think and understand. You accept the ups and downs, the bumps on the road, the wind, the rain and the sun, and all these experiences strike up a physical relationship between you and the land which is quite different from anything you will ever know as a motorist.

'Cyclist' is a word that covers a multitude of men and women – from a twenty-stone man who travels extremely slowly to the man I always thought of as the perfect touring cyclist. This book is dedicated to Michael Clarke who would knit spokes and rims together into a bicycle wheel while he listened to music, and commute by bike from southern Kent to London as easily as other people get on a train. I will always remember him turning up nonchalantly in the Cévennes, having cycled from Kent in less than six days at well over 100 miles a day – and he said he had taken it easy, stopping at markets and tourist sites en route. He was over fifty at the time. Though he was long and lanky, the right physique for cycling, he was not only a cyclist extraordinary, but an enthusiast for all the good things in life. He saw his cycling as a useful means of getting from one interesting place, one beautiful thing, one good meal to another. The sole purpose of his cycling was to enjoy himself to the full. He died too young, while this book was being written, which is one reason why I mention him, but the other is because of his gusto and tremendous enjoyment of the bicycle, which was an inspiration to me and, I hope, may now be a little to you.

Introduction

This is a book for people who love France. A trip to France is like visiting a brothel of illicit pleasures – five course meals, wines to wonder at, a countryside that can be pastoral, wild, romantic to the edge of magic. The space and variety are also among the reasons for it being the best cycling country in the world. However, you must choose the right roads to follow – as you can, since there are many byways rambling between the delightful places that flourish even on the verges of the subtopias and autoroutes, full of the timeless Frenchness of small-town life trickling on between market, café and *boulangerie*.

I am a romantic about France (and most other things), but in choosing the routes I and my wife, Sally, have been very much realists, because our idea of a good holiday is not going to France to suffer. Obviously, cycling involves some effort, but thankfully hills go down as well as up, which also makes things more interesting. Each basic ride has been calculated to be enjoyable and do-able by people with little cycling experience, though it is a good idea to get in a bit of practice beforehand, if you can, and to have reasonable bicycles. But even these aren't necessary for all of the trips, which are designed to be varied according to taste, anyway.

Each chapter is divided into two parts: the first being my description of the trip as I experienced it; the second being the details of the route and accommodation. It is impractical to list absolutely all the hotels and restaurants available on the routes, but we have tried to give an adequate selection and bear in mind that the bigger the place, the better the selection will be. We have avoided symbols as much as possible, but there are one or two: ⊨ for accommodation, ✗ for restaurant or café and H, M or L as a rough guide to the prices of hotels. This is a somewhat basic system, but at least it gives you an indication. L will average about 150F a room, M 250F and H 350F. Sometimes we might give further clarification, eg HH, to indicate that this is very lavish and expensive accommodation. Do also remember that a hotel designated H will have a restaurant, unless we say it has not. And the use of gourmet to describe a restaurant will mean it is not only special but expensive as well. But one of the principal pleasures of France is the food so do splurge at least once. The first hotel in each selection will give the postcode of the town in its address and any others will have the same code unless otherwise stated. This is important if you wish to confirm any booking in writing. For information about chambres d'hôtes see

p. 185. ⬦ represents a detour and **A** the possibility of doing an alternative route, details of which are usually given a bit further on. The final chapter contains practical information and tips.

In selecting six rides in different parts of France which people could do in a fortnight's holiday, we were spoilt for choice. But we decided to concentrate on regions we thought would best illustrate the immense variety of provincial France, though there are other regions as exciting as the ones we have chosen, and the permutations on routes are endless. We set out to choose small roads through interesting and not too difficult country. We made the selection ourselves because the bike routes produced by clubs and tourist organisations tend to go round in smallish circles and we wanted to go places. It turned out to be a very finnicky process that took many weeks, cycling bits here and there but mostly going back and forth trying alternative after alternative. In the end we feel proud of our six routes, each of which offers a variety of lovely countryside. They range from the fairly strenuous (the Cévennes and Burgundy) to the easier (Normandy-Loire), and include interesting tourist sites which are not the most crowded ones in summer. Do take time to cycle into the centres of villages and towns rather than bypassing them because that is where the most interesting parts are likely to be. Mostly they zig-zag in a general direction, though a couple are circuits, but even the general directional ones can be short-circuited to get you back to where you started (or you can return by rail). There is no need to treat anything as gospel: start later, finish earlier, strike off anywhere else you fancy – explore!

CHAPTER ONE

Earth's End

From Roscoff to Quimper via Cap Sizun and the Pays Bigouden

This journey starts on the north coast of Brittany, goes inland along the Morlaix estuary, and climbs into the pastoral countryside of the Monts d'Arrée and the Armorican Regional Park. Moving through a landscape of meadows, copses and tiny farms, it follows the general course of the river Aulne almost to the sea. Then it crosses the Crozon Peninsular and travels down the Bay of Douarnenez until it can head west once more to the tip of the Cap Sizun, the westernmost point in mainland France, beyond which lie only islands, among them the tiny, atmospheric Ile de Sein. It then makes its way south and inland through the Pays Bigouden to complete the crossing of Finistère. It finishes at Quimper on the river Odet. The route is quite hilly, but the stages have been kept quite short to compensate: and the largely unspoilt country and coastline make the effort worthwhile.

The essential Brittany (smaller than the present province) was the last part of France to be brought under central rule, with a history of opposition that was revived in the years following France's last mini-revolution, the Paris disturbances of 1968. Breton attitudes are not revolutionary so much as nationalist, with a great pride in the language and culture. The far west is where that pride flourishes most, where you may yet see the odd old woman who wears traditional costume sometimes because she has always done so and because when she was young everyone did. I cannot feel quite the same about the folk costumes and coifs that come out for high days, holidays, photographs and tourists – of which there are many. Brittany is a popular place, especially with the British. Its latest experience of diaspora is the British buyers of second, retirement or, indeed, permanent homes, who make up the largest ex-pat group in France, comfortable in a place in which quite a lot of people speak English and in which familiar legends, intermarriages, shared history and culture (even a shared Gulf Stream) almost out-number the seagulls flying across the water between one land's end and another.

There is a lot more to Brittany than Finistère, but Finistère is one of the best parts and this route of lanes and byways has been carefully chosen to offer the cyclist some hope of getting away from the worst of the tourist traffic in high season. Roscoff is a little place with some charm, not the least of which is its offshore island, the Ile de Batz. Traditionally, the islanders lived off fishing, farming and collecting seaweed to manure the fields – a way of life which the commune has tried hard to keep from disappearing. The seaweed gathering, which was once women's work after a storm, is now rolled up from the sea by a skoubidou, a rotating hook mounted on a boat, while skin-divers collect special varieties. This coast claims the highest concentration of different kinds of seaweed on the planet, with around 700 kinds found locally, and a seaweed therapy centre has been founded on the strength of it.

I came into Roscoff harbour at the same time as a small red and white fishing boat that bobbed against the waves like an angry duck. Like most harbours in Brittany, this is a port for work as well as for pleasure, and this being the beginning of January, the more frivolous sorts of boats were drawn up on shore, waiting for the summer. I cycled in a relaxed fashion, since my seaweed consumption had been low and my festive consumption high, and though I did not know it then, I had before my eyes the image which would be before me everywhere I went – a church spire, somewhat too grand, rising above low stone houses. There had been skilful stonemasons here. On the church doorway was a carving of a boat and, though the old houses were low, they had finely-cut lintels and doorways. There was blue in the sky and the sun gleamed on the roads, wet from the last rain, but overhead clouds were moving fast in a buffeting, contrary wind that tried to blow from all directions at once and howled in the characteristically French tangle of wires overhead. I took the main route out of town – there is no alternative for the first half mile – and by the time I was among open fields on the minor road to St-Pol-de-Léon, the blue sky had gone, and raindrops were coming. My first cycling Breton, a paysan with very muddy gumboots and an exceedingly genial set of false teeth, cast an eye at the slate-coloured stormclouds as he passed me and pedalled the faster, but two men distributing boxes in a field of statuesque cauliflowers seemed unworried.

Generally, the vegetation was nothing short of extraordinary – the cauliflowers you could put down to good farming, but I had already passed fuchsias in flower, gigantic bushes of camellias, and next year's japonica in competition with last year's roses. I had just decided that it was all obviously the effect of a beneficent Gulf Stream climate when a gale blew up out of nowhere, and the heavens opened. It would not have been too bad if it had been rain, but it was hail. I had never been hailed on while cycling before, but I quickly made the discovery that the two do not go together. There was not a scrap of shelter in the fields – some leafless trees and a house that might have acted as a windbreak lay a few hundred yards ahead, but I could not get to either. I turned my back to the storm and waited, but the hailstones bouncing off the road before me were enormous, and to judge from the pain, those bouncing off my head were even bigger. Meanwhile, my jeans had become sodden in about as much time as it takes to say *'Noye's Fludde'*, while my cape was flying up on all sides so that the hail could get at other parts normal weather cannot reach. It was most uncomfortable to be stuck on the verge like a misplaced cauliflower; and disturbing having to wonder whether the thunder and lightning were going to get much worse. It would not have been so bad if they had not been such big hailstones. This went on for twenty minutes, at the end of which I was soaking, cold and wondering how the camellias could stand it. Much of the sky was already blue again, but it was all too much meteorological excitement within the first five miles. It was plain that weather in Brittany was never going to be ordinary. As I set off, the two cauliflower men came out of the tractor cab in which they had been sheltering and looked at me as if I was mad.

Following the delicate spire of the cathedral of St-Pol-de-Léon, I came to the remnants of a market of dripping stalls in the main square, deserted by shoppers, which was just as well, since my casual glance at the *Toutes Directions* sign was suddenly obscured by the wind taking hold of my wet cape and gracefully folding up my head in it, so that I was forced to bump to a halt somewhere on the pavement. Even the stallholders were amused.

I went on out of town amid fields of more cauliflowers and artichokes, which were no ordinary artichokes. For one thing, a few of them had heads on them, which in January was very strange: for another, these or their forefathers were the front line in the Artichoke War of the sixties, when local growers united to take control of their own destiny, influencing Breton food producers of all kinds and giving the first push to a programme of economic reform which among other things brought an improved main road system to the region and Brittany Ferries to Roscoff. A militant young farmer, Alexis Gourvennec, was the leading spirit at only twenty-four and went on to become such a notable figure in civic life that he became known as the Prince of Brittany.

I had a small road to myself until I had to take to a bigger one for the approach to the only road bridge over the estuary of the Penzé, but even that was deserted – the Bretons being after all French and therefore seriously concerned with lunch. Climbing to the top of the hill, I looked back at the Roscoff peninsular with its spires and white houses, and the islands in the bay beyond and then turned and whizzed down to a tidal river where a line of sailing boats and a few small fishing craft lay peacefully at anchor. There was another climb ahead – a long and leisurely one, but it was quickly becoming apparent that there was no going anywhere in Brittany on the flat. I had the wind behind me – a gusty wind in which everything moved, shutters banging and tinkling, road signs creaking, wires shrieking and trees soughing. Coming through the hamlet of Kernady, a local cat executed a head-over-heels stepdance of being in love with it. And I descended steeply to the bay beyond, heading for Locquénolé, Morlaix and the hills of the interior.

After the ups and downs between coast and estuary at the start and the couple of brief entanglements with larger roads, the road is small, flat and pretty as far as Morlaix, winding along by the water with low hills, fields and a few houses over the narrowing bay. Morlaix is in a cleft with two viaducts above it: small boats come up almost to the centre, where the old town has tall stone houses with many shutters. It has an old centre with fine shop fronts and unusual pubs, old timber buildings with internal stairwells that rise up three storeys high through their middles. And it is home to Brittany's first experiment with real ale – the Coref breweries.

If you like it so much, you want to stay, then the best expedition for the following day is to Guimiliau via St-Thegonnec and your reward will be some of the most vivid stone carving in Brittany. You cannot go far in this region without encountering the *calvaire* (calvary) and these are outstanding examples from the sixteenth century, the golden age of the *enclos paroissial* (parish close). The *enclos* was a kind of life and death system around the church. For death, there was the cemetery and a charnel house to put the bones in when space ran short; for life, the church itself and the *calvaire*, whose central cross and the carvings below it were a continuing education in stone, based on the story of the Passion. The Guimiliau *calvaire* goes furthest towards being a kind of granite comic strip: over 200 figures range from Christ to Catell-Gollet (Catherine the Lost), a servant-girl who became the Devil's lover and got herself torn to pieces by demons. Not only is her story sexy, so is the carving.

From Morlaix, the road to Huelgoat climbs slowly up into the Monts d'Arrée along the valley of the Queffleuth river, which was brown and extraordinarily tumultuous when I saw it that wet winter, but is usually a clear stream of a twisty-turny character that takes it in almost all possible directions, which is quite an achievement for something that is supposed to go only in one. The landscape is very like north Devon, with rocks and lichened trees on the steep slopes to the left and pasture over on the other side. The noise of water is never far off, since as well as the river there are a multitude of rivulets. The climb is neither difficult nor unremitting but goes on a long time, after which the country is undulating and pastoral. Berrien is a small Welsh-type village with a china-clay pit, an *enclos*, a café and a centre for Celtic wrestling, if you feel inclined. The ruined church nearby stood in Benr'choat until 1955, when it was moved, having been struck by lightning. This was unfortunate since it was dedicated to Sainte Barbe who is supposed to protect you from this and it has been struck again since. But it has not been restored – perhaps people are beginning to lose confidence.

Huelgoat is pronounced 'Ewe-ell-gwatte', and means High Wood. It is a forest full of curious rocks and streams, including the river Argent which flows from the town lake and is a reminder of the silver and lead mine which was here in Roman times.

Lessons in morality carved in stone on the calvary at Guimiliau.

La Grotte d'Artus is yet another of the places where King Arthur is supposed to be slumbering. More significant, there are several places where you can slumber, since Huelgoat is in the Armorican Regional Park and is a modest tourist centre. There are quite a lot of new, little white houses up on the hill, but they are perfectly acceptable and the older town is straightforward and unspoilt – the square reminded me of rural Yorkshire. However, I did not stay there, being bound for one of the two hotels in the tiny hamlet of Locmaria-Berrien, a little further on.

The Auberge de la Truite is a strait-laced building that looks more like a private house than a hotel, until you are introduced to the large restaurant at the back, as I soon was, since madame had some difficulty in opening the front door, swollen after weeks of rain. I crossed the kitchens, whose grey enamel ranges were scarcely less perfect than they had been when they were put in some forty years before, and came into a bar that glowed with brass and polished wood; for the walls were panelled with the casings of the box beds that were once the pride of the Breton farmer's wife, ornamented with carvings and metal studs. These folk antiques date from the last century or before, but fell on hard times in the fifties and sixties when the lure of Formica relegated many of them to the lumber room or even the rabbit hutch, where fine pieces were sometimes to be found keeping in the bunnies. They were well-suited for the job, since the characteristic design involves a combination of brass studs and ornamented cut-outs, but it is doubtful that the rabbits appreciated them. More sensitive people kept what they already had in the family and added to them at knockdown prices, so that whole rooms could be panelled with craftsmanship 100 or 150 years old. My hostess, was a plump but minute old lady who had the gift of making you feel that you had come on a visit to a favourite aunt, and this an aunt with a large tank of salt water for lobsters in the cellar and bubbling spring water in the garden for the trout in the pool where they have always been kept since the days when Madame's grandfather ran the place as the station hotel on behalf of the wine merchant who had built it. The spirit of that wine merchant lives there still, for the cellar is reputed to be one of the best in Brittany, and both De Gaulle and Pompidou came here to eat and drink.

Alas, when I was there, the lobsters were off – they had gone off to the New Year's Celebrations and never come back, leaving one solitary specimen in a corner. The wine was not off, for I saw the list, containing a good many £50-bottles, but I could not get to see it.

'We never show anyone the *cave*,' said Madame. 'Never.'

Nor was there a cook, or a meal, for everyone was on holiday including Madame herself, except that since a strange cyclist had telephoned, she had opened up a room specially for him.

'I could get you an omelette or something, but I haven't much. It's only me here, you see,' said Madame, with a courtesy like the polish on old silver.

So it was that I made a mental note to go back when the restaurant was open, since the place was far too good to leave to politicians, and was driven to Carhaix which is not far off, to dine in the Restaurant des Gallois whose proprietor was not a Gaul at all, but a Corsican with a Bohemian chef's hat that flopped at the top like an artist's beret. José – no one calls him anything else – introduced me to a whole tureen of wonderful mussels cooked with white wine, shallots and cream, set a bottle of his best Rhone wine before me, and prepared a plate of ostrich. I could have had antelope, bison or crocodile, but the ostrich was local. I was surprised to discover it was red meat, like a light but extremely good and tasty rump steak. It turned out that the antelope and bison were local too, but the crocodile was imported. I was not sorry to learn this, since it has never been my ambition to cycle through a country full of crocodiles. What with the conviviality of the host and the good company at the next table, I was late to bed that night, but in my pocket was the name of the ostrich-farmer.

Carhaix is some 26 km (16 miles) and a moderately substantial hill beyond Huelgoat. In Roman times it was important enough to have its water piped in from the Black Mountains via an 18-km (11-mile) long aqueduct. Today it is a quiet and pleasant place with a charcutier whose wrapping paper lists the twenty-three medals and prizes he has won (so far). It is a useful centre though, and you can make your way down to the towpath that runs beside the canal. It is an unusual towpath in that it carries on after the canal joins the river Aulne, so that you have prolonged riverside cycling from Carhaix almost to the sea, providing you keep an eye out for mooring lines stretched across the path. And there are good places along the way: notably Châteaulin; Spézet, where they hold summer schools in Breton and sometimes religious services in a church which still has its Renaissance furniture and stained glass, and St-Thois, which is not in any guidebook that I could discover, but which had the merit of being close to the ostriches.

The ostriches lived at small stone farm with long, low outhouses – the smaller ones indoors, the larger padding round a field wearing the ostrich expression of perpetual astonishment, disapproval and indignation. I said to the ostrich farmer that I was surprised to see them outside in winter, to which he replied that he was in touch with a man in Quebec who kept them out in temperatures of $-35°C$ and 62.5 cm (25 in) of snow. He was a smart and efficient man, and now the French representative of the European Ostrich Association. He had a fine Celtic flow of speech, but became monosyllabic when I suggested that perhaps his ostriches ought to have some sand.

'Sand?'

'For their heads. Burying them, you know.'

The ostrich farmer was restored to loquacity, and gave me to understand that this was a lie and a slander. 'On the contrary, very much the contrary,' he added. 'A proud bird they are. Carry their heads high. They're more intelligent than other poultry. I know, I've kept them all.'

The ostriches looked indignant, as before. Try as I might, I could not get them to look intelligent. Conceited perhaps.

Like many Bretons, the artichoke is prickly with outsiders, soft within.

How many eggs the ostrich lays between late spring and beginning of winter seemed to be a bit of a fisherman's tale. Proud owners who may have paid as much as £4000 for a pair of guaranteed breeders may sell eighty in a season, when it is certain that some ostriches produce as few as twenty. That is the last the ostrich sees of them: the eggs go into an incubator and are scanned every day.

'Around the eighth day you hear a tap-tap: it's the heart beating. They hatch in five or six weeks – if they don't, my daughter blows them and decorates them.'

Every part of the ostrich is used: 15 to 18 kilos (33–40 lb) of meat, steak and fillet; the feathers for dusters, and the skin as leather.

I could not take the winding path along the Aulne: in the summer it would be tempting, but the recent long rains had ruled it out for now. Instead, I headed out across country from Huelgoat on an afternoon when the storm clouds were disappearing over the horizon, leaving the sun comfortable in what for Brittany in winter was an unusually permanent patch of clear sky. Heading west as I was, a second, softer sun gleamed before me from the wet road: and Brittany burbled with springs flowing from the hedgerows into ditches where the long grass streamed like coarse hair. Along the bank, I counted eight fountains in as many yards. Winter branches were very black and thin against the sky; the bracken brown, soggy and very dead and foxglove leaves hung floppy-eared. On the slope above, a small bunch of cows

Finistère's deep-sea fishing fleets are fighting for their lives.

grouped together for warmth, company and perhaps some philosophical meditation on the place of the Aberdeen Angus in the universe – you never can tell with cows. Around the village of Brennilis, I came to two notable works of man, both of which were obsolete, and both in their own way tombs. One was a *dolmen*, the other a nuclear power station. The *dolmen* was in the corner of a little field under trees. Two twentieth-century men with a tractor could have put it up in an afternoon, but for 3000 BC it was formidable. A notice said that it marked the transition between the *dolmen à couloir* and the *allée couverte* – you could say something similar about the French hotel and its bathrooms in the later twentieth century. The ancient object was facing some competition from twentieth-century moles, who were constructing their own *allées couvertes*, only longer. But covered with greensward and with a breeze springing up to rustle the dead beech leaves, it was really rather pleasant.

Being at the start of its 3000 years, the Centre Nucleaire was less attractive, though the big concrete lump of the reactor was looking more and more like part of the scenery as it acquired a motley collection of patternings, water streaks and the dull colours of lichens. It is, of course, in a very beautiful spot, like others against whose building the Bretons successfully campaigned – by a lake with the prettiest of hamlets just beyond – and is no longer in service.

With moorland above me, the lake below and fells beyond, the country was wild for a time: hills, water, sky merging in gathering greyness with the dusk. For an instant a stormcloud was turned dirty gold by the setting sun, but when that went the lake began to look chill, the hills to look blue – and I began to get a move on. The landscape of small fields returned with occasional cottages and farms, wood smoke rising very straight from their chimneys, mist steaming from their middens. The cows were all in at the last farm, turning their heads together like a chorus line to see me go by, amid a smell of milk, manure and dry chaff. I came down a long, exhilarating and bendy hill and up with a Celtic flourish into Brasparts where, as I was looking at my map, a British numberplate drew up behind me to ask if I wanted help. The result was that I soon found myself in the bar of Jacques Maz taking a glass of Christmas ale with Paul Stewart, formerly of Glasgow.

In Brasparts, do not pass by the bar of Jacques Maz. I cannot guarantee that you will find there the company that I did – or even any company at all, Brasparts being a small place, but it is a bar of peculiar warmth. There is another bar I would not have you miss either, the Ty Elise in Plouyé (not too far for a detour from Huelgoat) and which is a bar of peculiar heat. You will know it by the red dragon, for it is run by Byn Walters from Merthyr Tydfil, a Celtic tinderbox who sends fiery words flying from a long red lugubrious face. From him you may learn the place of Celts in the universe. There is a dirt floor to the bar and an atmosphere like the witches' cave in Macbeth after a slight spring-cleaning. A fine bar it is too, with people coming from hundreds of kilometres around at weekends because there is nowhere like it. But the bar of Jacques Maz is ruled by a quiet young man who knows plants and mushrooms in a way that no one stuck behind a counter all day has any right to do, and who has succeeded in creating an everyday place of good fellowship. Both men have made pubs, but Jacques has created a local – as he is able to do with the locals that he has around him.

If it does not seem such an extraordinary thing to have made a pub, then remember that France is the country of the café of separate tables, among which waiters dart like aristocratic water fleas. Cafés generate encounters, conversations and are often frequented by people of a certain sort of politics: but they lack the unassuming warmth of the good British pub. So the bar of Jacques Maz is a measure of how close the Bretons are to the British Isles – and not only because, like Ty Elise, it serves Coref, a draught beer of a British kind.

Among the people I met in that bar were Jacques and Gwen. He makes model dolphins for a living, which he sells to museums: she is young, but becoming a motherly woman. Gwen had been brought up in New York. (So many Bretons emigrated to the USA that in Gourin in the Aulne valley they have a glass-fibre Statue of Liberty in the market place, and are saving up for a stone one with Breton features, an ermine in one hand and a Breton bagpipe in the other.) In New York, her grandmother would wear Breton traditional costume to go to the supermarket. When she went to the Chinese supermarket where her language was Breton and the supermarket owner Chinese, they managed to communicate with each other at least to the extent that they both wore their national costume.

The road west from Brasparts is small, pretty and empty and at first rolling, but then it becomes more level and high. The first sign that the land is changing is a curl of blue-grey far off and far below: an estuary. In a few days you have come from one sea coast to another, and will soon meet a third. The estuary is that of the Aulne, another division in the jagged coast of Finistère. Above is the solid outcrop of northern Finistère with Brest and Cap St Mathieu: below, Cap Sizun and the Presqu'ile de Crozon. (A *presqu'ile* being land almost entirely surrounded by water.)

At Ty Jopic, a small place along the ridge road, you may choose to go further ahead along the top to Rosnoën and the suspension bridge at Térénez. (There is a viewpoint only a mile or so along which is worth a look with views of Ménez-Hom on the other side of the estuary.)

I went down to le Faou where I settled myself into the prettier of the two hotels as you come in (though the other was also recommended to me, being under new management) and ate more mussels – to which I was becoming addicted.

The next morning I set out along the estuary to the bridge of Térénez. Brittany continually brings reminders of Cornwall and Wales and the river Aulne was very like the Fowey estuary, with its woods coming down to the water and a sizeable ship here and there at anchor. Along here are a restaurant where water laps at the top step if you arrive at high tide, chambres d'hôtes and a café next to the suspension bridge, which is quite small with probably just enough space to ride on the footpath if you are a person with slim panniers. But there is no escaping the first part of the hill opposite, though here there is enough room to wheel a bike undisturbed. The hill goes up a long way through rather featureless country, so it is better to turn off. And the third left takes you into a side country of fields and farms, where the lanes should be peaceful when the main road from the bridge is full of lemmings.

For a while you lose sight of water, though there is another estuary below. Your lane goes up and down through a rural landscape until it eventually brings you out at Argol, which is a surprise, since the tiny village has a parish close altogether too big for it. Alas for the trees that were around it, which now exist only as a photo in the local *créperie* – Argol cut them down and left the place bald. The modern statue of the legend of Ys is no substitute, though it warns you what lies over the hill. The hill is slow at first: then it climbs steeply and ahead are curving arms of land and a sea of moving threads of white that must be breakers – and that is the empire of King Gradlon, whose daughter slept with the devil, gave up the keys to the kingdom and let in the sea, so that all the land of Ys was sunk beneath the waves and became, prosaically, the Bay of Douarnenez, the port that you can see on the far shore. After

Overleaf: The most westerly point of mainland France, the Pointe du Raz.

that, the lane leads downhill, twisting among the fields and bringing you out at a beach – Pentrez-Plage – where there is a hotel. If you keep parallel to the coast there are others at Pointe à Vagues and Ste-Anne-la-Palud and Tréfeuntec. In season, go inland to Plomodiern which is far enough away from the shore to offer a better chance of a bed, or better yet go on to Douarnenez. There are other things to see, however, apart from the seaside, which is comparatively unspoilt: the dark lonely church of Ste-Anne-la-Palud or, inland, Locronan, which is so picturesque that it stars in period films but is not too spoilt despite it all. (The best route is past the Manoir de Moëllien, now a posh hotel.)

However you pass your day by the sea, it is very likely that you will spend at least one night in Douarnenez, since that is the gateway to Cap Sizun. Douarnenez is not only very pretty in parts, with a wonderful bay and houses in pastel colours along the old waterside at Rosmeur, but it is a real place and a notable fishing port. The town began in the fish preservation business about 2000 years ago (if 'preserving' is the right word for making the Roman sauce *garum*, in which anchovies or other small fish were packed into casks with salt and left to ferment). The golden age of the sardine can brought the town great prosperity and a strong smell of fish for most of the nineteenth century, until the sardine decided to withdraw its cooperation from the unequal enterprise and disappeared from nearby seas for many years. This, and the hard times that followed, left Douarnenez a legacy you would never have expected from a sardine: the first French fishermen's union, created in 1902, and the first communist municipality in France, elected in 1921. If you head for the port when you come into town, the road along the bay offers very fine views and an excellent maritime museum run by enthusiasts at the end of it. The old harbour there is crammed with all manner of craft, including a light ship, and over it all is the bridge that next day will carry you to Tréboul, another part of the Douarnenez commune, and on to Cap Sizun.

There is no coast road here that offers you easy views of the cliffs and coves, but by taking smaller roads you can get nearer to the sea, escape the worst of the traffic and enjoy easy cycling through green landscapes most of the way. Pors Péron near Beuzec is a pretty beach and the nature reserve a little further on has fine views and dramatic cliffs. Perhaps there is an argument for not looking at the sea at all as you travel along the peninsula, since it will add to the effect when you get to the end and the Pointe du Van. I came to it on a grey day with spume flying white, crows black in the wind and the breakers crashing on to the shore of the Baie des Trépassés (the Bay of the Dead), named after drowned sailors. There, a little grey fifteenth-century chapel is attended by what seems to be a little grey fifteenth-century dog kennel. In fact it houses a spring and, since fountains were sacred to the Celts, it may be that the dog kennel is the more anciently holy of the two. The best thing about the Pointe du Van is that it is only the second most western point in mainland France. On the other headland across the bay, the Pointe du Raz, you see what happens when a place is the most western. I say nothing about the truly ghastly statue to Our Lady of the Shipwrecked, except that it really is time to pull some of these things down. But car parks and a commercial centre ruin it, though even their removal, which has been mooted, will reduce the torrents of visitors in season, for the Pointe du Raz is extremely fine, even if the only living plants are fenced off and everything else trodden out of existence. A little way inland is an old hotel, the Hotel d'Ivroas, standing straight and white quite by itself in this bare place, interestingly incongruous. Surprisingly that fits, or perhaps not surprisingly, since there is a statement about solitary buildings on the coast that says 'I stand alone' – and that is the mood of Cap Sizun.

To return along the other side of the peninsula is difficult, since all the feet that have trodden the Pointe du Raz into dust have to come and go somewhere, and it is on the southern side that they do it. You have to follow the main road to Plogoff, when you can strike off inland via Cléden-Cap-Sizun and Goulien before turning right at Quatre Vents. Or you can stay on the main road a while longer and head south through St-Tugen and Custrein.

Audierne, when you get there, is half resort and half port with houses ranged around a bay to start with and built up along the coast thereafter. The town has a slightly vacant look out of season, but is a pleasant place nonetheless, and contains my favourite hotel in Brittany. The Roi Gradlon is along the coast above the sea, has a manager who is so capable that there is not the tiniest seam in the running of his little empire and all done so gracefully that it seems no effort. It has lovely sea views and an excellent restaurant. One of the most interesting things about Audierne is that you take the ferry for the Ile de Sein from here except in certain weathers when it comes into Douarnenez. There is an office in the harbour, but the main ferry terminal is a couple of miles along the coast.

The Ile de Sein has enjoyed an exotic reputation for centuries, prophetesses, druids and wreckers included. Julius Caesar referred to the islanders as 'a nasty bunch', meaning he had failed to subdue them with whatever resources it was worth applying to a fragment of land which is 2 km (1 mile) and 100 m (328 ft) across at its narrowest. They were still fighters some 2000 years later at the start of the German occupation. When they heard De Gaulle's broadcast in 1940 from London calling the French to rally to him, every able-bodied man on the island took to his boat at once, leaving the women and children, the curé and the mayor (which did not prevent the remaining islanders from smuggling a further 3000 people across the Channel). Four great centres of resistance were honoured after the Second World War – Paris, Grenoble, Nantes and this one square kilometre of island. With remembrance ceremonies hosted in turn by each, it is rather a strain on the civic budget for the mayor to hobnob with such company, since the islanders do not like to accept charity (though they did accept an exemption from taxes from Louis XIV, which has continued ever since).

Traces of earlier Celtic beliefs are apparent in a typical Breton pardon.
Opposite: Quimper, where some old ladies still wear the coiffe.

The present-day mayor is also *le roi* – Alain le Roi – and quite easily able to survey all of which he is monarch, since the island is flat and treeless. Approaching it on the fast, modern ferry over waves which have all the clarity and almost, it seems, the solidity of turquoise glass, the Ile de Sein is a black blob which turns into a bit of squashed Scotland, with dour houses huddling together. The ferry is a sign, both of the island's special position and of the energies of an exceptional mayor. The two schools have three teachers for a dozen children and there is an expensive new de-salination plant. Many people have had to leave for the mainland in the years since the war, but there are still fifteen fishermen, and the mayor has started oyster beds. Sixty thousand day-trippers a year now come to the island, yet it is still unspoiled and

the mayor is determined to keep it so. There are a number of fascinating islands off Brittany, but the Ile de Sein remains a special place, well worth the hour-and-a-half's crossing from Audierne.

Audierne is at the northern limit of the Pays Bigouden, which is the country inland from the Bay of Audierne, and below Cap Sizun. If any traditional costume is to be seen in something close to the context of everyday life, it is here that you will see it. In terms of cycling, too, inland is best; for the western coast of the Penmarc'h peninsula has no simple route south and has had holiday houses scattered over it piecemeal, so that quite a small amount of building has done maximum damage to what was never an entirely wonderful landscape in the first place. From Audierne, therefore, it is best to go up the river Goyen – there is a riverside path which looks particularly charming and it is not three miles to Pont-Croix, which is a splendid small town whose houses cluster round a tall-spired church on a hill and straggle down to an old river crossing which was once a small port. From here I went by lanes and tracks up the left bank of the river. You can take either of two roads on the right to Mahalon, but they are duller and I found an irresistible attraction in the name Confort-Meilars, which sounds like a character in an English public-school story. However, the route does not go as far as the church and *calvaire* on the main road, but keeps to small ones until you near Pouldergat. Having passed the town on a larger road, it is little more than a mile till you turn off on to lanes again, crossing the valley and the river Goyen – which is now no more than a stream – at Pont-Meur, from where, with a little twisting and turning, you can make your way through the gateposts of the Château de Guilguifin. (I felt a little alarmed, but it is the road, not a private drive.) Then it is pleasant, easy cycling through Plogastel-St-Germain, where they have one of the first *pardons* of the year in April: a small event in comparison to the large-scale religious processions in the summer. A *pardon* is the one event for which traditional costumes are sure to come out, and is usually followed by celebrations in which traditional music – still a living presence in Brittany – has an important part.

The small roads continue till Tréméoc through woods and farmland – including one particularly fine avenue where the trees twist out of the banks like the arms of old men. Then the roads start to get larger and when you encounter a roundabout complete with an elaborate tourist office which has a full-size boat, you know you are back in the twentieth century. Still, the town centre of Pont-l'Abbé is old, and I was attracted by the flowery Hotel de Bretagne in the market square before I decided to go on to le Guilvinec on the coast.

Le Guilvinec is a small town, but a significant port which, with its neighbours St- Guénolé, Loctudy and Lesconil, makes up a major centre of small fishermen. I met one of them in the bar of the hotel in the evening, at lunchtime, and again the following evening. He was usually in port for three or four days after a trip he said, but this time it was a fortnight for the fitting of a new engine. I was intrigued to meet one of the fishermen so renowned for their militancy and find him so quiet, for he said little about himself and expressed few opinions, except that he had a little grin that came easily and sometimes seemed to be his comment on the world.

By the second evening, I had heard that he was an outstandingly successful fisherman with two boats in the family each worth a million pounds.

'You're a millionaire,' I said, when I saw him again.

'Yes, at the bank. In theory.'

'But a difficult, risky life?' He was not to be drawn.

'Don't get enough exercise, that's the problem.' (It was clear that he had a few of my centimetres about him.) 'Sedentary job nowadays, sitting in the wheelhouse all the time.'

'But there must be a lot of hard work still,' I said.

'Not if you're captain. And I'm smart – I'm the captain.'

I was still not quite certain how far to take him seriously, for he had that little grin.

You will find as you approach journey's end on a bicycle that its scenes flash before your eyes. And the river Odet with its winds and woods is the perfect setting for remembering. I headed for Quimper, which is a biggish town but an agreeable one. Turning off the main road, I came to a mill: a glade in which the grass grew in wonderful tussocks and the machinery was still moved by the gentle, eternal power of water.

'I like it because it's living,' the young miller said to me. He makes an obsolete system viable by grinding mostly *blé noir* (black flour) for *galettes*. 'Water, grain – living things I work with. It makes me sad to see a dead mill. And this one's been in the family a long time.'

You could say something like that about Brittany. It is very much alive. That is why it still has its tales and its music, even a little costume, and why it may yet not lose its language. It is also the reason why its enterprises flourish and why its farmers and fishermen do inconvenient, unrespectable things – even awful things – when they feel threatened. Here, hot blood and rebellion, independence of mind, warm friendship and good company have been in the family a long, long time. And the Celtic spirit moves it all, as the water moves the grasses in the mill pool.

Brittany 11 days 343.5 km (220 miles)

⊟ Accommodation   ✗ Places to eat   ◊ Detour   A Alternative route

Map ref: IGN Green Series 13, 14. (Note: Breton roads and names are so complex that even IGN gets them wrong).

To get there: Road, rail or ferry. Air to Brest from Paris.

To get back: Road, rail or air from Quimper.

Food and drink: No great regional cuisine. Galettes (savoury crêpes from black flour, sweet ones from white flour). Good fish and shell fish. Dairy products including the biggest camembert and butter factories in France. Good butter cakes. Lots of vegetables (cauliflowers, artichokes, etc), but sadly hotels make little use of them. Cider and calvados are popular, with mead (*hydromel*) or mead mixed with cider (*chouchen*), available at fêtes. There is Muscadet wine from the Brittany/Loire borders and Coref real ale in some pubs.

Weather: Mild winter and summer, can be wet and windy.

Useful address: La Maison de la Randonnée, (cycling and walking itineraries), M. Laden, 9 rue des Portes Mordelaises, 35000 Rennes. Tel: 99 28 44 30. *Le Télégramme*, the local paper, has useful Wednesday supplement with dates of musical events, eg Festnoz.

Day 1
Roscoff – Locquénolé
(19 km/12 miles)

Roscoff – St-Pol-de-Léon
(5 km/3 miles)

Roscoff A
A pretty old port with eminent marine biology centre.
⊟   Hotels: Hotel les Arcades (L), 15 rue Amiral Réveillière, 29680 Roscoff, 98 69 70 45, on front, central; Hotel Bellevue (M), rue Jeanne d'Arc, 98 61 23 38, on front between ferry terminal and centre of town; Hotel le Brittany (H), boulevard Ste Barbe, 98 69 70 78, château-hotel on front near ferry terminal.

◊   Visit the **Ile de Batz**, small island with seaweed industry, early vegetables and exotic garden. Other boats touring the estuary.

From Roscoff go out of town past the ferry terminal. Take D769 at roundabout then fork left.

St-Pol-de-Léon
Attractive market town.
⊟   Hotels: Hotel du Cheval Blanc (M), 6 rue Oaulin, 29200 St-Pol-de-Léon, 98 69 01 00.

St-Pol-de-Léon – Locquénolé
(14 km/9 miles)

Go through town and left on C3 after estate wall, towards Trégudon. Wind along above coast on little old road to escape the new main road D58. Return to D58 to cross Penzé Estuary. Turn left on D173, directions *'Locquénolé et Morlaix par la corniche'*, and right at T-junction on D73. Continue along the estuary.

Locquénolé
⊟   Hotels: Hotel le Bruly (M), 29670 Locquénolé, 98 72 21 11, faces estuary, good food.

The old port of Roscoff.

Day 2
Locquénolé – Locmaria-Berrien
(49 km/30½ miles)

Locquénolé – Morlaix
(6 km/3½ miles)

Continue along estuary on D73 and D769.

Morlaix [A]
Fine old town. Excellent pubs, some with real ale, many with roof-height inner stairwells.
- Hotels: Hotel d'Europe (M), 1 rue Aiguillon, 29600 Morlaix, 98 62 11 99.
- Restaurant le Bains Douches, 45 allée du Poan-Ben, 98 63 83 83, bistro in old baths; Brasserie de Deux Rivières, place de la Madeleine, home of Coref real ale.

In town centre go right on D769 direction 'la poste' Carhaix, then left at start of big hill. Go over roundabout towards Huelgoat and Carhaix. (NB: ignore old road signs which say this is the N169.)

[A] At **le Plessis** take short detour right to old abbey le Relecq. Continue on D769, then turn right on D42.

Berrien
Centre of Parc d'Armorique and Breton games (*ti ar goren*).

Berrien – Locmaria-Berrien
(8.5 km/5¼ miles)

At crossroads through village turn left back to D769, and right through pretty scenery.

Locmaria-Berrien
- Hotels: Hotel-restaurant Auberge de la Truite (L), Gare de Locmaria-Berrien, 29690 Huelgoat, 98 99 73 05.
- You will see other and many good churches on the route, but for a tour of the most outstanding *enclos paroissiaux*, leave the route at **Pont Pol**, 3 km (2 miles) out of Morlaix, and take small road right to **Pleyben Christ** following small roads and continue on to **St-Thegonnec**.
- Hotels: Hotel Auberge St-Thegonnec (M), 29410 St-Thegonnec, 98 79 61 18.
Carry on to **Lampaul-Guimiliau, Guimiliau, la Martyre, Sizun** and **Commana**. See prehistoric covered alley grave nearby.

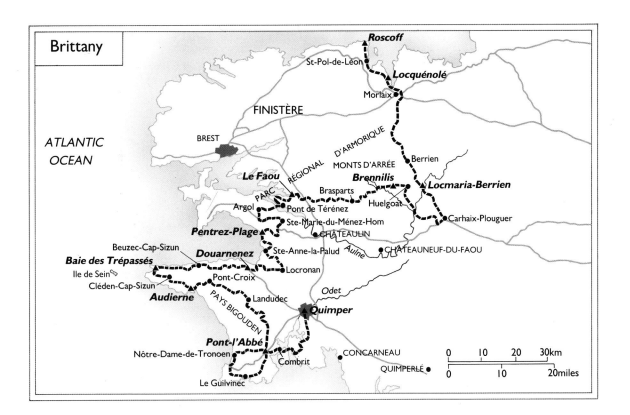

☒ Pub la Boule d'Or, 10 rue de Landivisiau, 98 78 00 05, with real ale.

Return on D111 via **Plouneour-Ménez** and the old abbey of le Relecq. For the strong-legged, return over the top of **Roc'h Trévezel** with views on a clear day to all the churches you have just seen. (NB: Tourist offices have excellent free brochures about the enclos paroissiaux.)

Day 3
Locmaria-Berrien – Brennilis
(43 km/27 miles)

Locmaria-Berrien – Carhaix-Plouguer
(14 km/9 miles)

Continue on D764 to **Poullaouen**. Turn left on to D54 at fork.

Carhaix-Plouguer
Old Roman crossroads, now Breton cultural and music centre.

⌂ Hotel Gradlon (M), 12 boulevard de la République, 29270 Carhaix-Plouguer, 98 93 15 22, big rooms, decent food. Chambres d'hôtes: M. Peter Novak, Manoir de Prevazy, 98 93 24 36.

☒ Les Gaulois, 9 rue Brizeux, 98 93 13 45, with extrovert Corsican patron with unusual meats (ostrich etc).

Carhaix-Plouguer – Huelgoat
(20 km/12½ miles)

Take main road D164 towards Chateaulin. Just outside town at **Moulin-du-Roi** turn right on little road D48 to **Kergloff** and **Penity-St-Laurent**. Turn right.

Plouyé
☒ Tavarn Ty Elise, bourg de Plouyé, 98 99 96 44, very genuine Welsh pub with real ale.
Continue north on little road D17.

Huelgoat
Visit the Forêt Dom de Huelgoat and le Gouffre, pretty rocky chaos with Arthur's camp, devils hole, fairy's bower, etc.

⌂ Hotels: Hotel du Lac (L), rue Général de Gaulle, 29690 Huelgoat, 98 99 71 14, lake side. If you haven't booked a bed at Brennilis, stay here. It is a long way to the next hotel at le Faou.

Huelgoat – Brennilis
(9 km/5½ miles)

Go left along lakeside on D179 (opposite direction to Locmaria-Berrien) into the Monts d'Arrée. Turn left on little road through **Kervinaouetizella** (Kervinaouet on IGN), over main road D764, to **Plouenez**. See pre-historic *dolmen, Maison des Fees.*

Brennilis
⌂ Chambres d'hôtes: Mme Gwenaëlle Le Lann, 98 99 62 36.
☒ La Menuiserie, 98 99 61 12, good simple lunch.

Day 4
Brennilis – le Faou
(33 km/20½ miles)

Brennilis – Brasparts
(14 km/9 miles)

Over crossroads to **Reservoir St-Michel** and lakeside camp site. Back and left round old dead nuclear reactor. After this there are many little roads and directions are not clear. The road bends to left on VC2, directions Foron, Locrafret, Brasparts. Go through hamlet, turn right towards Brasparts at fork – skirting lake and down the fairly steep side of valley on the left. Pass directions Kernamenez on left, go through a tumble-down farm, past a roadside calvary to hamlet of **Tenn-an-Vern**. Turn left at fork, ignoring road straight on, and up to top of hill. At T-junction descend to valley bottom and turn right towards Brasparts and le Faou.

Brasparts
See church with parish close.
☒ Drosera, 8 rue St Michel, 98 81 42 37, friendly pub; Auberge Chez Maurice, 98 51 41 55.

⌖ The Chapel of St Michel de Brasparts (7 km/4½ miles north along D785) is worth visiting. It is 300 m (984 ft) high, with good views. There is also a colony of artists and craftsmen back down the road on left and a small restaurant.

Brasparts – le Faou
(19 km/12 miles)

Brasparts
Go across town and right at church on D21 towards le Faou. Bear left at cross by right turn to Kroaz-Sebastien and turning to the Auberge du Meilh Squiriou. Go left towards le Faou through hamlet with snack bar.

⌖ See Menez Meur animal park to the north.

Continue through **Quimerch'**, **vieux bourg** (IGN has it as Vieux Quimerc'h). See ruined church, and go right on main road D770.

Le Faou
Pretty little port on estuary.
⌂ Hotels: Hotel Relais de la Place (M), place Mairie, 29580 le Faou, 98 81 91 19, recommended by Michelin as good value for money.
☒ Pizzeria next to hotel above, open late.

Day 5
Le Faou – Pentrez-Plage
(38 km/24 miles)

Le Faou – Pont de Térénez
(10 km/6 miles)

Go right on D47 to **Rosnoën**, then left on little road to follow estuary (fine views south over Aulne estuary to Menez Hom). Turn right on D47 to **la Croix Blanche**, and left on to small road to **Kergadalen** and D47.

Pont de Térénez

- Chambres d'hôtes: M. Stephane Brindeau, Ferme Agricole de Térénez, 98 81 06 90.
- L'Ermitage, passage Térénez, Rosnoën, 98 81 93 61, just before bridge, good, plain sea-food.

Pont de Térénez – Argol
(6 km/4 miles)

Cross bridge on main road D791.

- Detour first right down steep hill to pretty village of **Landévennec** with its old and new abbeys.
- Hotels: Hotel le St Patrick, rue St-Guénolé, 29560 Landévennec, 98 27 70 83, Irish with Guinness; Hotel Beausejour (M), 98 27 35 36.

From D791 turn left on little road to **la Fontaine Blanche**. Go left at unsignposted T-junction to **Kroas ar Glaz** and right on D60.

Argol
Fine *enclos paroissial* with unusual Roi Gradlon statue, and sculpture of the legendary Ys.
- Chambres d'hôtes: M. Louis Mevel, 98 27 78 13.
- Crêperie du Roy d'Ys, 98 27 77 69, very simple.

Argol – Ste-Marie-du-Ménez-Hom
(15 km/9½ miles)

All routes round Ménez-Hom are pretty. Take D60 towards Dineault. Before **Kerveou** take right fork on D47.

Ste-Marie-du-Ménez-Hom
- Chambres d'hôtes: Anna Jacq, 98 81 54 41.

- **Plomodiern**, nearby, is worth a visit.
- Hotels: Hotel la Cremaillère (L), 1 place de l'Eglise, 29550 Plomodiern, 98 81 50 10; Hotel la Mordandière (L), place de l'Eglise, 98 81 51 25.

Ste-Marie-du-Ménez-Hom – Pentrez-Plage
(7 km/4½ miles)

Take main road D887 towards Crozon.

- Detour on D83 to top of **Ménez-Hom** A (330 m/ 1083 ft), good views.

Continue on D887 to **Manoir Gueveur**. Go first left on small road to **Guern** and **St-Jean** (a pretty village), then take D63 to **St-Nic**. Continue on D63 past church, towards Plomodiern, Douarnenez, Quimper (Châteaulin and Ménez-Hom to left), then go immediately right on D108.

Pentrez-Plage
Good sandy beach.
- Hotels: Hotel de la Mer (L), 29550 St-Nic, 98 26 50 55.

- A The Aulne River valley is pretty. From **Ménez-Hom** go via **Dineault** to **Châteaulin**.
- Hotels: Hotel au Bon Acceuil (M), port Launay, 29150 Châteaulin, 98 86 15 77, pretty hotel on the estuary just beyond city.

- **Pleyben** with its parish close is worth visiting as is **St-Thois**
- Café de la Mairie, 98 73 83 29, good plats du jour. Follow towpath up valley to Châteauneuf-du-Faou. Easter folk music festival.
- Hotel le Relais du Cornouaille (M), 9 rue Paul Sérusier, 29520 Châteauneuf-du-Faou, 98 81 75 36.
- Le Chaland, Pont du Roy, 98 81 78 66, pizzeria-bar beside canal (friendlier atmosphere than hotel). Then go via **Spézet** to **Gourin** (see its statue of Liberty and museum of immigration).

Day 6
Pentrez-Plage – Douarnenez
(28 km/17 miles)

Pentrez-Plage – Ste-Anne-la-Palud
(12 km/7½ miles)

Go left along the beach to **Lestrevet**. Keep going on same road but inland to meet D63 at **Ploéven**. Take D63 for 1 km (½ mile) and turn right.

Ste-Anne-la-Palud
A striking church with sacred fountain where the biggest *pardon* is held at the end of August.
- Hotels: Hotel Sainte Anne (L), 29127 Plonévez-Porzay, 98 92 50 10; Hotel le Relais de Tréfeuntec (M), Tréfeuntec Plonevez Porzay, 98 92 50 03, 1 km (½ mile) south at Tréfeuntec; Hotel de la Plage (HH), à la plage de Ste-Anne-la-Palud, 98 92 50 12, with Michelin gourmet restaurant.

Ste-Anne-la-Palud – Locronan
(6 km/3½ miles)

Small roads here are badly marked. From the **Pointe de Tréfeuntec** head away from coast to **Kergonnec**. Go left and left again towards Plonévez-Porzay, cross the main road D107, and go immediately right.

- ⊨ Hotels: Hotel Manoir de Moellien (H), 29550 Plonévez-Porzay, 98 92 55 21, impressive château with gourmet food but good value for money.

Continue on same road.

Locronan
One of the designated 'prettiest villages of France', ancient, touristy.

- ⊨ Hotels: Hotel du Prieuré (M), 11 rue du Prieuré, 29180 Locronan, 98 91 70 67. Chambres d'hôtes: M. Fernand Jain, 98 73 52 41.

Locronan – Douarnenez
(10 km/6 miles)

Take D7 towards Douarnenez via **Kerlaz** (*enclos paroissial*), and **Kervignac** (good sandy beach).

Douarnenez
Lovely old fishing port and harbour, mecca of boat building and restoration with big sailing ship event in July. Visit the pretty Ile Tristan in the harbour with its château.

- ⊨ Hotels: Hotel Bretagne (L), 23 rue Duguay-Trouin, 29100 Douarnenez, 98 92 30 44, without food; Hotel de la Ville d'Ys (L), 39 rue des Sables Blancs, 98 74 00 87; Chambres d'hôtes: M. Jean Larour, 98 92 34 64; Mme Marie-Paule Le Floch, Manoir de Kervent, 98 92 04 90.
- ✖ Le Plijadur, quai du Vieux Port, pub with real ale.

Day 7
Douarnenez – Baie de Trépassés
(34 km/21 miles)

Douarnenez – Beuzec-Cap-Sizun
(16 km/10 miles)

Cross Tréboul Bridge and turn right into **Tréboul**. Take small road through **les Sables-Blancs**, go right on C4 at T-junction (Poullan-sur-Mer to left, Beuzec-Cap Sizun to right), and bend left with road (ignore turning to Lesaouvreguen). Go straight on through **Quillouarn** and **Kerdrel**. Turn-offs right all along road to high rocky sea cliffs.

- ⌕ Tiny detour to pre-historic tomb site at **Kermenir**.

Keep on same small road to **Pors-Peron**, turn right on D7.

Beuzec-Cap-Sizun
- ⊨ Chambres d'hôtes: Mme Christine Jade, 98 70 50 99.
- ✖ Bar, crêperie and tabac.

Beuzec-Cap-Sizun – Baie des Trépassés
(18 km/11 miles)

Continue on D7 towards Pointe-du-Van.

- ⌕ Turn off left to visit **Goulien**, or turn right to the rocky coast for Nature Reserve at **Goulien-Cap-Sizun**.

Carry on through **Meil Kerharo**.

Pointe-du-Van
Second most westerly point on mainland France with lovely chapel dedicated to St They and sacred fountain dedicated to Ste Anne (originally a pagan goddess). Good views to the left to Pointe de Raz, the most westerly point. Follow the road round.

Baie des Trépassés
A highly dangerous bay with miniscule harbours and peaceful inland lake.

- ⊨ Hotels: Hotel de la Baie de Trépassés (M), 29700 Plogoff, 98 70 61 34, big, modern hotel with good food; Relais de la Pointe du Van (M), baie des Trépassés, Plogoff, 29770 Cléden-Cap-Sizun, 98 70 62 79, 2 km (1 mile) from Pointe du Raz, same management.

Day 8
Baie-des-Trépassés – Audierne
(18 km/11 miles)

Baie-des-Trépassés – Cléden-Cap-Sizun
(6 km/3½ miles)

Go up past lake to junction with D784 (directions Plogoff and Audierne) into **Kerherneau**.

- ⌕ Visit the **Pointe du Raz**, with large sentimental statue of patron saint of drowned sailors, too many tourists. *Cité commerciale* with lots of bars and crêperies.

Continue on D784.

Plogoff
Go left down into the valley, up to **Lannoan**. Turn right on to V9 and D43, and right again at crossroads on V4.

Cléden-Cap-Sizun
- ✖ Restaurant l'Etrave, 98 70 66 87.

Cléden-Cap-Sizun – Audierne
(12 km/7½ miles)

Go through village on D43 towards Audierne via **Chapell-Langoas** and the **Manoir de Lezoualc'h** and turn right to **Goulien** and **les Quatre-Vents**. Turn right again on C3 towards Audierne. At crossroads with D784 turn left.

- ⊨ Hotel le Cabestan (M), 29770 Esquibien, 98 70 08 82.

Continue on D784.

Audierne
Old fishing port with harbour.

- Hotels: Hotel Roi Gradlon (M), 3 boulevard Manu-Brusq, 29770 Audierne, 98 70 04 51, our favourite in Brittany, friendly, modern, with good big rooms overlooking the beach and very good food, through town up estuary towards sea; Hotel du Goyen (H), sur le port, 98 70 08 88, Michelin gourmet restaurant.
- La Fillibuste, (on road round estuary past Hotel Gradlon), very good value lunchtime plats du jour, busy.
- Ferry service, starting at 9.00 a.m. to **Ile de Sein** small island, two hours by sea, no cars. (There is another ferry terminal 3 km (2 miles) further along the harbour.)
- Restaurant de l'Iroise, 31 rue Abbé le Borgne, 98 70 90 12, good plats du jour, excellent seafood.

Day 9
Audierne to Pont-l'Abbé
(39 km/25 miles)

Audierne – Pont-Croix
(5.5 km/3½ miles)

Follow riverside path inland along Goyen estuary (it parallels D765 and joins it briefly).

Pont-Croix
Old Pays Bigouden market town with striking church.

Pont-Croix – Landudec
(14 km/9 miles)

Go downhill to **le Vieux Port**, cross the river Goyen and turn first left on V12 towards Mahalon, Guiler-s-Goyen. Out of town turn right at T-junction on V2. Go past turning to Mahalon through **Guiler-s-Goyen** and on to T-junction. Turn right on to D143.

Landudec

Landudec – Pont-l'Abbé
(20 km/12½ miles)

Go left on D784 towards Quimper. At **Château de Guilguifin** turn right through gateposts. At T-junction turn left and then right on to D57 to **Plogastel-St-Germain**. Turn left at T-junction near church on D240 towards Pont-l'Abbé. Pass the **Chapelle de St Germain** with first *pardon* of the year, **Stang-ar-Bacol** and **Trémeoc**. At junction with main road D785 turn right, and go left at roundabout past tourist information centre.

Pont-l'Abbé
Market town where you may see the occasional *coiffe*.

- Hotels: Hotel de Bretagne (M), 24 place République, 29120 Pont-l'Abbé, 98 87 17 22, pretty-looking hotel; Hotel Château Kernuz (H), route de Penmarc'h, 98 87 01 59, 2 km (1 mile) to south-west, lovely old family home-turned hotel, good value for money.

Day 10
Pont-l'Abbé circuit of southern Bigouden
(28 km/17½ miles)

Pont-l'Abbé – Notre-Dame-de-Tronon
(9 km/5½ miles)

Go west on small road and cross the main road D785. Continue past **Chapelle-Notre-Dame-de-Treminou**. Continue to **St-Jean-Trolimon**, cross D57 and turn left through **Treganne**.

Notre-Dame-de-Tronoen
Church on the beach.

Notre-Dame-de-Tronoen – le Guilvinec
(8 km/5 miles)

Continue to seaside and turn left along beach to the **Point de la Torche** and **St-Guénolé**

- Hotels: Hotel de la Mer (M), rue F. Péron, 29760 Penmarc'h, 98 58 62 22.

Go on to **Notre-Dame-de-la-Joie**. See the tall lighthouse, Phare d'Eckmühl, and pretty **Kérity**. Turn inland on small roads to **Penmarc'h**, then return to coast on small roads.

Le Guilvinec
Pretty little fishing port.

- Hotels: Hotel du Centre (M), 16 rue Général de Gaulle, 29730 le Guilvinec, 98 58 10 44, friendly.

Le Guilvinec – Pont-l'Abbé
(11 km/7 miles)

Return through **Treffiagat**, past the Château de Kernuz (see above) to Pont-l'Abbé.

Day 11
Pont-l'Abbé – Quimper
(23 km/14½ miles)

It is possible to go by boat from Combrit as the route shows, or by road (see **A**)

Pont-l'Abbé – Combrit

(6 km/3½ miles)

Go north on D785 towards Quimper. Turn right at roundabout on main road D44 towards Bénodet. Turn left.

Combrit

Combrit – Quimper

(17 km/10½ miles)
Take D44.

Ste Marine

Three km (2 miles) south-east at tip end of Odet estuary.

☒   L'Agape, le Guen, 98 56 32 70, Michelin gourmet restaurant

Take the boat across the estuary.

Bénodet

⊨   Hotels: Hotel de la Poste (M), rue Eglise, 29950 Bénodet, 98 57 01 09. Hotel le Minaret (M), corniche de l'Estuaire, 98 57 01 13.

☒   Ferme du Letty, Letty, 98 57 01 27, 2 km (1 mile) south-east, Michelin gourmet restaurant.

◇   If you happen to be there in August, there is an outstanding local fête at Concarneau, to the east, the *Fête des Filets bleus*.

◇   There are boats to **Iles de Glenan**, **Loctudy** and up the Odet estuary.

Take the boat up the Odet estuary.

Quimper

Old city with cathedral, museums, china-making centre, etc. For railway, follow river past cathedral.

⊨   Hotels: Hotel de la Sapinière (L–M), 286 route de Bénodet, 29000 Quimper, 98 90 39 63, no food; Hotel Gradlon (H), 30 rue de Brest, no food, 98 95 04 39.

☒   Le Capucin Gourmand, 29 rue Reguaires, 98 95 43 12. Michelin gourmet restaurant; various pubs with real ale.

◇   If you prefer not to stay in Quimper try **Ty Sanquer** (7 km/4½ miles to the north).

☒   Auberge Ty Coz, 98 94 50 02, recommended by Michelin as good value; Bar le Lutunn Noz, real ale.

Ⓐ   To go by road to Quimper from Combrit, follow directions Quimper. Take D144 through **Quillien**. At **Kerlec**, go right at the crossroads on D20, across Anse estuary to chapel at **St Roch**.

◇   Turn right to explore **Sentiers de 'l'Odet** (*Henchoubale an Oded* in Breton), on **Odet Estuary** with Roman remains.

Follow estuary north via **Site des Vire Court**. Return to D20 and go north to **Kervilien** at outskirts of Quimper. For **airport Quimper-Pluguffan** take D40, then D56. Otherwise follow the river Odet into Quimper.

CHAPTER TWO

Half-timber and Horses

*From the Coast of Normandy to the Loire
via the Sarthe*

The old divisions of France have a geographical unity that the larger modern *départements* have lost. This journey from the coast to la Loire is very much through old Normandy, old Maine and Anjou; the orchard country of Auge and the riverland of Sarthe. It is truly *la France profonde*, a domestic landscape that is a pleasure to cycle in, with lots of little roads.

The route starts at the port of Ouistreham, heads east away from creamy coloured stone villages round Caen into the flat marshy country of the Marais, then goes south skirting the hills of the Auge Valley. If nothing else, there is always an animal to talk to with cows, sheep, horses.

Heading west, it crosses the Forêt d'Ecouves into the picture-book pretty Alpes Mancelles, then moves south through the more modest countryside of the old *département* of Maine with its fields and woods, crossing the pretty little Sarthe and Loir rivers.

Finally it reaches the great river la Loire. There is a distinct change of mood here. This is aristocratic France where much of French (and English) history has taken place. Vineyards, white tufa towns and villages, troglodytic dwellings, and fairy-tale châteaux make this a fascinating landscape.

Perhaps this route is best summed up as the *route des chevaux*. You cannot escape them: elegant thoroughbred racehorses, trotters, chunky Percheron carthorses, tiny Shetland ponies. I saw horses on my first day, and they were still in evidence when I reached Saumur, home to France's prestigious Cadre Noir – the National riding school.

I discovered that when you come off the ferry at Ouistreham, which is the port for Caen, you can have a last taste of Britain – if you are desperate for it. The café-restaurant la Phare serves ham and eggs for breakfast for 20F, while normal *petit-déjeuner* costs almost thirty. I noticed this with regret when it was too late – I was drinking my coffee and eating an apple tart and *pain au chocolat* from the *boulangerie* next door. Outside, the little fish market was bustling under its canopy; in the café I was alone.

At the double lock gates you are not allowed to ride over – and with good reason since they are full of gaps – so I walked my bike across, cycling up to the old gun emplacement beyond the lighthouse. Below the tall jetties, timbers festooned in seaweed, small fishing boats were penned in waiting for the tide. I looked out over the estuary with its sands, birds and beaches. A fringe of cloud was turning silver at the edge where it met the clear sky, blue but winter pale. The brown water of the estuary was returning to the sea with slow swirls, its mud banks streaked by currents and eaten into holes by eddies. In the mud, a wreck of a boat: farther out, an incongruously bright orange cargo ship was steaming in. Returning towards the lock gate bridge I began my journey and immediately attracted the good wishes of a white-haired old gent on a roadster who passed me at some speed crying out: *'Mais il est loupé – il est trop vieux!'* Out by the marina, I could have taken the towpath along the canal, which goes straight into the centre of Caen, but I was heading for smaller places on byways – though I had to rejoin the main route from the ferry for a hundred yards near the café which was making a considerable living out of being the first café liberated in the allied landings, reminders of which are everywhere here.

In the first small town, Ranville, there were two signs together; one to the post office, the other to the war cemetery, as if remembrance were just such an everyday necessity. In the town centre a plaque told me how the Lancashire regiment made this the first liberated village in France on 6 June 1944, a day which has even given its name to a hotel. Having had the first café and the first town, I looked forward to the first liberated baker, *charcuterie* and *bibliothèque municipale*. What I got was ornamental animals – an old factory, the *Poterie d'Art*, selling *animaux de toiture* and china creatures for gardens and parks. A bird sat on top of an impossibly large number of vases, with a huge workshop, with what looked like a former colony of worker's cottages next to it, stood to one side. On the top of the workshop's roof a large squirrel was sitting biting its fingernails while a cat arched its back lower down, looking at a fox climbing up the roof after a bird that sat on the crest. Everything you might want to put on your house (and a good many you wouldn't) was there – all manner of decorations: letters, ornaments, spikes, cockerels, parrots, even a peasant with a basket on his back. They were obviously running out of roof space since an apple tree in the garden was full of brilliant budgies and three cats. I would have bought one, but not with so many miles stretching before me.

I had left the stone villages of Caen and was now cycling past half-timbered farms, through orchards with sheep, cows, chickens and woodpiles. Piles of hay lay around for the cows who stared with portentous blankness in the way cows do. It struck me that for them summer and winter feed must be the difference between a salad sandwich and a dry biscuit. There were newly-born lambs with enormous ears that looked as if they had been born with them almost full-size. And among all these live

Close encounter with a bear: the potteries at Bavent.

animals two pottery swans stood stock-still as the brown fowls ran around them in the garden.

    I came to Eel Lane – *le Chemin d'Anguilles* – which itself twisted and turned. A succulent plop came from the ditch beside me as a water rat dived in, or something like a water rat. There were many old withies (there must have been a lot of basket-making there at one time), some of them hollow with age, others with ferns growing out of their crannies and varicose trunks with bark-like sinews.

    At the main road a sign told me that this was The Bog, for I was on the *route du Marais* (a picture of a toad emphasized the point). I crossed the river Dives, fast, muddy, and brown, with swirls in its current. Then suddenly I was heading for the hills and the toad and the *route du Marais* had become the *route de Cidre* with an apple. I turned to follow the road below the hills. Above me stood a fine half-timbered manor house and on the other side an old abbey. Stopping by a field with donkeys brought out a pair of furious dogs who seemed convinced that I was a scout for the donkey salami business, and their owner behind them. He told me this was Brucourt hill, where William the Conqueror achieved his first victory in one war, and where Rommel came in another.

There were signs for cheese and cider up in the hills, but I continued on the road below winding round under the hills before climbing gently to Putot-en-Auge, a pretty village with a good Norman church and much half-timbering. At a large horsey establishment, the Haras Logis St Germain, some very snooty-looking horses looked down at me from behind their posh white fence. No telling who they belonged to, but I heard later that the Aga Khan had a stud in the Auge.

Beuvron-en-Auge is almost entirely half-timbered and designated 'one of the prettiest villages of France'. There is a French association which has devoted itself to classifying them and awarding to rather fewer than a hundred of their favourites the right to put up a sign to attract tourists. There were various indications of summer visitors, including twin cottages competing for chambres d'hôtes on either side of the road as I came in. I stopped for a cup of coffee at the Café du Coiffeur, not absolutely certain that it was a café rather than a hairdresser, since all the old snippers and cutters were still in their places. The patron told me they had belonged to his father. After turning the place into a café, he had not been able to bring himself to throw them out.

Mid-coffee, a farmer brought in a foaming jug of cream sweet cream, not *crème fraîche*. Putting it in the fridge he turned to me, *'C'est pour le gâteau au riz,'* – rice and farm milk, slow-cooked in his old bread oven – a favourite Norman dessert. He made it sound like haute cuisine. I was sorry not to be there to taste it when it came out of his oven, especially with all the cream.

Norman half-timbering comes in all stages of dereliction, from the tumbledown barn to the less tumbledown barn, to the house slightly done up, to the pretty house which in the end becomes a hotel (layers of different periods leave you confused about its dates). Can a remnant restored be old? Is a collage of old pieces new? I was cycling along on the tiniest of roads, all potholes with grass in the middle, on the edge of the hills of Auge which are the heart of old Normandy's cheese and cider production. I had passed signs for *cru de Cambremer*, which had left me uncertain as to whether it was cheese or milk and turned out to be cider and calvados. And then I passed Monsieur Lemoine's sign for calvados which was a certain thing and I stopped – perhaps it was lunchtime.

In his parlour, his wife sat guarding a table neatly laid out with bottles. Auge calvados is double-distilled, the only calvados with an *appellation controlée*. We started with the five-year-old and went back till we reached an autumn eighteen years before. It is not common to find such old bottles and I was as mellow as the calva by the time

I'd finished tasting. I packed a bottle of the eighteen-year-old into my saddle bag. It was foolish, but it weighed less than a pottery cat and was more useful.

Calvados as a whole is twinned with Devon and there are lots of little *jumelages* between Devon and Norman towns. They have much in common, but one thing that is decidedly different is cider. Norman cider, bubbly and held down with a champagne cork is quite different from scrumpy from the mug and the barrel. In Normandy each *terrain*, each apple, makes a different cider. These differences are prized. Cider production increased when milk was cut back in 1985 and Norman farmers are now investing in new cider orchards with improved varieties of apples, and looking to their government to support them. This will enable them to go on living their old lives in their pretty old farms making their cider, pommeau and calvados in the same old barrels, some of which I saw dating from the seventeenth century.

St Pierre-s-Dives is a modest little market town with a fine medieval market hall that operates on Mondays with a big pig and veal section. It was off my route but I had a rendezvous with an English cycling enthusiast living in France. Geoffrey Roberts-Todd is one of an increasing number of English people who have settled in Normandy. He is beginning to make a living by combining his triple enthusiasms for his adopted country, cycling and his young family. Starting by renting bikes and fixing cycle itineraries, he now specializes in renting child-seats for bikes, enabling parents to carry their offspring round the Norman countryside in style (see p. 53). Geoffrey was very fit and I could see why.

The time had arrived to do battle with the hills, and fortified with the spirit of calva I turned towards them, winding slowly through their pretty valleys, inwards and ever upwards. At the top of the Auge hills, Livarot is brick-built instead of half-timbered. This is the land of Livarot cheese. It is hard to choose between a good Livarot and a good Camembert. Livarot is an earthy-tasting cheese with orange-skin. Perhaps the Camembert has a slight edge. I am still testing. The county town for Camembert is along the ridge at Vimoutiers, which has a Camembert museum and a statue of a large Camembert cow standing in the main square. Ironically, the mass production of Camembert now takes place in Brittany, but here it can still be found made by artisans.

On my way down from Vimoutiers I passed a farm of the old style, as picturesque as a child's toy with animals all over the road. Everywhere is pretty here. Just before the village there was a little château fitting snugly into its picture-book setting of hill and lake, then the tiny village of Camembert itself, its church with a good spire, its little *mairie* and a handful of old houses. Its one concession to tourism is an incongruous-looking modern building, the new Camembert Museum, to compete with the one at Vimoutiers. Seeing me hovering, a nice old man came out of his house.

'The Manoir de Beaumoncel, the house up there, just above mine, that's where Marie Harel first developed the cheese.' He added, not quite with a wink because he is a serious man, 'With more than a helping hand from her *curé*.' In his retirement,

The best-known Normandy carthorse: Percherons on the Lerouxel farm.

Monsieur Gouyet has taken on the duties of informal guide; he watches for strangers in the village, and dashes out like a welcoming farm dog to ensure that the glory of Camembert does not pass them by. He pointed out a black tomb in the churchyard:
'Calvados,' he said.
'I beg your pardon?'
'Filled with Calvados.'
'Died of drink, you mean?'
'Her coffin is filled with calvados – the wife of the mayor.'
I expressed my condolences. 'Was it recent?'
'1915.'
Following the valley I left Calvados for the Orne. The country here is a change from the Auge, flatter with forest, parkland and horses everywhere. The Haras du Pin is the French National Stud, run by the Ministry of Agriculture. The morning I passed by, neatly uniformed trainers were busy, either driving out into the forest with smartly turned out carriages drawn by perfectly manicured heavy horses, or perched high up on shiny, polished, long-legged racehorses. In their presence, as a man accustomed to riding a bicycle in scruffy sandals, I felt as if I had landed up in the middle of Ascot on a donkey. I always have a feeling that such horses are of a higher society than I am. They are certainly worth more at often over a million pounds. For this reason France has made horses a state concern. There are subsidies for them which makes owning them a possibility that anyone can consider. Here even I could get a subsidy to ride a horse, though it would need to be a pretty heavy one.

The Lerouxel family had just the thing – a farm with heavy horses. Madame is president of the Percheron Association and she and her husband have helped to start a spectacular annual cart rally which goes from Dieppe to Paris, and commemorates the races between the Dieppe fishmongers to get their catch to the Paris markets. She took me to meet some of the horses, which ranged from all colours of brown to the two creamy-coloured Percherons. 'Sensible animals with no biting or unnecessary temperament,' said Madame. And they did seem to be. They were all female, which might have helped: big, soft, intelligent animals. One even opened her stable door with her nose.

For the Haras du Pin, spring is the busiest time, with their stallions continually on the go. Mares carry their young for eleven months, which is not such a long time to produce something so many times the size of a human baby. And the foals are born in the early spring. I realized there were a lot of things in the world that I knew nothing about, such as how you go about making a foal. It seemed to be a variable business, because in the Auge they do it with artificial insemination and a pony, which is there to excite the fillies, gets kicked by them, and is always left frustrated. While in the Aude they go in for the real thing.

To find out more I went to Argentan, the centre of this horsey world, the ideal country for thoroughbreds. Like most Norman cities, Argentan was pulverized by the Allied forces during the liberation and there is not a lot left to look at there. After the war the French had to rehouse their people as fast as possible. Today Norman cities still display a bit of this post-war haste. Outside Argentan town hall, I bumped into

Calvados: land of apples, cider and dairy produce.

the mayor-*adjoint* and retired English school teacher, François Poulain, on his bicycle. He told me how after the war his town was redesigned by the local doctor who knew nothing about architecture, let alone had any idea about what might be needed for cities of the future. And he told me about Edouard Pouret, horse doctor extraordinary.

One of the first veterinary specialists to treat only horses, he has been instrumental in improving conditions of veterinary service and horse stock. He loves horses and invented the first horse operating table. 'Horses used to have operations on the stable floor which was very unhygienic. They are big, heavy animals. I had to work out a way of getting them to fall onto my table when they were anaesthetized and not hurt themselves; then to turn them over, which is not easy because they have pointy backs.' In his clinic he has a recovery room with a soft floor which can be kept dark to encourage the awakening horses to get up and head for the light outside.

He also breeds horses for other people including the King of Morocco. HM Queen Elizabeth has called him in too; on one occasion for an impossible job, to save the life of a prized steeplechaser ridden by her former son-in-law Mark Phillips.

Back on my route again, at Sées, I changed direction from east to west and went from half-timbering back into stone again. The Forêt d'Ecouves is in the Parc Régional de Normandie-Maine – hilly and pretty, full of ancient half-empty crumbling villages with an air of having been left behind by time. I took a turn to the north to visit St-Christophe where they have a ceremony of blessing automobiles, but all I saw there was a sulky, one of those strange flat things that looks like a toboggan tied to a horse. Perhaps if it were blessed it might turn into a Rolls-Royce.

Ecouves is here more open country than real forest, and, after traversing it, I came into a greener landscape at Carrouges where my hotel was my favourite of the trip. It was not that it was specially marvellous, but that it had real quality and was very French. As so often, I was the only guest and I wondered how it could be profitable to keep a hotel open here all winter. The patron was such a modest man that I did not know he was the boss until I saw him later, his gentle smile under a floppy cook's hat. The whole family was agreeable, even down to the hotel dog. My room was spacious and furnished with old things. Since there was no telephone in the room, they gave me theirs to make calls on, relying on my honesty to let them know for how long I was talking. The dining room was discretely furnished with white curtains and many much cherished plants: palms, even an orchid in flower. Mozart played in the background. The tables had white lace over maroon damask and were set with white plates with a raised pattern. From the 64F menu, I chose an avocado salad with crab, carrot and lettuce, followed by hoki (a hake-like fish on a trial run flown fresh from New Zealand) with a light sauce, leeks, carrots, broccoli, cauliflower, rice, peas and noodles. I ate it all because it was so good. The cheeseboard was excellent too, as were the home-made profiteroles to finish. I had a good half bottle of white Burgundy with a *pichet* of red to wash it all down and vowed I would return.

Carrouges has an impressive château which I passed down the hill on my way out of town, a Gothic and licheny old pile that is municipal now. In spring, a great carriage weekend is held here which must bring back a touch of the old glamour. I had passed the Château d'O a while back, still privately owned though not by the same family as before the Revolution. It, too, is being run as a business, perhaps the only way to run a château in France these days.

I came to Pré-en-Pail, a place which is simply all main street, with a frontier-town look and a frontier-town feel too. It seemed to offer opportunity, because here you can buy a whole village for next to nothing and there is even an English estate agent to help you do it. The French think the British are crazy to buy up ruins, then double the cost and more by doing them up.

I was now on the edge of the Alpes Mancelles, which are generally too much to cycle except by the hardy and enthusiastic, but whose hills help to make them interesting. (The Suisse-Normande to the north is even steeper and prettier, but even harder to cycle which is why I had decided to give it a miss.) St Céneri-le-Gérei, another of the specially designated 'prettiest villages of France', is the most attractive with an old bridge below it and a church above. St Léonard-des-Bois is almost as good, but spoilt by the modern hotel which someone foolishly allowed to be built right in the middle of the village. Here I stayed at the delightful Moulin d'Inthe. When I arrived, Monsieur Rollini had just succeeded in catching a giant trout which he was busy disengaging from his hook in order to return it to the river. Later he made me an impeccable meal and then got out his local calva. 'Better than the Auge,' he said. And I think I agree, but I can't remember very much after that. Next day I carried my hangover through a selection of saintly villages – St-Paul, St-Georges and St-Jean in quick succession. I had left Normandy for the old *département* of Maine and the Sarthe, named after the river which rises in the hills here (which flows through St Céneri). I would not see it again until it had been through le Mans and emerged the other side.

Once an area of hemp-growing, there is not much industry here nowadays, and not much else either. And judging by my experience of the Sarthian personality, the old hemp industry was strictly for sail-making – the toughest material available at that time. You can still see the old *four à champre*; the hemp ovens which were used for treating the material and, at Fresnay-s-Sarthe, the huge riverside mills.

Today the whole area seems to be in limbo; but the villages are not without charm, having old churches and winding streets. There was a pretty château at Sillé-le-Guillame – evidence of a gentler past – and St-Symphorien, Epineu-le-Chevreuil, Chassillé, with another château, Tassillé, Vallon-s-Gée, are all pretty, with such

Overleaf: One of France's 'prettiest villages': St Céneri in the Alpes Mancelles.

quiet roads they are made for cycling. But I missed the drama of big trees and important buildings, so I passed through quickly, reaching the river Sarthe again at Noyen-s-Sarthe.

I followed it down to Malicorne where, at the entrance to the town, there was a manoir surrounded by water, and a pretty mill on the bridge. This is where the old Tessier workshops are still producing the delicate frilly china with very French scenes which you always knew was French but never knew where it came from.

Further down the river at Solesmes is the rebuilt Cistercian abbey of St Pierre, the biggest centre of Gregorian chant in the world. I was there at dusk, intrigued by the cowled figures in the street and contemplating the neat white church with the grey-stone bulk of the abbey behind, when there was a clattering behind me like devils from hell. Turning, it was quite a shock to see a sinister figure in black, arms outstretched like a crucifix. It was the local priest throwing open his shutters. I wondered what the hierarchy and rivalries were between him and the monks. His job struck me as rather like having a sandwich stall outside the Dorchester.

La Flèche sits on le Loir, like the Sarthe, a tributary of the much bigger Loire. Here you feel you've come into a more benign country. The Loir is a pretty river which continues pretty all the way upstream to Troo where the famous cookery writer, Jane Grigson, chose to live (which would make an attractive and interesting detour if you have the time).

La Flèche is rather a fine town, with a military college which fills the streets with bright uniforms. It offered a breath of refinement after the stubbornly rural aspect of the country from which I had just come. I stayed at the Vert Gallant, a friendly old hotel with a curly staircase, an antique espresso machine and an interesting winter menu.

Next morning I meandered along the river via Luché-Pringé and le Lude, with its tufa cliffs, the soft white rock which was once much used for building. With tufa on your land, you were prosperous: it was dug out along the best seams to avoid shifting the stone above, leaving caves that might house livestock – or even people – and which nowadays mostly grow mushrooms in an industry which is centred here. Riding past, there is a smell of fungi on the air from huge tips of spent mushroom compost lying by the roadside. There is a great deal of hustle and bustle; a coming-and-going of little trucks in and out of the caves. I stopped to ask if I could buy some and was told the boss was below ground and would not be coming up for hours. It was just like mining.

Leaving the Loir through a wild, sandy pine forest, I found that I had not finished with pottery birds, a couple of which were sitting on gateposts at la Petite Rocherie. I was more surprised at les Cartes to come upon a whole roadside of paintings on concrete slabs. I had been vaguely aware that this was a land of amateur sculptors, some of whom had commercialized their enthusiasms, as with the roof-finial factory near Ouistreham. They were more or less obsessive; some gardens had one or two peculiarities, like the pottery birds, while others were packed with them.

Cautious after my experiences with Sarthians, I stopped rather tentatively at the little house that appeared to own the slabs to ask about them. I was met with great beams of pleasure, enthusiastic demands that I come and see the rest, which was in the Taugourdean-family back garden. It was a surprisingly big garden and packed with naïve art: cement canvases overlapped all along the walls, cement animals of every conceivable variety from pigs with piglets to big prehistoric beasts, coy married couples holding hands, a cow to fill with wine and milk and, if it was possible to be more bizarre, strolling casually amongst it all, live peacocks.

Taugourdean was the perfect name for such art and I designated all future examples of the kind by that name, which I hereby pass on as a useful new word generally. The Taugourdean family was sitting in the middle of its treasure trove, but as they pointed out, not a treasure to attract many thieves – for many of the works need several people to carry them. Monsieur Taugordean himself is now dead, but with his garden as his memorial, his spirit, and certainly his sense of humour, live on.

His grandson Dominique said he was the best of all possible grandfathers: 'A lot of these things were made for us. He was always making us wonderful new toys. We couldn't have a pony, so he made us one. Next week it would be a whole football team . . . you can imagine – magic!'

I decided that I must have got through the taciturn Sarthe and be out the other side.

It was true. I was on the home stretch now, downhill or, at the worst, flat all the way to Loire. At Mouliherne I hit a decent café, and at Vernantes a touch of real class, a restaurant fit for a government minister (the Economics Minister to be precise). Here, the tufa that I had so far seen only as a cliff with holes appeared in buildings for the first time in all its whiteness and, more importantly, I encountered my first vines. This put the seal on it, I was in a different world – out of cider, into wine.

Through woods and fields I came at last to a steep embankment and climbed to the road at the top. There was the Loire. It had the careless look of all big rivers, and a slightly neglected look as if now that it was no longer used for transport it was not going to bother keeping up appearances. I cycled along the road on top of the embankment marvelling at the quantity of water, more than usual after all the rain we had had.

Even the grandest Norman city cannot match white Saumur. It has quite a different sense of importance. Built from the silky tufa cliffs which line the river, it has a light and graceful southern look in keeping with the delicate wine the area produces – favoured by the English aristocracy for many years because of Edward VII's fondness for it. Saumur is the castle pictured for September, the most famous of the months in the *Tres Riche Heures* of the Duc de Berry. It is quintessentially French, the most aristocratic of castles, and nick-named 'the castle of love' for the Dukes of Anjou who were much given to that kind of thing.

Formal gardens at the château of Villandry on the Loire.

The Loire is a curious looking-glass world; two sides of the same mould. The grand houses and châteaux on the outside built from stones quarried out of the chalky rock, and the gruyère holes that were left behind, in which the lesser mortals used to live and work, that are being rediscovered by a new generation. There used to be whole communities, whole villages of troglodytes living in their hobbit homes. Fireplaces are carved from the naked rock, their chimneys emerging Peter Pan-like into the fields above. It knocks the normal problems of divided ownership into a cocked hat, though it has advantages too: troglodytes don't have to pay rates. There are miles and miles of underground caves, for living in, for keeping things like wine, or for growing things like mushrooms or snails. There are also the half-and-halfs – dwellings which start off as troglodyte and develop into windmills or châteaux above ground. There are strange things in troglodyte caves: sculptures which some people interpret as witchcraft and orgies, others as caricatures of the lives of the great and the good above ground. Rabelais, who lived down the road at Chinon and was not a troglodyte, would nonetheless have known the answer.

Alain Ludin, troglo-extraordinaire, found some strange things in his troglodytic home. He wanted to know what they were and so he went knocking on troglodyte doors, asking and talking to troglodyte dwellers, and thus he discovered the secret of *pommes tappées*: 'In two years of asking I found only four people who had any recollection of them. Not one man. The youngest woman was eighty-eight, the oldest ninety-eight.'

Gradually he pieced together the story of the dried apples, an extremely local business which replaced wine here after phyloxera wiped out the French vineyards. These whole apples, which would keep for ten years, were a huge success and sold in large quantities to the British navy. They became a matter of state concern when British apple growers felt so threatened they demanded the apples be banned. In fact their manufacture stopped quite naturally as strong new vines were introduced. People returned to the old business of making wine and *pommes tappées* were forgotten – until Monsieur Ludin.

Alain Ludin was born in a cave home and is therefore a real troglo. But his parents took him out into the world when he was still a child, and it was only when his grandparents died that he became fascinated by their troglodyte lives. Now thoroughly submerged, he has given up his work to restart the manufacture of *pommes tappées à l'ancienne*, even establishing an Association of Troglodytes with its own *confrérie*.

He showed me his troglo museum with its *pommes tappées* ovens, and I had one of his dried fruits, which re-establish their shape when cooked with cinnamon and wine. They are delicious, but I will never eat my fill of them because they are too expensive at something like £70 a kilo. As to their secret, apart from showing me the tools he uses, including the special hammer used to tap them with, he would reveal no more. 'It has taken me a long time to find the perfect apple. Now I've found it I don't want to lose it.'

The museum and workshop where Alain Ludin makes pommes tappées.

It seems a shame to come to the Loire and not get more than a tantalizing hint of the treasure-trove of châteaux along the river. The aristocrats of French architecture, they were not only the homes of dukes and duchesses, kings and queens but the inspiration behind many a story of fairy-tale princes and princesses. Though the French revolution cut off the aristocracy in its over-blown prime, the Loire has kept alive a dream of those elegant days. All the Loire area makes easy, though not traffic-free, cycling and two extra days will get you to Tours with its main railway station and enable you to see a little more of this historic countryside.

Chinon is just down the road from Saumur. The castle there is where Joan of Arc recognized the Dauphin hidden amongst his courtiers. Richard the Lionheart and other Plantagenet kings and queens are buried in the great abbey of Fontevraud, just behind Saumur. These real figures of history are as much the stuff of our dreams as Monsieur Perrault's Sleeping Beauty (inspired by the château of Ussé), or Rabelais' *Gargantua*, a satire on the lives of his Anjou neighbours. There were even miracles. In the fourth century the funeral bier of Martin, an early Christian saint, passing down the river turned the autumn countryside green (giving the French their idiom for an Indian summer). The church of Candes-St-Martin where he is laid to rest is but a few kilometres east of Saumur. Next door to it is Montsoreau whose castle inspired Dumas' celebrated novel of infidelity and revenge, *La Dame de Montsoreau*. Today, both places are listed amongst the Prettiest Villages of France. But casting a shadow over the river near Montsoreau, there is a more frightening story-in-the-making, the slumbering giant of a not quite dead nuclear power station.

Normandy – Loire 10–11 days 441 km (259½ miles)

▭ Accommodation   ✕ Places to eat   ⃟ Detour   **A** Alternative route

Map Ref: IGN Green Series 7, 17, 18, 25, 26

To get there: Road, rail or ferry to Ouistreham.

To get back: Road or rail from Saumur, or Tours.

Food and wine: Normandy is apple and dairy country, so there is delicious cream, butter, cheese and lots of things cooked in cider or calvados. They include Normandy's classic dish, *tripe à la Normande*. Normandy is famous for its boudin, blanc and noir, and for its cheeses which include Camembert, Pont l'Evêque and Livarot. There are many interesting wines on the Loire: at the luxury end there are Sancerre and Pouilly Fumé, while at the more modest end, Vouvray, Borgueil and Chinon. Saumur-Champigny can compete with champagne and is a fraction of its cost. The tufa caves are home to the biggest production of fungi in Europe (not only the humble *Champignon de Paris*), as well as snails which are called *lumas*.

Weather: Generally warmer and sunnier than Britain.

Useful addresses: *Calvados Cycling* is run by Lucy and Geoffrey Roberts-Todd who can organize everything for you including an addition for bicycles to transport babies. St-Pierre de Mailloc, 14290 Orbec (tel: 31 63 09 04). For the Loire area there are extensive circuits for cyclists with good maps available from: CRT, 9 rue St-Pierre-Lintin, 45041 Orléans, Cedex 1.

Day 1
Ouistreham – Beuvron-en-Auge
(35.5 km/22 miles)

Ouistreham – Ranville
(7 km/4½ miles)

Ouistreham
A rather down-market seaside resort with plenty of accommodation and food, a fish market and nice old centre.

✕ Au Coin du Port, 90 avenue Michel Cabieu, 31 97 15 22, up market routier recommended by *Le Monde*.
From the ferry terminal cross the narrow lock bridge by the lighthouse.

⃟ Detour to **Caen** by continuing down between the canal and the river Orne for accommodation, Norman history, Friday and Sunday markets, or big city life.

▭ Hotels: Hotel de France (M), 10 rue de la Gare, 14300 Caen, 31 52 16 99, with big comfortable rooms, no food.

✕ Ho-Fei, 45 Avenue du 6 Juin, 31 84 54 53, excellent Chinese food.
Take road between the canal and the river past the yacht harbour.

At T-junction go right over the site of the famous Pegasus Bridge into **Bénouville** which has a château. This is where the Normandy landings got their first foothold.

▭ Hotels: Hotel la Glycine (M), 14860 Ranville, 31 44 61 94, small rooms with good food; Manoir d'Hastings et la Pommeraie (H), 18 avenue de la Côte de Nacre, 14970 Bénouville, 31 44 62 43, very good rooms, but expensive restaurant.

⃟ See bird sanctuary at north-east corner of estuary. (Maps and information available from la Maison de la Nature, 14121 Sallenelles, 31 78 71 06.) To reach Sallenelles, follow the D514 on east side of Orne towards coast. (Tourist office at Ouistreham has a simpler leaflet and map.)

To continue route, return over the bridge and go past T-junction to roundabout. At roundabout turn second left out on **D37** towards Ranville and Troarn.

Ranville
See château and remnants of old town.

▭ Hotels: Hotel 6 Juin 1944 (L), 14860 Ranville, 31 78 69 79, on D37. Chambres d'hôtes: Marcel and Andrée Calbris, 31 78 78 53.

Ranville – Robehomme
(5.5 km/3½ miles)

Go through the village and turn left on to a narrow unsignposted road, D224.

⃟ Detour to **Troarn** 7 km (4½ miles) ahead on D37, old abbey and accommodation, a little Saturday market and several bigger annual *foires*.

Turn left onto main road D513, past the Poterie du Mesnil de Bavent to the right (see extraordinary roof fantasies [*épis*]. Take the first right, D37b towards Troarn, then first left to **le Prière** and **Bavent**.

▭ Hotels: Hostellerie du Moulin du Pré (M), route de Gonneville-en-Auge, 14860 Bavent, 31 78 83 68.
Then take the D224.

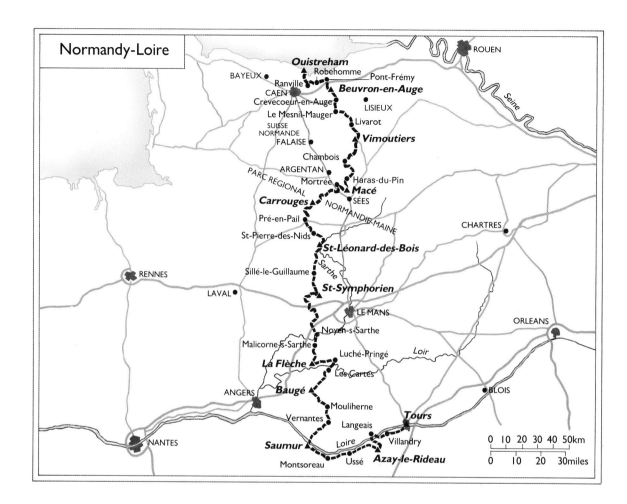

Normandy-Loire

Robehomme

Part of the Hameau de Bricadil.

▱ Chambres d'hôtes: Jacques and Annick Marie, 31 78 01 74; Mme Konecewiecz, 31 78 84 90.

Robehomme – Pont-Frémy

(17 km/10½ miles)

Going out of the village fork left onto the Chemin d'Anguilles, a narrow road in the marais (fenlands) past **le Hom** to T-junction at the D26.

↻ Can visit elegant old seaside resorts with plenty of accommodation, **Cabourg**, **Dives** and **Houlgate**. Turn left at the D27, then first right on a tiny road through marais. Cabourg is the resort made famous by Marcel Proust as Balbec.

✕ Restaurant Pied de Cochon, 31 91 27 55, 2 km (1 mile) on D514 at Hôme.

Turn right at the main road D27, crossing river Dives, canal and main road D400. Turn first right on D49 past **Brucourt** to the left.

Pont-Frémy

▱ Hotels: Auberge du Pont Frémy (L), Criqueville-en-Auge, 14430 Doculé, 31 79 21 35.

↻ Detour to **Criqueville-en-Auge** by going back to where you turned right on D49 and continuing up hill. Château where Rommel stayed during the war.

▱ Chambres d'hôtes: M. & Mme Alexis, 31 79 20 01.

Pont-Frémy – Beuvron-en-Auge

(6 km/3½ miles)

Continue on D49 under motorway and over main road. Follow the line of hills left to **Putot-en-Auge**, past tiny half-timbered *mairie* and Norman church. (Do not miss the pretty château-haras.) Carry straight on.

Beuvron-en-Auge

Designated one of the prettiest villages in France and considerably touristy.

▱ Hotels: Auberge Boule d'Or (M), 14430 Beuvron-en-Auge, 31 79 78 78. Chambres d'hôtes: Jacqueline Fouquet (L), 31 39 02 57; Marie-Therese Duval (L), 31

79 23 79; M. & Mme Jacques Marie (L), 31 79 23 01;
Mme Monique Hamelin (L), 31 39 00 62.

☒ Pavé d'Auge, 31 79 26 71, Michelin-designated gourmet
restaurant; Café du Coiffeur.

☐ For quieter accommodation go to **Hotot-en-Age**.
☐ Chambres d'hôtes: Mme Marie Gallot, les Vignes, 31 79
22 89.

Day 2
Beuvron-en-Auge – Vimoutiers
(41 km/25½ miles)

Beuvron-en-Auge A – Crèvecoeur-en-Auge
(13 km/8 miles)

There are several possible routes from here. This one is
the quickest, but has a section of main road between
Livarot and Vimoutiers. The others are slightly longer.
Leaving Beuvron, take the D49 past the Haras Dem,
bending round in the direction of the hills past the
Manoir de Victor Pontfol. Cross the D16 onto a small
road with grass and pot-holes. At T-junction go left on
D50.

Notre-Dame-d'Estrées
☐ Hotels: Hotel Au repos des Chineurs (HH), chemin de
l'Eglise, 14340 Notre-Dame-d'Estrées, 31 63 72 51.
Chambres d'hôtes: M. Patrice Nudd-Mitchell (L), 31 63
06 86.

Half-timbering at Beuvron-en-Auge.

Go first right, almost turning back, on a tiny road with
bad surface. At fork take directions 'cidre, calva, cru de
Compremer'. Turn right on to an un-metalled road to
join main road, N14 past pretty château.

Crèvecoeur-en-Auge
This area is stuffed with pretty manoirs and châteaux.
☐ Hotels: Auberge du Cheval Blanc (M), 14340
Cambremer, 31 63 02 28.

Crèvecoeur-en-Auge – le Mesnil-Mauger
(3 km/2 miles)

Turn right on main road D511 past signs for 'Fromagerie
Domaine de St-Lourd', cross two bridges, then turn left
on D154.

Le Mesnil-Mauger

☐ Go right round the church and straight on D154 for
more cider, pommeau and calva at level crossing, then
just over crossroads with D47 for butter and cream.

Le Mesnil-Mauger A[2] – Livarot
(16 km/10 miles)

From Le Mesnil-Mauger go right over the railway on
D269 to **Carouges** and **Caparmesil**.

☐ Take a short detour left on D180 to Haras de
Bonneval owned by the Aga Khan. Grandchamps le
Château had a delightful château (a short detour up the
road left).

Then carry on to **St-Julien le Faucon, Coupesarte** (its
manoir is just the other side of the railway), and **le
Mesnil Durand**. At the main road D85 turn right.

Livarot
A striking brick-built town with a famous orange-skinned
cheese.
☐ Hotels: Hotel du Vivier (L), place de la Mairie, 14140
Livarot, 31 63 50 29; Hotel de Normandie (L), 12 rue
de Lisieux, 31 63 52 36.

Livarot – Vimoutiers
(9 km/5½ miles)

Follow the main road D579.

Vimoutiers
Another cheese town, with a camembert museum.
☐ Hotels: Hotel le Soleil d'Or (L), 15 place de Mackau,
61120 Vimoutiers, 33 39 07 15; Hotel de la Couronne
(L), 9 rue du 8-Mai, 33 39 02 62; Hotel de Lisieux (L),
avenue Maréchal-Lyauley, 33 39 03 04; Hotel l'Escale
de Vitou (M), 33 39 12 04, plenty of recreational
facilities.

A This alternative route from Beuvron-en-Auge is 63 km
(39 miles). It is prettier, but longer and best broken
into two days.

From Beuvron, take the D146 to **Gerrots**.

- Chambres d'hôtes, M. Montqais, 31 63 01 79.
Turn right and then left to **Rumesnil**.
- Chambres d'hôtes: M. Flajolet, 31 63 05 35; Mme Lesuffleur, 31 63 01 08.
Go through village to T-junction with main road and turn left to **Léaupartie**. At entrance to village turn left on D117 to **Montreuil-en-Auge**.
- Chambres d'hôtes: Mme Duval, 31 63 06 48; M. Gesbert, Ferme du Manoir, 31 63 00 64.
Continue through woods towards **la Roque Baignard** and turn right onto D59 at pretty half-timbered château with moat. Go past old abbey, la Val Richer, and le Manoir de Gosset to main road N13 at **la Potèrie** (15 km/9½ miles).
- Auberge de la Boissière (M), 31 32 24 56.
At la Potèrie turn left on main road, then first right to **la Boissière**.
- Chambres d'hôtes: Mme Monique Delort, le Manoir, 31 32 20 81.
Keep right on tiny road past church and château and right again on D180 to **Lécaude**. Keep on D180 through **St-Crespin** to **Carrouges**, and right on D269 to **le Mesnil-Mauger**. Then follow details of
A[2].

A[2] Beuvron-en-Auge – Croutttes (51 km/31½ miles). This route is longer and harder, but does not use any big roads. The first part follows the original route to le Mesnil-Mauger (16 km/10 miles). From le Mesnil-Mauger follow D154 across railway, then turn right on D47, and left to **Ste-Marie-aux-Anglais**. More a commune than a village. Turn right at T-junction and right again to **Vieux-Pont**. Ancient church and manoir.
- Chambres d'hôtes: Mme Allison Nash, le Boquet, 31 20 30 62; M. Michel Sady, Les Coutures, 31 20 21 54.
Continue on D154 and turn right at fork into **Boissey**. Interesting old manoir.
- Detour west along D4 to **St-Pierre-s-Dives**. Monday morning market in wonderful old covered hall.
- Hotels: Hotel des Agriculteurs (L), 118 rue de Falaise, 14170 St-Pierre-s-Dives, 31 20 72 78, grotty accommodation, decent cheap meal; Hotel de France (M), place du Marché, 31 20 74 66 by old *halles*.

Turn right on D4, then left to **Ecots** (see manoir and church with lonely Irish war grave). Take the D40 to **St-Martin-de-Fresnay**. In the village turn right, then left to **Notre-Dame-de-Fresnay**. Turn right on D39 through **Peulvey** to turn off left just before **Ammeville**. Climb into the scattered **Commune du Renouard**, past **Mesil-Imbert**, **le Renouard** and the rather special **Prieuré St-Michel** to **Crouttes** (11 km/7 miles). Music and other cultural activities.

- Chambres d'hôtes: 33 39 15 15; Mlle Leconet, le Haut Bourg, 33 39 22 16. Ferme-auberge: M & Mme Guidez, le Haut de Crouttes, 33 35 25 27, specializes in game, must book.
- Can go left 8 km (5 miles) along main road D916 to Vimoutiers for accommodation if need be (see above).

If staying at Crouttes join the following day's itinerary at Camembert. Go down to main road, turn left and then immediately right on small winding road descending between farms, then steeply down to small lake and on into Camembert.

Day 3
Vimoutiers – Macé
(43.5 km/27¼ miles)

Vimoutiers – Chambois
(19 km/12 miles)

Go south on D26, then right up Viette valley on D246. After 3 km (2 miles) turn right.

Camembert
Home of Marie Harel who developed the cheese during the eighteenth century. Her manoir now the Ferme de Beaumoncel, is on hillside behind church. Also little camembert museum.
Return to valley and D246.

- At fork, go right for local cheese-makers: Durand, opposite Haras Bonnerie, or further along on left-hand side, Delorme. For eating then and there ask for old cheeses.

Return to fork and go right up through **Champousoult** and the **Commune de Coudehard** to **le Hameau Sorel**. Go steeply up left to **Mont-Ormel** (lovely views and where decisive battle of the Liberation took place, fought by the Poles). Turn right on D16 and descend.

Chambois
Pretty little town with an old castle.
- Chambres d'hôtes: Mme Clapeau, le Château, 33 36 71 34.
- A couple of kilometres west on D143 at **Aubrey-en-Exmes**,
- Chambres d'hôtes: Mme Maurice, 33 36 82 36; Mme Lebouteiller, Château de Crennes, 33 36 22 11 further along at Urou-et-Crennes.

Chambois – Haras-du-Pin
(11 km/7 miles)

From Chambois turn left on main road D13, then go right just before **Avenelles** to **Omméel** (picture-book haras). Keep right past the Château de Villebadin.

Villebadin

⌂ Chambres d'hôtes: M. du Mesnil du Buisson, Château de Champobert, 33 39 93 61.

⌂ **Exmes**, (3 km/2 miles) south east.

⌂ Hotels: Hotel du Commerce (L), Grand-Rue, 61310 Exmes, 33 39 93 04.

Go over the crossroads at main road D14, then right and immediately left past **la Passière**, **Launay** and **la Frenaie** to **la Tête du Loup** on main road N26. Turn right.

Haras-du-Pin

France's 300 year old national stud and training centres. Many events throughout the year, see them exercising or go on guided tour.

⌂ Hotels: Hotel Auberge Pin Fleury (M), 61310 le Pin au Haras, 33 39 97 77, with restaurant; Hotel du Pavillon de Gouffern (M–H), 61310 Silly-en-Gouffern, 33 36 64 26, very luxurious, good value for money in Forêt de Petite Gouffern, big park with menhirs, lake and recreational facilities just to the west.

Haras-du-Pin – Macé
(13.5 km/8¼ miles)

Go back along D14 and take D26, the first turn right, to **la Cochère** and **Almenêches** (see abbey-church). Go straight through the village and on to D16 to **Medavy** (pretty château and chapel). Turn left down D240.

Macé.

⌂ Hotels: Hotel l'Ile de Sées, Vandel, 61500 Macé, 33 27 98 65, one of our favourite hotels.

Day 4

Macé – Carrouges
(27 km/16½ miles)

Macé Ⓐ – Mortrée
(5 km/3 miles)

⌂ Try a 9-km (5½-mile) round trip from Macé to **Sées** Ⓐ[2] and back. Sées is a pretty old city, with cathedral, old market hall and glass-making centre.

⌂ Hotels: Hotel du Cheval Blanc (M), 1 place St-Pierre, 61500 Sées, 33 27 80 48; Hotel le Dauphin (M), 31 place des Halles, 33 27 80 07, has been recommended. Chambres d'hôtes: Mme Darraidou, château le Bois Hue, 33 28 74 82.

Turn left and right through Macé to **Vandel**, **le Mesnil** and **la Planche**. At T-junction D26 turn left past Château d'O (one of prettiest châteaux in Normandy, with an annual classic car rally and expensive restaurant [33 35 35 27]). Continue on D26 to main road, N159 and turn right.

Mortrée

☒ Restaurant la Ferme d'O, 61570 Mortrée, 33 35 35 27.

Mortrée – Carrouges
(22 km/13½ miles)

Continue on main road to **la Buissonerie**, then turn left on D16 to **Montmerrei**. See ancient church on Celtic necropolis and standing stones.

⌂ Gîte d'étape: Saint-Yvière, 33 35 31 75.

Continue on D16 over crossroads.

⌂ Detour right to **Sassy**, with its château, and beyond to **St-Christophe-le-Jajolet** (church holds annual benediction of cars).

⌂ Chambres d'hôtes, Mme Jean, 'les Marais', 33 36 51 28.

Passing turn offs to **Franckeville** and **la Bellière**, go on to **la Perdrière**. Turn left past priory ruins to **Goult** (wonderful old church and village). Behind village climb on foot to **Chapel St-Michel** and good viewpoint. Go back to road and turn right. Continue on tiny road going right at fork to **St-Sauveur-de-Carrouges**, then left on D754.

Carrouges

Magnificent château with annual carriage fête. See Maison du Parc for information about whole Normandy-Maine Regional Park, gîtes d'étapes, etc (tel: 33 27 21 15).

⌂ Hotels: Hotel St-Pierre (M), place Charles-de-Gaulle, 61320 Carrouges, 33 27 20 02, very friendly with good food. Chambres d'hôtes and gîtes d'étapes: M. Pierre Bugnot, la Gringorière, Ste-Margarite (2 km/1 mile to north), 33 27 22 96.

Ⓐ Go and explore the pretty Forêt d'Ecouves in the Parc Régional de Normandie-Maine (see Carrouges, below, for Maison du Parc information centre) with its 417-m (1313-ft) high centre at the Signal d'Ecouves. Then take D536 (30 km/18½ miles via **le Bouillon**, **Fontenai les Louvets** and **Livaie** to rejoin route in **Carrouges**.

Ⓐ[2] Jump a day and go on from Sées through **la Roche Mobile** following the Sarthon through **St-Denis-s-Sarthon** (accommodation available) to rejoin the route in the Alpes Mancelles. Alençon has lots of accommodation too.

⌂ Hotels: Hotel le Grand St-Michel, 7 rue Temple, 61420 St Denis-s-Sarthon, 33 26 04 77, has been recommended, English spoken.

Day 5

Carrouges – St-Léonard-des-Bois

(38 km/24 miles)

Carrouges – Pré-en-Pail

(16 km/10 miles)

Take D16 out of Carrouges, past Maison du Parc and château to **Lignières** and **Orgères**. Go left on D221 through the Forêt de Monaye and down into **St-Samson**.

Pré-en-Pail

- Hotels: Hotel de Bretagne (M), 145 rue Aristide Briand, 53140 Pré-en-Pail, 43 03 13 00, good rooms, so-so food.
- Robin Hood's Tavern, 43 rue Aristide Briand, 43 03 13 34. Pub Anglais, Anglo-French couple, live music Saturday night.

Pré-en-Pail – St-Pierre-des-Nids

(11 km/7 miles)

Go south on D144 beneath the Mont des Avaloirs (400 m/1312 ft)

St-Pierre-des-Nids

- Hotels: Hotel le Dauphin (M), route Alençon, Mont des Avaloirs, 53370 St-Pierre-des-Nids, 43 03 52 12, a Michelin-recommended good value restaurant which we thought poor value.

- Detour to **Etang du Tour**, fishing lake with pretty picnic area, just out of St-Pierre on D121 towards Alençon.

St Pierre-des-Nids – St Léonard-des-Bois

(11 km/7 miles)

Take D144, crossing river. This is part of the pretty but hilly Alpes Mancelles. (It is 6 km/3½ miles directly to St-Léonard following the river Sarthe on D270.)

St Céneri-le-Gérei

On river Sarthe, one of France's designated prettiest villages, only moderately touristy. See old church with murals.

- Gîtes d'étapes: Moulin de Trotte, *Mairie* 43 03 50 13.
- Auberge de la Vallée, route de St-Pierre, 33 26 57 98. Cross river a second time, bending round up hill on D146 and returning to river Sarthe.

St-Léonard-des-Bois

- Chambres d'hôtes: M. Rollini, Moulin d'Inthe, 43 33 79 22, old mill on the riverside, very comfortable with superlative food.

- Short detour along Sarthe valley for pretty ride on D270.

Day 6

St-Léonard-des-Bois – St-Symphorien

(37 km/23¾ miles)

St-Léonard-des-Bois – Sillé-le-Guillaume

(23 km/14½ miles)

- Detour 12 km (7½ miles) to **Fresnay-s-Sarthe**. See château, old hemp mills on river.
- Hotels: Hotel Ronsin, 5 avenue Charles de Gaulle, 72130 Fresnay-s-Sarthe, 43 97 20 10.

From St-Léonard take D112 past Vallée de Misère and Pont de la Folie, then turn right on D146 to **St-Paul le Gaultier**. Cross D15 onto D105 to **St-Georges-le-Gaultier**. Then take D168 and go right at church on D105 to **Mont St-Jean**. Cross the Forêt de Sillé, taking the right side round the Etang du Defais (swimming), and leaving the Parc Régional Normandie-Maine. Go straight on.

Sillé-le-Guillaume
Château.

- Hotels: Hotel du Pilier Vert (L), 72240 Sillé-le-Guillaume, 43 20 10 68.

Sillé-le-Guillaume – St-Symphorien

(14.5 km/9¼ miles)

From Sillé follow main road D304, directions Le Mans, down to bottom of hill, then take D45, second right. At **Rouez**, bear right on D101 and over crossroads at **Bruy**.

St-Symphorien

- Hotels: Relais de la Charnie (M), 72240 St-Symphorien, 43 20 72 06.

Day 7

St-Symphorien – la Flèche

(49 km/30½ miles)

St-Symphorien – Noyen-s-Sarthe

(26 km/16 miles)

St-Symphorien A
Leaving St-Symphorien, continue on D101 to **Epineu-le-Chevreil** (pretty village on the river Vègre). Cross the river and turn left at main road D21.

The little river, le Loir, a tributary of la Loire, near la Flèche.

Chassillé

Pretty château. Cross main road N157, then under motorway and turn left immediately to **Tassillé**. Go left and right in village to **Vallon-s-Gée**. Take D69 through **Pirmil** and under motorway.

Noyen-s-Sarthe

Old hemp mills on river.

⊟ Hotels: Hotel Manoir de Kerveno, 43 95 76 06.

Noyen-s-Sarthe – Malicorne-s-Sarthe
(7 km/4½ miles)

🚲 Detour of 20 km (12½ miles) along river Sarthe to **Solesmes**. See Abbaye St-Pierre with its Gregorian chant library and masses.

⊟ Hotels: Grand Hotel (H), 72300 Sablé-s-Sarthe, 43 95 45 10, opposite abbey.

🚲 Or you can go 5 km (3 miles) north east to **Asnières-s-Vègre**.

From Noyen follow river on D41.

Malicorne-s-Sarthe

Centre of the old Tessier china manufacturing. It has Emile Tessier's museum and two workshops still in production. See pretty moated manor and church.

⊟ Hotels: Hotel la Boule d'Or (M), 2 place de la République, 72261 Malicorne-s-Sarthe, 43 94 73 64; Hotel le Cheval Blanc (M), 2 rue Carmot, 43 94 80 21; SNCF château, Domaine de Rive Sarthe, 43 94 80 04.

Ⓐ From Chassillé go south via **Loué** (10 km/6 miles)

⊟ Hotel-restaurant Laurent (M), 72540 Loué, 43 88 40 03, Michelin-rosetted.
Then take D101 to **Rocher de Pissègre** and D57, past ruined château de l'Isle to **Chevillé**, **Fontenay-s-Vègre**, and **Asnières-s-Vègre** (pretty old village).

⊟ Chambres d'hôtes et gîtes d'étapes: M. Jean Anneron, Manoir des Claie, tel: 43 92 40 50; or Mme David, 'la Tuffière', 43 95 12 16.
Continue through **Bijottière** to **Avoise**.

⊟ Chambres d'hôtes: Mme du Peuroux, Château de Dobert, 43 92 01 52.
Cross river at pretty **Parcé-s-Sarthe**. Turn left along it to **Malicorne-s-Sarthe** to rejoin route.

Malicorne-s-Sarthe Ⓐ – la Flèche
(16 km/10 miles)

Go south on D4 to **Villaine**, **Aubinière**, and **Verron**, then left on D169 through **Vau** to **St-Germain du Val**, and right on D12.

La Flèche

Situated on the Loir river with château, military college, and Tertre Rouge Zoo which saves animals at risk.

⊟ Hotels: Hotel du Vert Galant (M), 70 Grande Rue, 72200 la Flèche, 43 94 00 51, nice rooms, good food, unpretentious decor; Relais Cicero, 18 boulevard Angers (M), 43 94 14 14.

✕ La Fesse d'Ange, place du 8 Mai 1945, 43 94 73 60 recommended by Michelin as good value.

Ⓐ A 19-km (12-mile) short-cut from Malicorne to Luché-Pringé: take D8 to **le Chevalerie** and **Courcelles-la-Forêt**. Then take D54 to **Ligron** (pretty château and old farms). Continue through **St-Jean-de-la-Motte** (centre of the *boule de fort*, an Anjou game) to **Luché-Pringé** on the river Loir.

Day 8
La Flèche – Baugé
(42 km/26½ miles)

La Flèche Ⓐ – Luché-Pringé
(15 km/9½ miles)

From la Flèche, return to St-German du Val, turn right on D160 to **la Transonnière**, then left on main road N23 to **Clermont Creans**. Turn right on D13 through **Pringé**.

Luché-Pringé

⊟ Hotels: Hotel Auberge du Port des Roches (M), 72800 Luché-Pringé, 43 45 44 48; 2 km/1 mile along the river at le Port des Roches, alas not as pretty inside as out.

🚲 Detour to **le Lude** (13 km/8 miles). Follow D214 along river via **le Port des Roches** (punts on river). See tufa caves and mushroom growers. Trying to keep near river, turn first right on small road, right again, and right at T-junction on D307. Cross river Loir to **le Lude** Ⓐ[2]. See impressive château (summer-time *son et lumière*).

⊟ Hotels: Hostellerie du Maine (M), 17 avenue Saumur, 72800 le Lude, 43 94 60 54.

✕ La Renaissance, 2 avenue de la Libération, 43 94 63 10, recommended by Michelin as good value.
Return along south side of river on main road D306 towards Laval. Turn right on D54 to river crossing (directions Luché Pringé right).

Ⓐ Short cut from **la Flèche** direct to **Baugé** (18 km/11 miles) on D938.

Ⓐ[2] For short cut home, from le Lude continue along river Loir to **Aubigné-Racan** (12 km/7½ miles) and railway.

Luché-Pringé – les Cartes
(8 km/5 miles)

To continue the route from Luché-Pringé go over river on D543. Turn right, as above on D158, crossing D306.

Thorée-les-Pins

Turn left on 224 through a wild sandy forest.

Les Cartes

See extraordinary cement garden sculptures.

Les Cartes – Baugé
(19 km/12 miles)

Continue on D224, then turn right on D104 and immediately left on D195 through pine forest to **Vaulandry** and **St-Martin-d'Arcé**. Turn right on D817.

Baugé
Lovely old town with château and church.
- Hotels: Hotel Boule d'Or (M), 4 rue Cygne, 41 89 82 12; Hotel le Grand Turk (L), 41 89 10 36. Chambres d'hôtes 1 km (½ mile) south west at Vieil-Baugé: M. Raphael Moreau, 41 89 13 43; Mme Duperray, 41 89 72 98; Mme Chantal Reveu, 41 89 25 59.

Day 9
Baugé – Saumur
(40 km/24½ miles)

Baugé – Mouliherne
(13 km/8 miles)

From Baugé take D58 through Forêt de Chandelais to **le Guédéniau** and continue.

Mouliherne
- le Cheval Blanc, good value plats du jour.

Mouliherne – Vernantes
(10 km/6 miles)

Mouliherne
Continue on D58 through **le Carrefour** and **le Loroux** (see ruined abbey).

Vernantes
Civilization again with château, interesting nineteenth-century church and vineyards.
- Hotels: Hotel Pelican (L), place du Pelican, 49390 Vernantes, 41 51 50 20.

Vernantes – Saumur
(17 km/10½ miles)

Turn right on main road D53 (towards Longue), and immediately left (before château) on D206 to **Jalesnes**, **Boulaye**, **Beaucornu** and **Mesanger** to **Blou**. Keep left on D129 (directions Neuillé). At T-junction just before Neuillé, turn right and cross main road at **l'Oucheraie**. Go straight on and over river Aution to **le Gué d'Arcy**. Bear left to **la Croix de la Voulte**. See Boumois château on D229 right and carry on to **les Rosiers**.
- Hotels: Hotel Jeanne de Laval (H), route nationale, 49530 les Rosiers, 41 51 80 17, Michelin gourmet restaurant.
- La Toque Blanche, route Nationale, 41 51 80 75, recommended by Michelin as good value.
Turn left on D229 alongside railway line via **les Roches** to railway station.

St-Lambert-du-Lattay
- Chambres d'hôtes: M. & Mme Andre Renou, 41 78 36 78; M. Remy Rabouan, 41 78 48 05.
Turn left over river Loire with views of Saumur's château.

Saumur
The 'castle of love' of the Dukes of Anjou was illustrated in *September* in *Les Très Riches Heures* du Duc de Berry. Saumur has good food, wines, museums and a crystal tradition. There is the underground world of troglodytes including *pommes tappées*, mushrooms, snails, and most important of all, wine caves including their excellent sparkling wines. Nearby le Cadre Noir, the National Riding School, puts on acrobatic displays. Note: excellent booklet, *Promenades, Saumur et sa Région*, published by local tourist board.
- Hotels: Hotel l'Esperance (L), 453 quai du Jagueneau, 49400 Saumur, 41 51 10 00; Hotel le Clos des Benedictins (M), 2 rue des Lilas, St-Hilaire-St-Florent, 41 67 28 48. Chambres d'hôtes a little way east down the Loire: Mr & Mrs Judd, Castel du Petit Hureau, 41 67 22 47; M. Marc Deheeger, Château de Beaulieu, 41 67 69 51, warm welcome, lovely rooms, excellent food; Mme Goumain, Domaine du Marconnay, Parnay, 41 67 60 46, with pool.
- Restaurant les Caves de Marson, troglo-restaurant, Rou-Marson, a couple of kilometres west of Saumur, 41 50 50 05 (must book).

Day 10
Saumur – Home

You can either take the train back to Caen via Tours and le Mans or carry on and do the two-day extension to see more châteaux of the Loire.

Day 10
Saumur – Azay-le-Rideau
(51 km/32 miles)

Saumur – Montsoreau
(11 km/7 miles)

Saumur
Follow the south side of the Loire on the main road, D947 to **le Val Hulin**.

- Turn right to visit Troglotap, a troglodytic *pommes tappées* museum.

Continue on D947.

Montsoreau
One of the prettiest villages of France with lovely views of Loire and its château. The sand banks in the river are bird sanctuaries with many rare birds.

🛏 Hotels: Hotel Bussy et Diane de Meridor (M), 49730 Montsoreau, 41 51 70 18; Hotel Loire (M), 41 51 70 06.

Montsoreau – Ussé
(21 km/13 miles)

Montsoreau
Go on from here to **Candes-St-Martin** (famous old church where the fourth-century Saint Martin was laid to rest. His bier passing down the river turned the autumn countryside green giving the French their term for 'Indian summer'.)

📷 The Abbey of Fontevraud – at the top of the hill above the river, to the south – is the Plantagenet royal mausoleum, where Richard the Lionheart is buried.

📷 **Chinon** is a beautiful town down the Vienne river in whose castle Joan or Arc recognized her Dauphin. Nearby at **la Devinière** is the home of Rabelais, whose extremely earthy imagination seems rather at odds with the delicacy of the Loire landscape.

Stay on D7 on south side of Loire going past France's oldest nuclear power station (as dead as is possible for a nuclear power station).

Ussé
See Perrault's sleeping beauty château.
Turn left on small road towards river and follow river on little road D16 to **Bréhemont**.

🛏 Hotels: Hotel Castel de Bray et Monts (M), 37130 Bréhemont, 47 96 80 49.

Ussé – Azay-le-Rideau
(19 km/12 miles)

Turn right on D19 crossing river Indres and back to D7. Turn right and right again on D17. Take first left after crossing the D751, go over the bridge.

Azay-le-Rideau
Exquisite moated château (*son et lumière* in summer).

✖ Les Grottes, 47 45 21 04, troglo restaurant.

Always have your punctures in charming places.

Day 11
Azay-le-Rideau – Tours and home
(38 km/23½ miles)

Azay-le-Rideau – Langeais
(10 km/6 miles)

Follow the Indres on D57. Cross the Loire.

Langeais
See its château.

🛏 Hotels: Hotel Hosten et Restaurant Langeais (H), 2 rue Gambetta, 37130 Langeais, with Michelin gourmet restaurant.

Langeais – Villandry
(13 km/8 miles)

From Langeais cross back over river and turn left on little road D16 along Loire.

Villandry
Beautiful château and gardens.

🛏 Hotels: Hotel Cheval Rouge (M), 37510 Villandry, 47 50 02 07.

Villandry – Tours
(15 km/9½ miles)

Villandry
Go back to little road and at **Savonière**, cross the river Cher and turn right on small road past **le Grand Moulin**.

Tours
Cathedral, museums and many gourmet restuarants.

🛏 Hotels: Hotel Balzac (L), 47 rue Scellerie, 37000 Tours, 47 05 40 87.

CHAPTER THREE

Cream with Everything

From Strasbourg and back via the Northern Vosges

The first thing that strikes you about Alsace is that it is not like France. It is stubbornly Alsatian with its own separate language and culture. It is also beautiful and tidy, with strict conservation laws to keep it that way. The Vosges mountains run north–south separating Alsace from the rest of France and the river Rhine separates her from Germany. The region is sub-divided into two Rhine *départements*: the north, perversely called the lower (*Bas*) and the south, the upper (*Haut*). This route concentrates on *Bas Rhin* because there are fewer big industrial centres and fewer tourists – which is not to say that there are none. Way off most British holiday-makers' agendas, Alsace is definitely a holiday place for the centre of Europe; so if you want to visit the most touristy parts of *Haut Rhin* (especially the southern wine route where the Alsatian vineyards run along the foothills of the Vosges Mountains, or the *route des Crêtes* on top of them) try to avoid July and August – or take camping gear.

This trip starts in the flat plains following the Rhine north, then goes inland through half-timbered pottery villages to the borders of Germany. It gets hilly as it enters the Vosges Regional Park, a huge area of forest and châteaux. It dips briefly into Lorraine along the Marne-Rhine canal, then joins the wine route. You can go back to Strasbourg along the Bruche canal, or continue south following the wine route to Selestat. This enables you to visit two of Alsace's most striking sites: Mont Ste Odile, the sacred place of Alsace's patron saint, and the fairy-tale castle of Haut Kœnigsbourg. Both are a steep climb, but worth it. Afterwards you return to Strasbourg through the flat Ried, part of the old flood plains of the Rhine preserved from drainage and the intensive cultivation of sweetcorn.

Alsace is a well-organized place, and especially so for cyclists. The forerunner for a national campaign to encourage cycling, it has many specially designated cycle tracks, tarmac towpaths along the canals, and a network of delightful small forest roads.

Strasbourg has a tiny airport and I was out of it in a flash on to small roads running through the middle of fields – none of the misery of motorways that one is used to round airports. At the little Bruche I turned towards the city following its towpath. Large bunches of mistletoe were hanging in the trees, the sunlight getting progressively more golden as it reached the tips, by which time it was quite gold. I was lucky. It had been raining for weeks before I arrived.

Wolfisheim is a little village just before Strasbourg. There I passed a battered old synagogue and stopped. A man who was packing things away in a car told me proudly it was the oldest synagogue in the area: 'Built in 1870. I look after the key. Would you like to see inside?'

We went into the gloom. He showed me the Scrolls of the Law behind the altar, ornate, ancient and dusty, and told me how he used to come in as a boy to turn on the lights for the congregation.

'For them it was work on the Sabbath. They've got a time-clock now,' he said, 'but before I used to do everything like that for them.'

In the middle ages, Strasbourg passed a law allowing Jews to trade but not to live in the city. (They traded particularly in hops, and what is called here the Brewer's Star is the Star of David because of this.) When the bell rang and the gates closed at 10.00 p.m., they had to be out, which is why Strasbourg is surrounded by villages with diminishing Jewish communities (despite the influx of Moroccan Jews after the war) and ever more abandoned synagogues as the Jews have moved in to the city. I asked if the synagogue was Orthodox.

'Orthodox? Women in the gallery, men below, is that orthodox?'

Strasbourg is a delightfully higgeldy-piggeldy old place, half-timbered houses tilting over the streets, steep roofs set with tiers and tiers of tiny gabled windows. When I arrived it was in chaos: a combination of roads up for new tram lines and frenetic Christmas activity. Traffic was stalled everywhere and I was grateful to be able to walk my bike. Christmas trees lined the streets setting off the magnificent displays in shop windows. The splendid cathedral was completely buried under the avalanche of a Christmas market as noisy and bustling as anything out of medieval times. The little chalet shops were stuffed like a Christmas stocking with craftwork and glitter of every description; stalls of sweet and savoury snacks that would make a glutton of the thinnest man, along with hot punch steaming out of huge cauldrons. An ornately decorated chestnut roaster was doing a brisk business, more perhaps because its operator was a ravishing blonde than because anyone really wanted hot chestnuts.

The city has a considerable air of prosperity and well-being, women elegant though well padded, men in expensive coats and hats and everyone cool and collected, none of that Gallic gesticulating or the hugging and kissing, and they were all speaking Alsatian, which is like German only different.

I had booked my first night at the Hotel Couvent des Franciscans, and was grateful I had, because Strasbourg was packed and my hotel full. I had an amazingly big attic room with delightful views over gabled rooftops, and none of the discomforts that its name might have hinted at. Like a lot of hotels in French cities it had no restaurant and I ended up in an old inn at the back of the hospital which was cosy and distinguished like one of the older Soho restaurants. My first Alsatian meal was very different from the French food I was used to but very good: lots of different kinds of well-prepared vegetables, a rather vinegary salad dressing and no cheese course. It included an escalope rolled up with ham and cheese with a light sauce made with cheese and cream, and a scrumptious cake for dessert also made with lots of cream. The Pinot Noir was served out of a pretty little glass jug with a green handle into a glass to match. If this was Alsatian cuisine I decided Alsace and I would be able to live quite harmoniously together.

Next day I headed north, following the river Ill. The plain between the Vosges and the Rhine was formerly a flood area with a quick crop or a bit of grazing snatched off it in summer. Now much of it has been ploughed-up, which has changed the delicate balance of nitrates in the soil, and been transformed into expanses of tobacco, maize, sunflowers, cabbages, sugar beet, and always in bigger and bigger fields. Hops were growing in the hedgeless fields but they had none of the charm of Kent. I suppose medieval strips must have suffered from the same problem – a patch here, a patch there and no real identity to any of them. Put a hedge round a field and it is a field, put a frame round a picture and it really is a picture. The cabbage fields in particular were no pleasure to pass: most were at least partly harvested, and the trimmings rotting among the furrows sent bad vegetable breath rolling across the road.

At la Wantzenau the river Ill looked like the Cam in Cambridge, with punts and swans bobbing together and lots of riverside inns: the water brimmed from the rain that had been falling for weeks. Most of the riverside hotels were closed, but in summer, I thought, it would be a good first night stop-over if one wanted to avoid negotiating the big city.

It is often very difficult to get a snack at lunch time: the custom of the country is that one eats heartily at midday, so if one stops that is what one does. The Restaurant Schaeffer was open with a 55F menu and I went in. A smiling lady in black came forward, and another, beaming even more but in yellow (like a wasp that had come apart at the seams and lost all its malice in the process), offered me a choice of tables as if it were an international negotiation. They would cede me the little one in the middle, unless it was the round one. 'Lots of couples want the round – it's very pretty.' In the end I had the round even if I was not a couple, and if it was not pretty, it was not the ladies' fault. There were Christmas balls hanging from ribbons like bright seaweed; confections of cedar twigs with dried flowers; pink candles; cacti furiously in flower and fresh flowers (pinks and daisies) as well as pot plants. This is a land of compulsive flower-arrangers, I thought.

Lunch was a comfort (as Alsatian food usually is): a cream of cauliflower soup, with none of the over-cooked taste cauliflower can have and very creamy; veal-knuckle stew with vegetables and more cream and a little pottery jug of Riesling. The two madames (who I thought of as the Schaeffer sisters) mothered me into having a pudding I did not really want and certainly did not need, and after much too long, I staggered out into a day where the gold was already fading fast into grey.

Trying to keep as nearly parallel to the river as possible I went to the end of the road (where there was a pub with an outdoor skittle alley which reminded me even more of Cambridge). Following a tiny white road on my map, I got inextricably lost, ending up in a boggy field. I came to a stop and an official-looking man in a van said there was no point going on, so I didn't. I returned the way I had come and headed for the main road I had been trying to avoid just as it started to rain.

The road was busy and I was grateful for the cycle track alongside the railway. I eventually found myself in Kilstett – a slightly more up-market sort of place – then Gambsheim with suburban outskirts and more closed hotels and restaurants. Following directions to 'Achern' and 'Allemagne', I turned right on a huge empty road. I was alone but during the rush hour thousands of Alsatians poured back and forth from their work in Germany, which is how Alsace succeeds in having such a low unemployment rate.

The Rhine is a river of majestic proportions, a creature with such ebbs and flows

Traditional life is preserved in Hunspach.

Soufflenheim has been making cooking pots for centuries.

that it developed a mythology which Wagner elevated to universal status. Blocked and barricaded from its periodic floods, the river has been tamed and mostly stays within its man-made banks – probably as well in view of the amount of rain which had fallen recently. But the great days of the Rhine transport are over, the lock at Gambsheim being the last big engineering project associated with it. Here is a ship's lock fit for a destroyer, with something like an airport control tower for a lock house. I peered nervously into the depths feeling like a rather tiny man on a bicycle. Cycling over what remained of the Rhine, I reached the German border post which was quite deserted. I cycled round a couple of times waiting for something to happen but nothing did, and with a sense of anti-climax I rode back. After the Second World War the border was set on the eastern side of the river, making this part of the river wholly French.

The road along the Rhine would have been perfect for cycling if the weather had been more benign, a splendid empty road with massive embankments on one side and a marshy woodland with alder, willow and lots of mistletoe on the other (a remnant of the old Rhine forests which used to line the river). Once in a while it was interspersed with gravel workings and very blue lakes, or ploughed avenues of sweetcorn stumps. Because of the sheer volume of the river's water these flat lands beside the Rhine have their own temperate micro climate (like the other big European river the Danube), and lots of animals and birds.

I rode up the embankment to a big car park for a last view of the river, which was imposing even in the rain, vast and still with a dramatic back-drop of mountains. Then I turned inland towards the more domestic landscape of the village of Sessenheim, a sacred place for German poetry-lovers. Here in the eighteenth century, Goethe, the greatest of all German poets, fell in love with Fredericke, the pastor's daughter. This love inspired his first great outpouring of lyricism, but like many great loves, it ended in tears. A pretty little restaurant, the Auberge au Boeuf, celebrates their relationship with an exhibition of memorabilia.

Scattered here and there among the fields are picture-book half-timbered villages. Village houses in Alsace do not cling to each other in the usual promiscuous French way, but are separated from each other like a child's picture of village houses. Even the inns are independent, upright sorts of buildings, raised well off the ground, twin staircases rising grandly from either side to meet at a central door. (If you quarrel over a drink you can go off in different directions.) This part of the country is centred on the great forest of Haguenau, France's biggest and a timber manufactory of impressive efficiency. On my map it showed a feature called 'oak' as if oak was a very rare thing indeed. It turned out to be an 'old oak', an even rarer thing.

One of the great charms of Alsace is that it cherishes its small local industries, and the Haguenau forest supports an age-old craft in two villages entirely devoted to pottery. South of the forest, Soufflenheim has streets lined with pottery shops, many with cafés and tea shops attached. There have been potteries here since the Bronze Age (though probably not tearooms). Pots in folksy blue, folksy brown, folksy green, and mostly with flowers on. Some houses were made of pottery, covered in green and yellow tiles, or covered in pottery murals. Everything in the village seems old, but so well cared for it looks new. These people are compulsive decorators and titivators – probably tidiers too and certainly keen on house repairs. What with the Christmas decorations, it was all a bit much.

Whereas the Soufflenheim clay is light and slow-fired at 1000°C to produce pots you can put in the oven, at Betschdorf, on the northern edge of the forest, the clay is denser and fired at a higher temperature. Its pots are resistant to acids, making them ideal for such things as pickling; and the characteristic blue and grey designs are more refined. In the little pottery museum you can see the work of the local potters without having to visit them all. Though you may want to go anyway. Some potters are happy to continue in the traditional ways, perfecting their skills, others take new initiatives.

Just to the north, Hunspach is one of ninety-six *plus beaux villages* of France, as decided by an association set up for that purpose. It is also 'a flowery village' as designated by another association. Hohwiller, Hoffen, Seebach, are all pretty, flowery villages; Alsace seems to be so filled with them that you are soon spoilt and begin to wonder why the rest are not.

The 600 inhabitants of Hunspach are proud of their *maisons à columbage* (half-timbered houses) and their heritage, and are happy to spend the 2000F per household per year it takes to maintain their position as a flowery village 'They have good hearts,' said pretty Sylvie Heiby, who was born here and now runs the village *gîte*. 'They feel pride but they don't boast about it. They keep it inside. Twenty years ago you did not see flowers on the postcards,' she added. 'People couldn't afford them, it was just a simple agricultural community.'

Ninety per cent of the village is still made up of the same old village families, only one house is a second home. This is not very unusual in Alsace, but unheard of in the rest of France. The village has also kept most of its services going, even if people have to run them on the side: it has a Protestant church, school, post office, baker, butcher, ironmonger, restaurant, café and even a railway with two or three trains a day. It also maintains its folklore group and brass band: 'People often sing their Alsatian songs in the bistros and we still have old women who wear national costume. In fact all the villages guard their local ways and individual accents.

German influences are inevitable. For a lot of its history Alsace has been German, and today Germans are Alsace's most numerous tourists. Many come just for the weekend (which is the hardest time to find a room). Alsace is the ideal, the unspoilt place they would like Germany to be. And there are lots of German second homes in Alsace, so there are not the quantities of empty houses you find everywhere else in rural France, but planning regulations are very strict.

I set off towards the forests on the northern borders lost in my thoughts about the uneasy position Alsace has sandwiched between Germany and the rest of France, when suddenly I came face to face with what looked like a giant helmet sticking up out of the forest floor in front of me. I had a fleeting desire to fall off my bike into a ditch, then remembered the Maginot Line.

Maginot was the French defence minister who decided after the First World War that France needed better defences. He spent a fortune in the thirties building this truly French system of fortifications, so complex you have to go on guided tours or you get lost. The round-topped roofs are shooting posts and 30 m (100 ft) down is a whole self-supporting underground world: wells, electricity, trains, hospitals, air conditioning, the lot. I wondered if anyone had thought of a modern use for them – mushroom growing perhaps?

I had a good lunch at the very pretty Hotel au Tilleul at Cleebourg. *Tilleul* is the French for linden, France's tree of the revolution, and a symbol of liberty. During the war the Germans cut most of them down. I toyed with the idea of stopping but wanted to make more headway, so I went on to Wissembourg, passing the first vines I had seen. The countryside is very pretty and hilly, rising gently up to Wissembourg in the extreme north of Alsace on the borders with Germany, on the edge of the Vosges mountains. And it has officially recognized its 'borderness' by creating the first international lycée where German pupils can come to school.

Opposite: The Rhine plain from the grand folly of Haut Kœnisbourg.
Above: Wissembourg, on Alsace's northern borders with Germany.

I cycled round the old town admiring its fine buildings, its church and old salt house which had the wonkiest roof I have ever seen. A builder's nightmare, I thought and was glad it did not belong to me. The little canal which cuts through the town has lots of over-hanging houses, which in Alsatian are called *schlopf*. (Alsatian is not a literary language, but a gutsy one.)

Christmas preparations were as prominent as ever with bad *Père Fouettant* and good *Père Nicolas* competing for space in window displays and the whole gamut of fairy-tale figures stuck round the church. Alsace is a place made for the festivities of Christmas (some people even think they were invented here), because it is a place where people like bright and pretty things, and things that are good to eat. Chocolate-makers and *patissiers* are part of this fantasy world, and their confections made my mouth water. I ended up being drawn into a *charcuterie*, attracted by a life-size cut-out of a pig in an apron inviting me in to buy his sausages – after all sausages are what Alsatian cuisine is supposed to be all about. There were black puddings and white puddings, smoked deer sausage and chestnut sausages, but much as I might have liked to there was no way I could cook a sausage in my hotel room, so I left them where they were, deciding that the next meal I ordered would be the real Alsatian thing: sauerkraut and sausages.

As it turned out my next meal was Alsatian, but not sausages. The Ville de Paris is a very ordinary pub but with a very extraordinary barman, Joseph, an ex-sailor who spoke English. Joseph made me my first *tarte flambée*. I expected a dessert flamed with alcohol. I was disappointed to discover it was a savoury thing, but it was so delicious that I decided to forgive it. By the time I had finished, I had decided it would be my lunch for the rest of the trip. It is really the perfect lunch snack, just a piece of thinly-rolled bread dough scattered over with pieces of bacon and sliced onion and lots of sour cream on top. The trick is to cook it in a sizzlingly hot oven – it is done almost instantly. If its edges are not a trifle burnt you know the oven was not hot enough. Compare it to the humble Breton *gallette*, which you now find masquerading as something special in all corners of France, and you are left wondering how the Alsatians have guarded its secret for so long and why the *tarte flambée* has not swept the world like pizza.

I cycled away from Wissembourg through orchards and vineyards to look for the border post. I found it, a tiny sentry box by the side of the road, as deserted as the bigger one at Gambsheim. Truly there seems not to be a border between France and Germany any more. I continued up into the Vosges National Park and its forests, at Lembach I encountered the old Maginot Line again. But I was looking for an earlier Maginot line because here in these northern Vosges there were an amazing 110 castles, all built in the twelfth century. There used to be even more, the most impressive collection of defensive castles in Europe. In those days Alsace was a collection of city states. When Louis XIV made Alsace part of France he ordered the destruction of her castles, which is why they are all in ruins. Nonetheless Alsace has kept special privileges from those days and has other special laws from its later German days: for instance, hunting is strictly controlled, not a free for all as is the case in most of France, and clergy are paid by the state despite the fact that France has been officially atheist since the revolution.

The forests are very pretty, like Canada they say, and certainly it had the nip of Canadian cold in its air when I was there. The little forest roads were perfect for cycling, but started to go up quite steeply.

Alsatian forestry combines management of the natural oak and beech trees with stands of Christmas trees. If it is never a really wild wood, it still manages to guard its natural aspect (much of French forestry is totally industrial). I passed a little group of woodsmen sitting in a circle round a fire, the hot breath streaming from their mouths as they laughed together. It was a kind of life, I thought, which must have gone on more or less the same for centuries, though not the Christmas trees which were stacked up by the side of the road concertina-ed into huge packing cases ready for the markets of Europe.

I was still hunting medieval castles in the middle of the forest when I met François de Pourtales, a count who lives in a family house only 25m (82 ft) from the Maginot Line. His house was built as a summer shooting lodge, and during the war was occupied by four different armies including the Free French. In 1945 when he returned from Indo-China it had been reduced to a shell. Slowly he has rebuilt it, making it beautiful and comfortable. Today the count lives entirely off his trees which he loves – 1700 hectares (4201 acres) of forest which his son and a dozen estate workers manage for him. The count is no longer rich: 'I have nothing to leave except atmosphere and trees,' he told me, and he seemed quite happy about it.

'Our contact with the forest is much more personal in Alsace. A tree has a memory, you read its life when you chop it down. There's a big difference between chopping down timber and growing trees.' He also loves the hunting which starts in May.

I found a hotel on the main road near Wœrth, though it was probably not the one recommended. Everything in it was over the top including Madame who was gilded like a birthday cake; and the food was such a continuous disaster that it could have made a script for *Fawlty Towers*. Sugary carols emitted continuously and 'Silent Night' got stuck several times, to my huge enjoyment, but nobody else noticed. The dining room appeared to be entirely full of Germans, blissfully unaware of the strangeness of either the food or the decor. When Madame stopped to ask if everything was all right it was on the tip of my tongue to remark on the chef's love affair with the *cube de bouillon* and a suggestion that he be put out of doors. Instead, I said 'yes' in the usual cowardly English way. Later I was glad I had been reticent,

Overleaf: A typical village on Alsace's wine route.

for on seeing the chef, a grim-jawed, scantily-haired man, it was plain that he was madame's husband.

The country was undulating as I got back to my route the following day. At Nehwiller there was an old steel works, one of many such remnants of a once prosperous industry here. It is strange to feel romantic about a factory, especially when you know about the working conditions in the last century, but the idea of working in your home village is more appealing than joining the daily exodus to work in a factory the size of a small town in Germany. These small factories feel more like workshops than the dark satanic mills we know from the north of England.

Jaegerthal is deep in the forest and its old factory is now a ruin. It really is romantic, straddling the stream which used to power it, and overlooking a deep green lake. This was the original de Dietrich forge, 300 years old. From this little factory started an empire which is still the biggest employer in Northern Alsace. I saw the house the family still keep here, a pleasant, unpretentious looking place for a rich family I thought. I passed another de Dietrich factory on the outskirts of the old spa Neiderbronn-les-Bain at Reichshoffen which makes France's high-speed train, the TGV. Neiderbronn has a new industry too now, a sparkling new water plant, Source Celtique, with crystal clear glass walls through which you can appreciate the long steel shaft busy pumping water from the bowels of the earth. And just down the road another drill was going even deeper, 3 km (2 miles) or more, to hot, dry rocks which may yet become the source of our future energy.

From Oberbronn, a cobbled and fortified village, I skirted the edge of the hills through pasture and other quaint half-timbered villages. With the ring of an incestuous theme-song they all seemed to end in 'willer', but I discovered it only meant village (like the German *weiler*).

Back in the forest I saw my first family of deer. There seem to be more wild animals and birds in Alsace than elsewhere in France, perhaps a result of the strict laws about hunting. Here too there are carp ponds, which are simply large squares cut out of the ground and filled with water. Once a year they are drained and their fishy harvest collected in baskets. The smaller ones go into a new pond and the bigger ones are eaten. Carp are tough, tolerant creatures who can stay out of water a long time. Fried carp is really a specialty of the south of Alsace, but I had some in the north and it was nice and crispy, if a bit dry. Not a patch on a good cod and chips, though.

Then it was a steep climb up to Lichtenberg and the church bells were going like a fury as I arrived. Monsieur Schmutz lives just below the castle. He is a Lutheran pastor and has a rambling house filled with his family and lots of musical instruments. A delightful man he told me he had cycled to Oslo and back when he studied there as a young man. His family had once been German and Lichtenberg was the last village where they still spoke German rather than Alsatian. 'In German my name, Schmutz, means kiss, but in Alsatian it is not so nice,' he said laughing.

He showed me his alpenhorns; some so long you could only get breath for one low burp. 'Northern Alsace is largely Protestant and music is important in the Lutheran tradition. I have always had a brass band,' he told me. When he discovered the Vosges alpenhorn it rather took over. Now he has over thirty players and they perform all over the world.

I was now going into the prettiest part of the Vosges but tough cycling. I followed the Mittlebach valley on little forest roads heading up and up towards la Petite-Pierre. It was a beautiful landscape of mixed forest, helped by a fine day, and if my bicycle was heavy, my spirits were light. I went past a party of hunters eating and drinking together in a clearing and would have loved to have joined them. Instead I wound my way slowly up past a forest farm with highland cattle to Erckartswiller. There at Chez Annie I ate a late lunch, and was very grateful for it. The soup came in a huge bowl, to which I helped myself, accompanied with great wodges of bread. If it was no gourmet treat it did not matter. A group of locals clustered round the bar gossiping, while I looked out of the window at a gentle pastoral scene of meadows with more highland cattle and a little chapel. It was cold but the sun was shining and it was all very agreeable.

La Petite-Pierre is the centre of the Parc Régional des Vosges du Nord, and is in the most beautiful part of the forest. It is a gem of a place and the locals know it, but have not spoilt it. The views down over the valley as you come into the village are quite lovely, a tiny half-timbered chapel folded into the hillside. There are hotels, of course, a château and a couple of little museums, but little else. The church is shared between Protestants and Catholics with, until recently, a moveable altar which ran forward on rails to conform to the habits of the different denominations. Alsatians have learnt to be tolerant.

I went down through the forest on a minor detour, past more fish ponds until I reached Graufthal where a little row of troglodytic houses is set into the chalky cliffs. It was nothing compared to the great works on the Loire, but was in the process of restoration nonetheless. A charming girl was busy helping an old woman into a car and both were happy to stop and answer my questions. The last of the families who lived there, she told me, had died in 1958. The houses had been empty ever since. Now a local association was going to restore them. It was going to be expensive. 'But we have to look after our heritage,' she said.

Graufthal is very near the borders of Lorraine. From there I headed back through the forest to Dossenheim. And did a minor detour back into the 'willers'. Bouxwiller is the classic Alsatian village and not to be missed. Its synagogue is going to become a cultural museum of Alsatian Jewry. There seems to be a lot going on around here because just down the road in the little village of Kirrwiller there is an international nightclub. I did not get a chance to go, but the locals told me people come from far and near. They said the owner was just a simple café proprietor . . . it seemed rather unlikely, but no more unlikely than moving a synagogue to Israel, which I had heard was happening in Balbronn. Alsatians are nothing if not dauntless.

Hugging the edge of the Vosges I headed south through Neuwiller with its wonderful square, fortified abbey, and a church of all sorts of styles and periods (including a baroque bit with figures sculpted on its roof). Then I was into the lego-land of Saverne's suburbs and I followed the canal straight into its old centre. Saverne is a big maker of all manner of things from Kuln scales to watches. There was a lot of hypocrisy after the war and the French did not care to invest in Alsace, so now there are a lot of Swiss and German firms here. Apart from factories Saverne has some impressive buildings, including a bishop's palace fit for a king, where things went on to bring a blush to a well brought-up catholic cheek. It makes you appreciate the Reformation. Saverne also has a very grand town hall which, when I was there, had a very large sculpture outside it – an entire orchestra of life-sized musicians. They were made from off-cuts from the local wheel-barrow factory, and the same factory had donated works of wheel-barrow-art to other local establishments including the supermarket. There were also various craftsmen and a smallish brewery (*brasserie*),

Below: Foie gras was introduced into Alsace by Jews from Hungary.
Opposite: The Ried. The Rhine plains used to flood naturally every winter.

Karlsbrau, which does tours in summer. I was tempted by a glass engraver, but doubting the future of any piece of glass in my panniers, I settled for a *tarte au pomme*, the craftsmanship of whose pastry was at least the equal of Monsieur Norbert's glass, and which had the advantage that it could be consumed on the spot. It was simply the best tart I've ever eaten, and on account of that special tart Saverne keeps a warm place in my memory.

This is the narrowest section of the Vosges and here the Marne-Rhine canal slices neatly through the mountains. On the other side is Lorraine which many people, wrongly, lump with Alsace in the general category of half-German. In fact only the Moselle *département* was ever part of Germany, and the look and feel of the place is very different. Not only is French the language everywhere, even the houses look different, the half-timbering all gone. The northern forests of Lorraine are pretty with a fine glass-making tradition, but this Lorraine is industrial with coal mines. It was a late flourish of its engineering heritage I wanted to look at. I cycled along the canal passing its little string of lock houses one after another, just the occasional trickle of smoke coming from a chimney to indicate that there was life in them. The Plan Inclin is a great ship lift, built in the 1960s to replace the twelve locks which took a barge all day to pass through. Now there are no barges but there are cruisers in summer which will take you through, lifting you the 40 m (131 feet), and giving you a meal at the same time. But when I was there in winter there were no boats of any kind and it was a bit desolate, so I followed the canal towpath back to Saverne.

Next morning in a small burst of sunlight I went to look at a final piece of industrial archeology – the Chappe telegraph, the world's first. The road climbs to 463 m (1519 ft), a haul that only an enthusiastic cyclist would contemplate. The telegraph which dates from Napoleonic days is of course no longer working, but here, in the eighteenth century, a series of signals was transmitted at 10-km (6-mile) intervals all the way to Paris.

By the time I got up there the sun had gone and a deep frozen fog was settling in. Visibility was more like ten metres than ten kilometres and I wondered if Chappe had had the same problem. It was also getting very cold. I had a look at the old ruined castle of Haut Barr which was evocative in the mist with its soft pink sand-stone and ancient battlements. In its middle a curious half-timbered house-cum-restaurant was snuggled like Thumbelina inside her walnut. It looked more convivial than it turned out to be and I left without a coffee.

In the plains again the fog had disappeared and I set off south along the edge of the hills. The trouble with the geography of Alsace is that it is like Jack Sprat and his wife: all plains or all Vosges, and for the cyclist, the one is a bit uneventful while the other is too exciting by half. So he/she is more or less confined to the route that follows the foothills, and a lot of that is the Wine Route, and being vines there is not a lot of variety there either. But to start with, the route I chose went through pasture with animals and cherry trees and very pretty too. These orchards have a medieval look

– sparse, a couple of rows of trees loosely planted down the middle of a field, and the trees are allowed to grow big and old, which is very different from the custom in the south of France. It must be lovely in spring with the blossom. I passed through delightful sleepy little half-timbered villages: Marmoutier, Hengwiller, Allenwiller, Wasselonne, Westhoffen, where in the summer they hold a famous cherry festival. At these fêtes people eat cherry tarts which are cooked communally in the village oven, and cherry pancakes which are cooked outdoors, and they drink cherry schnaps.

Coming down through Balbronn and Bergbieten, I was into vineyards on the *route du Vin.* I headed down the main road into Molsheim, a centre of the wine industry. Wine is big business in Alsace, forty per cent of its total agricultural product, a fifth of all French wine, and by no means the cheap end of the line. This can be very posh stuff, single grape wine made by independent *vignerons*. It is endearing however that the industry has not wiped out the little home producer (as it has in most of the south) perhaps because it is so expensive. I saw many farms with just a couple of rows for their own consumption.

Molsheim is full of wine caves, but its spiritual fame comes from Bugatti who lived, worked and died here. Molsheim is Bugatti-ville. The whole town is crazy about him and most public places have a picture of one or more of his cars. There is a Bugatti museum, a Bugatti fan club, and once a year, an assemblage of Bugatti fans and their cars from all over the world. Italian by birth, Bugatti came to work for de Dietrich. He soon had his own factory (which is still here, though now it makes airplane parts). He died as he lived, in his car in a motor-racing accident.

I found the Auberge de la Chartreuse tucked out of the way round a corner of the impressive town square, set within the equally impressive town fortifications. I entered by a door that had once been used for delivering wine barrels and the dining room was the old wine cellar. Madame was the essence of Alsatian charm and hospitality, a combination of warmth and politeness. We shared the mutual bond of a generous waist-size and when I learnt her name was Munch we got off to a good start. At last I had my *choucroute garnie à l'alsacienne* – thick slices of boiled ham, fat pork chunks, a whole heap of different sausages all piled up with boiled potatoes on a mountain of sauerkraut; a plate of food so great that even I was daunted by the sight of it. But with help from my delicious jug of Tokai I eventually reached my last potato.

Many such dinners later, I realized that this was a very superior example of its kind. Monsieur Munch was the chef, thin as a rake, but also a charmer, and with an accent so strong I thought he must be foreign (though he was as Alsatian as they come). The Alsatian-French accent is remarkable: it sings like Welsh, concentrating its emphasis into the first syllable rather than the last, and rising at the end of a sentence.

It was over my sauerkraut that I discovered Madame's chambres d'hôtes, and there I ended up, and a great treat it was too. My room had antique furniture and a big bathroom, with a kitchen I could use if I wanted, all for 160F a night. So I stayed for two days and the next night I ate *biche* (which is venison), this time with the family, and heard some more war stories. By the third day I had to drag myself away.

It had been my idea to follow the Bruche back to the airport at Strasbourg. After talking to the Munches I decided to extend my trip to take in two major tourist attractions to the south: Mont Ste Odile – the holy mountain of Alsace's patron saint – and Haut Kœnigsbourg Castle. Both would be insufferably packed in the middle of summer, but it was a shame to miss them now, they said.

Here I was moving into the more touristy parts of Alsace. All the villages along the wine route are too pretty by half. If you thought you'd seen it all before – the half-timbering, the fortified villages, the Romanesque churches, etc, they will be more abundant and quainter than ever.

Mont Ste Odile, 761 m (2497 ft) high, is built on an ancient sacred site (there are still several kilometres of very old Celtic fortifications, known as the Pagan walls). This was the convent to which in the early days of Christianity, a duke's blind and unloved daughter escaped, and where her sight was restored by a miraculous spring. There are chapels, ancient and more recent, with some fine decorations, and her tomb is a major pilgrimage centre. The sacred spring is still expected to perform miracles for people with eye troubles. There is also a nice-looking hostel, but you will need to book in March if you want to stay in July. For a moving memorial to the horrors of the Second World War, go west across the Champ du Feu to le Struthof with its concentration camp and gas chambers. The camp was placed in the coldest part of Alsace, 700 m (2296 ft) high facing the winds of the north east. Here more than 10 000 Alsatians were murdered. A beautiful chapel has been built as a memorial to so many *patriotes resistantes.*

I wouldn't have wanted to miss the picture-book villages of the wine route, or Sélestat, that elegant old cultural centre, with its wonderful competing churches. From Sélestat I climbed the long hill to Haut Kœnigsbourg castle which is now more a dream castle than a real one. At the turn of the century it was transformed by the German Kaiser Wilhelm II, no expense spared. It may be a touch Hollywood, but its craftsmanship is superlative. Alsace has a long tradition of artists and craftsmen and has been producing masterpieces fit for emperors for centuries.

Coming back through the Ried I found much of it under water. It looked like a flood disaster, but I learnt that this was the natural course of events here – even when it was not raining all the time. And I discovered another side to Alsace. Not just serious about protecting their architectural heritage, Alsatians are increasingly worried about their landscape too, and ecologists have a lot of political clout here, as in Germany. There is a lot of re-education going on, in government circles and at grass-roots level. Even wild things are gaining their rights, and verge-cutting, for instance, has to wait until after the orchids have finished flowering in the spring. A cheerful young farmer to whom I stopped to talk told me: 'My family has always farmed here. This is very special land, the only prairie like it in France.'

The last thing I did before leaving Strasbourg was to buy a small plate with a Henri Loux design, one of those bitter-sweet pictures of Alsatian country life towards the end of the last century which are now collectors' items. It seemed to say something important about the continuing traditions of life in Alsace. I got it back safely, intending it for a present but ended up liking it so much I kept it.

A stone mason, Raymond Keller, summed up his Alsace: 'God created Alsace first, then all the rest. We have the privilege of being here at the centre of civilization. We're pig-headed and prickly, but we can be big-hearted too. We don't want an easy life. We struggle and work hard, and the greater the challenge the more we like it.'

Alsace 8 days 232 km (144½ miles) or 12 days 384.5 km (240 miles)

⊟ Accommodation   ✗ Places to eat   ◊ Detour   A Alternative route

Map Ref: IGN Green Series 12 and 31.

To get there and back: Train, plane or drive to and from Strasbourg.

Weather: Cold in winter (skiing in the Vosges). Can be humid and hot in summer. The Rhine plain has its own temperate climate. Spring is lovely with the fruit trees in flower.

Food and drink: Alsace is a place made for gluttons: it has the best of everything. It tries to compete with Burgundy in terms of cuisine and like Burgundy, lots of dishes are cooked in wine, but in Alsace these are white wines (*coq au vin* becomes *coq au riesling*) and they have cream with everything. There is a lot of game and river fish, like carp, are popular. Alsatian foie gras is legendary and its sausages are world famous. Don't forget the hearty peasant dishes (which Alsatians really like) such as *choucroute garnie à l'Alsacienne* (sauerkraut and porky things) or *baeckaoffa*, a collection of meats slow-cooked in a casserole with potatoes, onions and wine. Add their fine *patissiers* and *chocolatiers* and you will understand that Alsace is no place for a diet. *Tarte flambée* (a kind of pizza classically topped with cream, onion and bacon) must not be missed. Alsatian wines are usually single grape wines produced by independent *vignerons*. They can be very expensive. For normal meals ask for a jug of Riesling. Otherwise there is pinot gris or Tokai, pinot noir and Gewürztraminer which is stronger and sweeter. Fruit alcohols are delicious, among them pear, cherry and plum, and marc de gewürz can also be a delicious ending to a meal.

Useful addresses: Office départementale du Tourisme du Bas-Rhin, 9 rue du Dôme, 67000 Strasbourg, tel: 88 22 01 02. Ask for the useful map of cycling routes, *plan des pistes cyclables*, Strasbourg and other cycling information.

Day 1
Strasbourg Airport – Strasbourg
(10 km/6 miles)

Strasbourg airport/Entzheim A
⊟   Hotels: Hotel Père Benoit (M), 34 route de Strasbourg, 67960 Strasbourg, 88 68 98 00, old inn. Chambres

d'hôtes: M. Reibel, Ernolsheim-sur-Bruche, 88 96 04 32, château-farm; M. Schaefer, Duppigheim, 88 50 70 81; M. Spitz, 88 85 54 51; M. Spitz, 88 85 51 63; M. Georges, 88 85 52 57.

Turn left out of airport. Turn right beside railway station and cross line going towards Hangenbieten. At the Bruche canal turn right and follow its towpath all the way to Strasbourg. There are many ways into the city. This is only one. After **Eckbolsheim**, continue along the canal under the railway. Cross the canal and continue on other side over another railway. At junction with the Ill river, turn left along it, keeping as close as possible. A cycle track takes you under the motorway behind a school still alongside the Ill. Just before the Hotel du Département, turn right over bridge towards it, then left behind it. Cross left on les Ponts Couverts. You are now in the old quarters. The tourist office is near the cathedral.

Strasbourg
Lovely old city, magnificent cathedral, museums, etc.
⊟   Hotels: Hotel Ecluse du Rhin (M), 50 quai Jacoutot, 67000 Strasbourg, 88 61 40 57, near Rhine on canalside, has garden; Hotel Couvent du Franciscan (M), 18 rue Fg. de Pierre, 88 32 93 93; Hotel des Rohan (H), 17–19 rue du Maroquin, 88 32 85 11, near cathedral.
✗   Cerf d'Or, place de l'Hôpital, 88 36 20 05, also a hotel (M), but not as comfy as the above; Au Rocher du Sapin, 6 rue Noyer, 88 32 39 65, is recommended by Michelin as good value; Buerehiesel, parc d'Orangerie, 88 61 62 24; la Crocodile, 10 rue Outre, 88 32 13 02; Julien, 22 quai Bateliers, 88 36 01 54 (the last three are Michelin-designated gourmet restaurants); or one of the little restaurants off the cathedral square.

A   To bypass Strasbourg, go north and east round it. From **Hangenbieten**, cross the canal on D221 to **Breuschwickensheim**, and then take the D622 to **Ittenheim**. Then take D222 to **Hurtigheim** and from there the D341 to **Statzheim-Offenheim**. Continue on the D41 and the D64 to **Pfulgreisheim**, **Lambertheim**, and at the refinery take the D301 to **la Wantzenau**.

Day 2
Strasbourg – Soufflenheim
(38 km/23½ miles)

Strasbourg – la Wantzenau
(12 km/7½ miles)

The simplest way out of Strasbourg is to follow the river Ill behind the Palais d'Europe and take D225, route de la Wantzenau, or go right and left through the Orangerie to the canal. Turn right along it, then left over the bridge and go straight on.

La Robertsau
See Château de la Robertsau and park. The area north-east is a big wilderness of natural lakes and forest. There are paths through it for cycles which re-join the route de la Wantzenau.

☒ Restaurant Château de Pourtalès (H), 161 rue Melanie, 88 31 37 40; simple café by gate.

From Robertsau go through the park and continue past la Ferme de la Bussièrre on tiny road. At T-junction, turn left to re-join the route de la Wantzenau going right.

La Wantzenau
⊟ Hotels: Hotel le Moulin de la Wantzenau (M–H), I impasse du Moulin, 67610 la Wantzenau, 88 96 27 83, old mill with garden; Hotel Relais de la Poste (M–H), 21 rue du Général de Gaulle, 88 96 20 64, old inn.

☒ Au Soleil, Restaurant Schaeffer; I quai Bateliers, 88 96 20 29.

La Wantzenau – Dalhunden
(18 km/11 miles)

There should be a route to Kilstett, but it is not easy to find. Alternatively, cross level-crossing to D468, turn right and cross back again to **Kilstett** and **Gambsheim**. Go right on D94.

⏍ Detour to Barrage de Gambsheim (ships' lock) on Rhine. Go right on D2, directions 'Achern' and 'Allemagne'.

Continue straight on on D29 to **Offendorf** and **Hertisheim**. Carry on on D468 and D737.

Dalhunden
⊟ Hotels: Hotel la Couronne (M), 24 route du Rhin, 67770 Sessenheim, 88 86 97 16.

Dalhunden – Soufflenheim
(8 km/5 miles)

Continue on D737. Turn away from the Rhine and go left over the river Moder. Cross railway.

Sessenheim

🛏 Hotels: La Croix d'Or (M), I rue Goethe, 67770 Sessenheim, 88 86 97 32.

✗ Auberge au Boeuf, 88 86 97 14, pretty restaurant and Goethe museum.

Cross motorway and railway and continue on D737.

Soufflenheim
Pottery town, with oven ware.

✗ Le Pichet, 88 86 66 79.

🔄 **Haguenau** (14 km/8½ miles) if needed for accommodation, etc.

🛏 Hotels: Hotel les Augustins (M), 6a rue de l'Etoile, 67500 Haguenau, 88 73 51 52.

✗ Barberousse, 8 place Barberousse, 88 73 31 09, recommended by Michelin as good value.

Day 3
Soufflenheim – Wissembourg
(30 km/18½ miles)

Soufflenheim – Betschdorf
(10 km/6 miles)

Take the D344 through the Forêt de Haguenau.

Betschdorf
Pottery village with decorative pottery; pottery museum, fine church with early murals.

🛏 Hotels: Hotel la Couronne (L), 28 rue du Docteur Deutsch, 67660 Betschdorf, 88 54 42 49. Chambres d'hôtes: Mme Joelle Krumeich, 88 54 40 56, speaks English and Christian Krumeich is a potter.

✗ Au Cygne, 88 54 42 43.

Betschdorf – Hunspach
(8 km/5 miles)

After detour through village, return to D344 and go north towards Soultz and **Kuhlendorf**. Flowery village with half-timbered church. Turn left on D28 to **Hohwiller.** Flowery village and church with early murals. Turn right on to D199 and continue to **Hermerswiller**. Turn right on D52 to **Hoffen**. A designated 'pretty village'. See town hall, old mills, linden tree. Turn left under railway and main road, then right on D76.

Hunspach
Another 'pretty village'.

🛏 Chambres d'hôtes: Sylvie Heiby, Maison Ungerer, 88 80 59 39; Mme Lehmann, 88 80 42 25 (NOTE: neither available July or August).

🔄 Detour on D49 to Seebach, another pretty village.

🛏 Chambres d'hôtes: M. Daniel Trog, 88 94 74 99.

Hunspach – Wissembourg
(12 km/7½ miles)

🔄 Make short detour north on D249 towards Schoenenburg, to visit Maginot Line. Tours on Sundays only.

From Hunspach go north on D76 to **Bremmelbach**. Turn right into village. Turn left through village and right then left towards Cleebourg. Turn right.

Cleebourg
Alsace's old wine area with *cave co-operative* from 1946.

🛏 Hotels: Hotel Au Tilleul, 94 rue Principale, 67160 Wissembourg, 88 94 52 15, a pretty hotel which has been recommended. Chambres d'hôtes, Finck, 88 94 50 90. (At Drachenbronn, a ferme-auberge with beds: Moulin des Sept Fontaines, 89 94 50 90, has been recommended. Also at Birlenback, a ferme-auberge and riding centre, 88 80 48 76.)

Go left, then right on D77.

Rott
Another wine village.

🛏 Hotels: Hotel la Cave de Cleebourg (M), route de Lobsann-Rott, 67160 Wissembourg, 88 94 52 18.

Carry on along D77.

Wissembourg
Northern capital. See abbey, churches, fortifications, Maison d'Ami Fritz, etc.

🛏 Hotels: Hotel la Walck (M–H), 2 rue de la Walck, 67160 Wissembourg, 88 94 06 44, comfortable mill outside fortifications; Hotel au Cygne (H), 3 rue du Sel, 88 54 38 28, old inn in centre.

✗ Restaurant de l'Ange, rue de la République, 88 94 12 11.

🔄 Detour east into forest for pretty **Lauter Valley** on German border.

Day 4
Wissembourg – Niederbronn-les-Bains
(35 km/22 miles)

Wissembourg – Lembach
(15 km/9½ miles)

Take the D3 and climb through rolling hills and steeply up to **Col du Pigeonniers**.

Europe's old cultural centre, Strasbourg.

Climbach

The hills here are under-cut by the Maginot Line, some parts of which are still used by the military.

🛏 Hotels: Hotel à l'Ange (L), 10 rue de Wissembourg, 67510 Lembach, 88 94 43 72; Hotel Cheval Blanc (M), 2 rue de Bitche, 88 94 41 95. Gîte d'étape: Mme Jautzy, 88 94 44 38, dorms and rooms.

Continue along D3 (hilly).

Lembach

See Maginot Line's *Four à Chaux*.

🛏 Hotels: Hotel Gimbelhof (LL), 67510 Lembach, 88 94 43 58; Hotel le Relais du Heimbach (M), 15 rue de Wissembourg, 88 94 43 46; Hotel Vosges du Nord (M), 59 route de Bitche, 88 94 43 41. Chambres d'hôtes: M. Lienhard, 88 94 40 11.

✖ Auberge du Cheval Blanc, 88 94 41 86, Michelin gourmet restaurant; l'Arbre Vert, 2 rue de Wingen, 88 94 42 56.

↻ Detour north-west along pretty valley on D3 and D925 to **Château Fleckenstein** on German border. Carry on to **Niedersteinbach**.

🛏 Hotels: Hotel Cheval Blanc (M), 27 route de Bitche, 67510 Lembach, 88 09 55 31, has a restaurant recommended by Michelin as good value. **Obersteinbach**, 2 km (1 mile) beyond on D3 has interesting museum of the border chateaux.

🛏 Hotels: Hotel Anthon (M), 67510 Lembach, 88 09 55 01, good food. Gîtes d'étapes: Mairie, 88 09 55 06; Mme Berring 88 09 55 26. Fermes-auberges: Domaine de Steinbech, 88 09 50 25, duck specialist.

Lembach – Neiderbronn-les-Bains

(20 km/12½ miles)
Follow the river Sauel on small forest road, then go away from river to **Mattstall** and **Langensoultzbach**. Go on and turn right just before **Nehwiller**.

↻ Detour to **Merkwiller-Pechelbronn** for museum and site of the world's earliest petrol exploitation. New experimental thermal power site and spa, to be major health and recreation centre.

Continue on D121 (hilly but mostly down).

Jaegerthal

Original de Dietrich factory. (For accommodation see Windstein below.)

↻ Detour north-west on to more castles including **Châteaux Falkenstein** and **Windstein**.

🛏 Hotels: Hotel Windstein (L), 8 route d'Obersteinbach, 67110 Niederbronn-les-Bains, 88 09 24 18; Hotel Jaegerthal (L), 1 route d'Obersteinbach, 88 09 02 40. Gîte d'étape: Mme Hausberger, Dambach, 88 09 20 6919.

From Jaegerthal take the D653.

Neiderbronn-les-Bains

Old spa. See baths, casino, Celtic water source, etc.

🛏 Hotels: Hotel de Hochscheldt (L), route de Jaegerthal,

67110 Niederbronn-les-Bains, 88 09 10 72; Hotel Muller (M), 16 avenue de la Libération, 88 63 38 38; Hotel Bristol (M), 4 place de l'Hotel de Ville, 88 09 61 44, very friendly, good food.

✖ Restaurant les Acacias, 35 rue des Acacias, 88 09 00 47, gourmet food.

Day 5
Niederbronn-les-Bains – La Petite-Pierre

(37 km/23 miles)

Niederbronn-les-Bains – Rothbach

(10 km/6 miles)

Go right on N62 and then left D28 in middle of town, out past de Dietrich factory. Continue on D28.

Oberbronn

Pretty with cobbled streets.

🛏 Gîte d'étape: Camping municipal, 88 09 71 96.

Go down through town. Continue on D28 (hilly) to **Zinswiller**, through old **Offwiller**.

Rothbach

Another old village.

Rothbach – Lichtenberg

(7 km/4½ miles)

Turn up off D28 on to RD198 and go along Rothbach valley. Turn left just before carp ponds, towards Lichtenberg, (the road rises all the way.) Carry straight on.

Lichtenberg

See castle and views.

🛏 Hotels: Hotel au Château (L), 4 place de l'Eglise, 67340 Ingwiller, 88 89 96 11; Hotel au Soleil (L), 2 place de l'Eglise, 88 89 96 13; Hotel au Boeuf Noir (L), 58 rue du château, 88 89 90 44. See also Reipertswiller below. Gîte d'étape: Mairie, 88 89 95 86.

↻ Detour north into glass-making area of Lorraine.

Lichtenberg – Wimmenau

(6.5 km/4 miles)
Go back down on RD198 and then turn left.

Reiperstswiller

🛏 Hotel la Couronne (M), rue de Wimmenau, 67340 Ingwiller, 88 89 96 21, comfortable, good food. Chambres d'hôtes, Schwebel, 88 89 96 17. Gîte d'étape: M. Wolff, 88 89 98 87.

Take D157 up through woods and down to the Moder Valley. Cross railway and turn right on D919.

Wimmenau

🛏 Hotels: Hotel l'Aigle (M), 55 rue Principale, 67290 Wingen-s-Moder, 88 89 70 41. Hotel Wenck (M), rue Principale, Wingen-s-Moder, 88 89 71 01.

Wimmenau – la Petite-Pierre
(13.5 km/8½ miles)

From D919 turn left by *Etang de Koosthal* on forest road. Wind round and up.

Erckartswiller
- Chambres d'hôtes: Helmlinger, 88 70 44 60.
- Restaurant Chez Anny

Take D813, then turn right on D7, continues hilly.

La Petite-Pierre
Pretty village, centre of good food and the Northern Vosges Regional Park. See fortifications, château, shared church, museums of seals and biscuit moulds.
- Hotels: Hotel des Vosges (M–H), 30 rue Principale, 67290 Wingen-s-Moder, 88 70 45 05, speaks English, includes *Winstub La Charrue* in *Cave*; Auberge d'Imsthal (M–H), (at **Etang d'Imsthal**, to south-east), 88 70 45 21, speaks English. Gîte d'étape: tel: Mairie 88 70 45 30.

Day 6
La Petite-Pierre – Saverne
(27 km/17 miles)

La Petite-Pierre – Graufthal
(8 km/5 miles)

Go down on D178, through the forest past the fish ponds. Turn right on D122.

Eschbourg
- Hotels: Hotel au Cheval Blanc (L), 67320 Eschbourg, 88 70 17 11; Hotel au Vieux Moulin (M), 67320 Drulingen, 88 70 17 28.

Continue on D122.

Graufthal
See troglydytic houses.

Graufthal – Dossenheim-s-Zinsel
(10 km/6 miles)

Return east on D122 down Zinsel valley through **Oberhof**, then turn left on D133.

Dossenheim-s-Zinsel
- You can do a long detour (26 km/16 miles) round an interesting collection of villages at the foot of the Vosges. Turn left on D14 to **Neuwiller-lès-Saverne** with its fortifications, churches and château.
- Hotels: Hotel au Chasseur (M), 8 rue du 22 Novembre, 67330 Bouxwiller, 88 70 33 19; Hotel Du Herrenstein (M), 20 rue Général Koenig, 88 70 00 53. Carry on along D14 to **Weiterswiller**.
- Hotels: Hotel Relais Irlandais, 7 rue du Château d'Eau, 67340 Ingwiller, 88 89 42 60. Take D56 to **Ingwiller**, an old village. See church, synagogue, botanic walk, Hoki shoe factory.
- Chambres d'hôtes: M. Ehrhardt, 88 89 61 86.

Go along D106 via **Uttwiller** to **Bouxwiller**, a wonderful old village with Jewish museum.
- Hotels: Hotel Au Soleil (L), 71 Grand-Rue, 67330 Bouxwiller, 84a Grand-Rue, 88 70 70 06; Hotel Heintz (L), 88 70 72 57. Take D17 to **Kirrwiller**.
- Restaurant/nightclub Adam-Meyer, 20 rue de Hochfelden, 88 70 71 81. Return to Dossenheim-s-Zinsel.

Dossenheim-s-Zinsel – Saverne
(9 km/6 miles)

Take D219.

Ernolsheim-lès-Saverne
- Ferme-auberge: M. Clauss, 88 70 01 63.

Turn right on D219.

St-Jean-Saverne
- Hotels: Hotel Kleiber (M), 37 Grand-Rue, 67700 Saverne, 88 91 11 82, good food.

Turn left and cross the motorway to **Monswiller** and follow canal right.

Saverne
Château des Rohan (Bishops Palace) museums, château, church, small machine factories, Karlsbrau brewery. Centre of good food. (Glass-engraver, Norbert Carabin, 2 quai du château.)
- Hotels: Hotel Boeuf Noir (M), 22 Grand-Rue, 67700 Saverne, 88 91 10 53, with restaurant recommended by Michelin as good value.
- Winstub Taverne Katz, 80 zone Piétonne, 88 71 16 56, good food, in historic building.

Day 7
Saverne – Molsheim
(41 km/25½ miles)

Saverne – Hengwiller
(10 km/6 miles)

- You can do a detour of 11 km (7 miles) along the towpath of Canal Marne-Rhine to **Lutzelbourg**. See the castle above. From there you can take a three-hour boat excursion (200F), food included, through ship-lift and tunnel.

- Detour along to **Haut Barr** (5 km/3 miles), 458 m (1502 ft) high. See château, views, Chappe telegraph. Return on D102 to re-join the route at **Haegen**.

From Saverne, cross canal and take D102 to **Haegen**. Bear left.

Thal-Marmoutier
- Chambres d'hôtes: Couvent Soeurs Franciscaines, 88 91 18 16.

Follow directions Marmoutier through **Sindelsberg**.

Marmoutier
See abbey-church with old tombs, fifteenth-century triptych in cemetery, chapel, and folk museum.

- Hotels: Hotel à la Couronne (L), 1 rue du Gal de Lattre-Tassigny, 67440 Marmoutier, 88 70 60 32; Hotel aux Deux Clefs (M), 30 rue du Général Leclerc, 88 70 61 08.

Go right on small road D229 to **Dimbsthal**, then bear right on D117.

Hengwiller
Lovely old village.

Hengwiller – Wasselone
(11 km/7 miles)

Turn left on tiny road.

Birkenwald
See château and old church.

- Hotels: Hotel des Vosges (L), 59 rue Principale, 67440 Marmoutier, 88 70 61 06; Hotel au Chasseur (M), 8 rue de Cimitière, 88 70 61 32.

Go straight on tiny road, rising through forest.

Allenwiller
See church. Turn right on D817 (still hilly).

Romanswiller
See church, château, mills.

- Chambres d'hôtes: M. Bochart, 88 87 22 49 at **Cosswiller** (to south).

Go through village bearing right on on D224.

Wasselonne
See fortifications and castle.

- Hotels: Hotel a l'Etoile (L), 1 place du Maréchal Leclerc, 67310 Wasselonne, 88 87 03 02; Hotel Au Saumon (L), 69 rue du Général de Gaulle, 88 87 01 83 good food; Hotel le Relais de Wasselonne (M), route de Romanswiller, 88 87 29 10; Hotel le Cerf (H), 67520 Marlenheim, 88 87 52 73, at **Marlenheim** (pretty village to south-east), with Michelin gourmet restaurant.

Wasselonne – Molsheim
(20 km/12½ miles)

Take D75.

Westhoffen
A fortified village and important Jewish settlement. See château, June cherry festival. Continue on D75 up out of town into vineyards and bear right to **Balbronn**, whose synagogue is to be moved to Israel. Turn left on D275 down to **Bergbieten**, then go on up to **Danglosheim** and turn left on D275 to T-junction and then right on main road D422.

Soultz-les-Bains
- Chambres d'hôtes: Schmitt, Ferme de Biblenhot, 88 36 21 09.

Go left in village on D45.

Wolxheim
An old wine village with canal.

Continue on D45 to **Ergersheim**, then go right on main road D30 and follow the Bruche past **Dachstein**. Go into charming little fortified village. See Château de Turkheim. Continue on D30.

Molsheim
Fortified town with bishops palace, Jesuits College. See Bugatti's museum. Wine centre.

- Hotels: Hotel Cheval Blanc (L), 5 place de l'Hotel de Ville, 67120 Molsheim, 88 38 16 87; Hotel Bugatti (M), rue de la Commanderie, 88 38 51 59, outside centre, big modern. Chambres d'hôtes: M. Munch, 88 49 34 39 (or ring restaurant), very comfortable, good value for money.
- ✗ l'Auberge de la Chartreuse, 88 38 30 97, M. Munch as above, just off central square.

You can either make Day 8 your last day or extend the trip to twelve days.

Day 8
Molsheim – Strasbourg Airport
(14 km/9 miles)

Return along the Bruche towpath.

Ernolsheim-s-Bruche
- Chambres d'hôtes: M. Reibel (M), 88 96 04 32, in château-farm.

Continue along the towpath to Hangenbieten and the Airport. For hotels see Entzheim on Day 1.

Day 8
Molsheim – Andlau
(27 km/17½ miles)

Molsheim – Rosheim
(11 km/7 miles)

Go west along the Bruche valley on D30.

Mutzig
See château, beer factory.

- Hotels: Hotel Felsbourg (L), 21 rue avenue Général de Gaulle, 67190 Mutzig, 88 38 13 28.
- For those who like something more strenuous, make a detour further up valley to **Dinsheim**.
- Chambres d'hôtes: Wetta, 88 50 03 79. Then turn right up the Hasel Valley on D218 to **Oberhaslach**.
- Chambres d'hôtes: M. Andre, 88 50 91 48.

Molsheim, where Bugatti lived and died.

Carry on to **Château** and **Cascade du Nideck**. You can go even further to **Wangenbourg**, with its castle.
- 🛏 Hotels: Hotel Parc (M), 39 rue Général de Gaulle, 67710 Wangenbourg, 88 87 31 72, with restaurant recommended by Michelin as good value.
  (NOTE: You can make this detour from **Haut Barr** near Saverne, and come down to **Molsheim** via the Bruche Valley, but you will miss all the lovely little villages in the Vosges foothills.)

From **Mutzig** take D392 under railway, and go through **Hermolsheim** to **Dorlisheim**. Turn sharp right inside village and cross main road N420.

Rosheim
Pretty old double fortified village with old abbey, lovely church, and Norman house.
- 🛏 Hotels: Hotel Alpina (L), 39 rue du Lion, 67560 Rosheim, 88 50 49 30; Hostellerie du Rosenmeer et Winstub (M–H), 45a avenue de la Gare, 88 50 43 29. Chambres d'hôtes: Mme Ichtertz, 88 50 44 53.

Rosheim – Ottrott
(5.5 km/3½ miles)

Continue on D35, the Wine Route, through hills and orchards, Vosges ahead, all the way.

Boersch
Another old fortified village. See early church frescos. Many wine *caves* to visit all along the Wine Route, or stay with them (*see chambres d'hôtes below*).
- 🛏 Chambres d'hôtes: Mme Richert, 88 95 81 45; M. Muller, 88 95 82 23, *vigneron*; Mme Huck, 88 95 82 31, *vigneron*.
- ✗ Restaurant le Chatelain, 41 rue Monseigneur Barth, 88 95 83 33, expensive, pretty place.
- 🖄 Detour down to **Obernai** (4 km/2½ miles) on main road. Delightful old fortified village where Alsatian artist Henri Loux came from. Many tourists.
- 🛏 Hotels: Hotel-restaurant de la Cigogne (L), 49 rue du Général Gourad, 67210 Obernai, 88 95 52 35, good food; Hotel du Parc (H), route d'Ottrott, 88 95 50 08.

Continue along D35 to **St Leonard** a tiny fortified village. See Spinder's wood-marquetry workshops, and other artisans.

Ottrott
Old village with unusual red wine. (Can detour up to Mont Ste Odile, but easier ride from Andlau.)
- 🛏 Hotels: Hotel Ami Fritz (M), 8 rue des Châteaux, 67530 Ottrott-haut, 88 95 80 81, pretty, with a restaurant recommended by Michelin as good value; Hotel Domaine le Moulin (M), 32 route de Klingenthal, 88 95 87 33, quiet, pretty site; Hotel les Châteaux (H), 11 rue des Châteaux, 88 95 81 54. Chambres d'hôtes: M. Ruthmann, 88 95 81 52; Mme Hoffbeck, 88 95 81 72; Mme Maurer, 88 95 80 12; M. Schwendimann, 88 95 80 74.

Ottrott – Andlau
(11 km/7 miles)

Continue on D35, through vines and orchards.

Heiligenstein
- 🛏 Hotels: Hotel Relais du Klevener (L–M), 51 rue Principale, 67140 Barr, 88 08 05 96, pretty. Chambres d'hôtes: M. Bossert, 88 08 14 05; M. Boch, 88 08 97 30; M. Ruff, 88 08 10 81; M. Vogel, 88 08 94 77; M. Boch, 88 08 41 26.

Continue along the rolling Wine Route.

Barr
Châteaux, Musée de la Folie Marco.
- 🛏 Hotels: Hotel Du Parc (L), 11 rue du Général Vandenberg, 67140 Barr, 88 08 92 91; Hotel Maison Rouge (M), avenue Gare, 88 08 84 40; Hotel la Couronne (M), 4 rue des Boulangers, 88 08 25 83, small; Hotel du Manoir (M), rue St Marc, 88 08 03 40, old manor, no restaurant. Chambres d'hôtes: M. Beyler, 88 08 03 23; M. Bachert, 88 08 95 89, *vigneron*; M. Ball, 88 08 10 20, with food. Gîtes d'étape: M. Bachert, 88 08 95 89.

Continue on Wine Route (or GR5 through vineyards).

Mittelbergheim
Old village. See forge, church with frescos, *caves*.
- 🛏 Hotels: Hotel Winstub Gilg (M), 1 route du Vin, 67140 Barr, 88 08 91 37, good food.

Take D62 (rather undulating) or D425 (easier).

Andlau
- 🛏 Hotels: Hotel Relais du Sorbier (L), Sperbaechel, 67140 Andlau, 88 08 33 38; Hotel Kastelberg (M–H), rue du Général Koenig, 88 08 97 83.
- ✗ Restaurant au Raison d'Or, rue Principale, 88 08 93 54.

Day 9
Andlau – Otrott via Mont Ste Odile
(27 km/17 miles)

- 🖄 Detour up to **Mont Ste Odile**, round trip 20 km (12½ miles). (NOTE: this is a long slow climb to 760m [2493 ft].)

Take D425 along the Andlau valley.

Le Hohwald
- 🛏 Chambres d'hôtes: Relais du Sorbier, Mme Lieber, 88 08 33 38; Lilsbach, M. Romain, 88 08 31 74. Gîte d'étape: tel Mairie, 88 08 33 47.

Take advantage of being in the Vosges to try a farm meal, *marcaire*, in a ferme-auberge.
- ✗ Fermes-Auberges: Wittertal-Hof, M. Hazelmann, 88 08 31 24, has beds too; Lindenhof, M. Deissler, 88 08 31 98; Kreutweg, M. Conrad, 88 08 32 84.

Take D426.

Mont Ste Odile
See tomb of patron saint of Alsace. Chapels with wood marquetry by Spindler, (*see St Leonard workshop above*), sacred fountain, 11 km (7 miles) of old Celtic fortifications called the Pagan Walls, busy in summer.

🏨 Hotels: Hotel du Mont Ste Odile (L), 67530 Ottrott, 88 95 80 65, book three months in advance at least.

🔲 Detour 22 km (13½ miles) over high **Champs du Feu** plateau for moving memorial to German atrocities at **Struthof** concentration camp.

Return from Mont Ste Odile on D426 past **Château d'Ottrott**.

Ottrott
For accommodation see above.

Day 10
Ottrott – Sélestat
(28 km/17½ miles)

Ottrott – Eichhoffen
(10 km/6 miles)

Continue on Wine Route as before via **Barr**, but bypassing **Andlau**.

Eichhoffen
Important old village with ancient chapel. See storks' nest on tannery chimney on D425.

Eichhoffen – Dambach-la-Villé
(9.5 km/6 miles)

Carry straight on on D35.

Itterswiller
🏨 Hotels: Hotel La Cave aux Souveniers-Kobloth (M), 73 route du Vin, 67140 Barr, 88 85 50 68; Hotel Arnold (H), 98 route du Vin, 88 85 50 58. Chambres d'hôtes: M. Hoffman, 88 85 52 89, *vigneron*; M. Hungerbuhler, 88 85 50 57, *vigneron*.
Continue on D35 undulating through **Nothalten**.

Blienschwiller
🏨 Hotels: Hotel Winzenberg (M), 46 route du Vin, 67650 Blienschwiller, 88 92 62 77.
Go right and left through town and up.

Dambach-la-Villé
Pretty Medieval fortified city. See ancient chapel.
🏨 Hotels: Hotel aux Deux Clefs (L), 1 rue des Ramparts, 67650 Dambach-la-Villé, 88 92 40 11; Hotel au Raisin d'Or (M), 28 bis rue Clémenceau, 88 92 48 66. Chambres d'hôtes: M. Hauller, 88 92 41 19; M. Nartz, 88 92 41 11. Gîte d'étape: Mme Hausberger, 88 09 20 69.

Dambach-la-Villé – Sélestat
(8.5 km/5½ miles)

Continue on Wine Route out of village, then first right onto small road in vineyards.

Dieffenthal
Pretty old wine village.
🏨 Hotels: Hotel les Châteaux (H), chemin de Scherwiller, 67650 Dambach-la-Villé, 88 92 49 13.
Take the first right out of the village and return to Wine Route.

Scherwiller
Old village with linden trees on canal, castle above.
🏨 Chambres d'hôtes: M. Dillenseger, 88 92 87 49.
Turn left at T-junction in village. Go past one moat and continue to second moat. Turn right over it, directions Chapel Wolfgang. Go left towards Sélestat.

🔲 Detour up **Val-de-Villé** and **Geissen** towards Villé. Here *eau de vie* is made from all sorts of wild fruits: pears, cherries, plums, and wild raspberries.

Go on under motorway to city.

Sélestat
An elegant old city. See Cathedral St Foy, St Georges church, other fine old buildings, humanist library.
🏨 Hotels: Hotel de l'Ill (L), 13 rue des Bateliers, 67600 Sélestat, 88 92 91 09; Hotel Vallant (M–H), place de la République, 88 92 09 46; Hotel Abbaye de la Pommeraie (H), 8 avenue Foch, 88 92 07 84. Chambres d'hôtes: M. Heintz, 88 82 51 04.
❌ Restaurant à la Vieille Tour, 8 rue de la Jauge; Restaurant Edel, 7 rue Serruriers, 88 92 86 55, Michelin gourmet restaurant; au Pied de Boeuf, 17 rue Poincaré, 88 92 11 29.

Day 11
Sélestat – Haut Kœnigsbourg – Sélestat
(30 km/19 miles)

Sélestat – Kintzheim
(9.5 km/6 miles)

To avoid negotiating main roads return to Scherwiller. At D35 turn left along Wine Route. Cross main road N59.

Châtenois
Old village. See church.
🏨 Hotels: Hotel Beysang (M), 67730 Châtenois, 88 82 29 48; Hotel Donteville (M), 94 route de Maréchal Foch, 88 92 02 54. Chambres d'hôtes: Mme. Idoux, 88 82 06 75; M. Sonntag, 88 82 19 57. Gîte d'étape: Mme Wassler, 88 92 26 20.
Continue on D35, along Wine Route.

Kintzheim

⊟ Hotels: Hotel au deux Clefs (L), route de Général de Gaulle, 67600 Sélestat, 88 82 31 42, pretty; Hotel Parc au Cigognes (M), route de Sélestat, 88 92 05 94.

Kintzheim – Haut Kœnigsbourg

(6 km/4 miles)

Turn left up D159 towards Haut Kœnigsbourg. It is a steady climb.

🔲 Detours: **Volérie d'Aigle** (exciting eagle display) on road up to Haut Kœnigsbourg in ruined castle; **Montagne des Singes** (apes) further up along same road; and **Parc des Cigognes** (stork breeding centre) is on the route back towards Sélestat.

Haut Kœnigsbourg
Fairy-tale castle 720 m (2362 ft). Good views, very crowded in summer.

Haut Kœnigsbourg – St Hippolyte

(6.5 km/4 miles)

Return on tiny road D1b¹ to Wine Route.

St Hippolyte
Pretty medieval city, belonged to Dukes of Lorraine.
⊟ Hotels: Hotel à la Vignette (L), 66 route du Vin, 68590 St Hippolyte, 89 73 00 17; Hotel au Ducs de Lorraine (H), 16 route du Vin, 89 73 00 09.

St Hippolyte – Sélestat

(8 km/5 miles)

Turn left on D1b¹ and left again.

Orschwiller
Old village. See customs house.
⊟ Hotels: Hotel au Vieux Tonneau (L), 5 route du Vin, 67600 Sélestat, 88 82 03 51, looks pretty; Hotel Guillaume II (M), 20 Grand-Rue, 88 82 10 92; Hotel du Haut Kœnigsbourg (M), P.B. 150, 88 82 50 04, good food. Chambres d'hôtes: M. Schwetterle, 88 92 11 31, *vigneron*.
Return to D1b and take D210 to join D159. Turn right on it and take D210 motorway and main road to Sélestat.

Day 12
Sélestat – Strasbourg

(55 km/34 miles)

Sélestat Ⓐ² – Sand

(23 km/14½ miles)

Return through the flat Ried. Take D21 to **Mutters-holtz**, (Remy Meyer's farm sells excellent cheese).
✖ Restaurant la Couronne, rue Sélestat, 67600 Baldenheim, 88 85 32 33 to the south on D21, Michelin gourmet restaurant.

Turn left on D211 to **Hilsenheim**. Go through village and bear right at fork on D682 to **Witternheim**. Turn right and then left on D82 to **Rossfeld**. Then bear right on D782 to **Herbisheim**. Turn left on to D5, then right on to D282 and cross river Ill.

Sand
⊟ Hotels: Hotel la Charrue (M), 4 rue du 1er Decembre, 67230 Benfeld, 88 74 42 66.

Sand – Nordhouse

(8 km/5 miles)

Sand
Continue on D282 to Matzenheim. Turn right on D288 through Osthouse.

Erstein
See Erstein nature reserve along the Rhine.
⊟ Hotels: Hotel à l'Agneau (L), 50 rue du 28 Novembre, 67150 Erstein, 88 98 02 12.
Continue on D288.

Nordhouse
You should actually bypass the main village.

Nordhouse Ⓐ – Strasbourg Airport

(23 km/14½ miles)

Cross motorway on D207 to **Hindisheim**. Continue on D207, bearing right and left. Then turn left on D161 to **Blaesheim**. Turn right on D84 to **Geispolsheim**, and left on D221 to **Entzheim**. (*See Day 1 for accommodation.*) This is the back of the airport and you have to make a tour to get into it. Turn right on D392, then left on main road D400, take the slip road right and turn left under D400, following the railway right to the airport entrance to the left.

Ⓐ To Strasbourg city centre (17 km/10½ miles). From **Nordhouse**, turn right on D788. Cross the Canal Rhône-Rhine and turn left on D468 to **Plobsheim** and **Hetzlader Farms**. Turn left towards Eschau, cross the canal and follow tarmacked towpath right along the tree-lined canal all the way into the city. (Work is in progress on tarmacking the towpath all the way south.) Go through **Illkirck-Graeffenstaden**.

✖ Restaurant Au Foyer des Pecheurs, chemin du Routoir, 88 66 14 85, a Michelin-designated gourmet restaurant.

Ⓐ² If you have more time you can continue down through the pretty villages of the Wine Route from St Hippolyte through Haut Rhin, into the little known area of carp-fish lakes known as **Sundgau**, to finish at **Basel** just inside Switzerland. On the Wine Route do not miss **Bergheim**, **Ribeauville**, **Kayserberg**, **Turkenheim**, **Ruffach**, **Guebwiller**. After this cross through the plains via **Wittelsheim** to **Altkirch** (*capital of the Sundgau*), then follow small roads towards **Basel**. Its international airport is just before the border.

CHAPTER FOUR

Heart of France

From Dijon and back via the Morvan

From Dijon this route crosses the plain to begin with a taste of some of the fine wines that have given this part of Burgundy its name of the Côte d'Or. It climbs to the historic city of Autun and crosses the Morvan, the heart of Burgundy. At Clamecy it starts to circle round to the north-east past the hilltop basilica of Vézelay and follows the valley of the river Cousin to Avallon, from where it continues through pastoral country past the romantic town of Semur-en-Auxois and hills where Caesar fought his decisive battles against the Gauls. The road is peaceful through the river valley of the Oze, descending to the Canal de Bourgogne and returning along it to Dijon.

Burgundy has a history which stretches far back and it was once a centre of power and culture. Indeed the spiritual and economic power of the Abbey of Cluny extended far beyond the village where it began, across Europe and brought about an extraordinary flowering of art and Romanesque architecture. It is this kind of past that leads present-day Burgundy to define itself as more than a region, more 'a state of mind' or, as one woman put it to me, 'Burgundy has heart but no borders. It is old France, a way of life, of enjoying things without stress – culture, countryside, fine food and wine.'

I began my journey at Dijon, the centre of both mustard and wine, which would be no better to get in and out of than other large cities but for one thing: the Canal de Bourgogne passes through the town and then comes so close to the small airport that within a mile you can be on the towpath heading south through the plain towards the river Saône. There, the junction town of St-Jean-de-Losne is a major inland port with bargees in blue jackets and peaked caps greeting their friends in bars or eating solitary Saturday night dinners in the most agreeable Auberge de la Marine.

Generally the Bressian plains are intensively cultivated and uninteresting. Upland Burgundy, though, looks quite reasonable even under intensive cultivation because the shape of the land sometimes gives it an almost sculptural quality, but a plain is a plain, and not even the Abbey of Cîteaux compensates for that. The Cistercian movement was founded here in 1098 as a return to the traditions of St Benedict, in particular following his insistence on the importance of manual labour. Always noted for their work on the land, the white monks founded the vineyard of Clos de Vougeot on the slopes some kilometres distant, and became great farmers, credited with inventing not only their own Cîteaux cheese which is rare and excellent, but also the more generally known Epoisses.

It is best to cut away from the canal early on at Longecourt-en-Plaine, whose château can be seen in the distance. When you get to its gates in the middle of the village you will be greeted by the geese on the green, unless they have been eaten since I passed by, and can cross the plain among woods and fields till you come to Vougeot and Vosne-Romanée.

Cycling on the Côte de Nuits is like a trip down an expensive wine list – a litany of labels few people can afford but which, repeated over and over, become names of legend: Gevrey-Chambertin, Nuits-St-Georges, Santenay, Pommard, Aloxe-Corton. It feels slightly strange. Not that the Dijon-end of the vineyards looked at all legendary. On the road out of Dijon at Marsannay there are suburban villas on one side of the road and vines on the other.

Like Cîteaux Abbey, the world's most exclusive vineyards do not breathe past glories: rather, they breathe money, successful commercialism and sometimes a feeling of the *nouveau riche*. In winter the vineyards are as stark as cemeteries, walled and gated; the great names hanging over the gate-posts like the names of the dead. There is something Dickensian about the formal enclosure of such tiny but immensely valuable pieces of land, and the fact that many of the *clos* are ruinous only adds to the bizarre effect.

Even stranger was the aftermath of the St Vincent celebrations in one village. He is the patron saint of wine growers, and his *fête* at the end of January brings in many people to drink and buy (there is always something for sale on the Côtes de Nuits). Coming through one village, it was suddenly spring, a blossoming of paper flowers – bright puce blooms on conifers, elaborate poppies on a creeper, yellow blossom on fruit-tree branches that would be bare for many weeks to come. There were figures, too – at first you thought them villagers working in the fields, then they turned out to be dolls.

In the bar of the Hotel de l'Etoile (literally so, since one star is what it had) in the centre of Nuits-St-Georges where I chose an attic room with no view, except stars, the patron served a good glass of Nuits-St-Georges for 14F: and added not only cassis to the delicious white Bourgogne Aligote to make kir, but also offered peach or raspberry liqueur (the peach being the better). There is a local industry making these, a hangover from the days of the phylloxera when local winegrowers, whose vines were destroyed, turned to the growing of blackcurrants and the making of cassis. Kir was popular in the early 1900s, and is named after Canon Kir, a celebrated mayor of Dijon, who served it at official receptions. It is one of those simple things that are made or marred by the quality of the ingredients and the hand that pours them. If you have had your fill of cheap white over-sweetened with cheap blackcurrant, you may find that a kir made in Burgundy itself restores your respect for the mixture.

Nuits-St-Georges is the heart of the Côtes de Nuits, which lies north of the Côtes de Beaune, with the Hautes-Côtes above both. It is an overgrown village with something of the contrasts of a gold-rush town between those whose claim is rich; those who deal and those who have no land or the wrong land and are hangers-on. The whole area is a patchwork of parcels of land, like claims. As with prospecting, chance has ruled which land bears gold and which does not, for the soil varies greatly here and the line of an *appellation controlée* may be drawn between apparently identical vines, with one side said to be worth a million pounds an acre and the other a fraction of that. You do not need a big claim to become rich. Not far away, the legendary Romanée-Conti comes from no more than four and a half acres owned by two proprietors, whereas one Nuits-St-Georges family owns 101 hectares (250 acres). Should land be for sale, it is not for sale to anybody. In one celebrated case the central government itself ruled against a Japanese offer – the minister was Burgundian.

What I found striking was the way in which wine permeates local culture, with the most ordinary people as discriminating as the most expert British wine taster. I had dinner at the Hotel des Cultivateurs, only a few yards up the road, in the company of a bottle of Gevrey-Chambertin, two travelling champagne corkers, and a workman who told us that he had trodden the grapes only the year before.

'Naked,' he said. What you wear for grape-treading was something I had never thought about before, but given that you are not walking on a thin layer but floundering around in a vat, nudity was only logical.

'No women allowed in. Hard work it is, hot because of the fermentation, and you get grapes stuck everywhere,' he said, and told us where. 'You have to watch out too, 'cos of the gas.'

'Gas?'

'Carbon dioxide lying at the bottom of the vats. Never work alone: slip and it's a quick death.' It all added a new flavour to the contents of my glass. The champagne corkers bought a round of ratafia, sweet fortified wine; I bought a round of *marc de Bourgogne*, and was late to bed.

Next day, trekking through the wine cellars which were part of the family estates of the Comtesse de Loisy, I saw the rope above the vats to which workers could hook themselves for safety. At seventy-six, with only one daughter interested in running the remaining 7-acre vineyard, the Comtesse had given up most of the cellars, but nothing could diminish the authority of her steps as she showed me her former empire. An intelligent and capable woman, she had a matter-of-fact but deeply-polished courtesy, and it was easy to see that she had been a beauty. She had spent her life with wine and perhaps owed her life to it, she said:

'When I was three there was a great typhoid epidemic, but my nurse, who had worked on the battlefield in the First War, boiled the water for my bottle and mixed Burgundy with it to be sure. As a baby I knew I lived in France, and in Burgundy. We made wine in my Burgundy and were north of Beaune: south of Beaune was different. But really, I think my family was here forever.'

At the bottom of the vine-slopes there are rather too many means of transport for cycling comfort – motorway, railway and another large road. The only reasonably coherent route to Beaune runs close to the railway. Other options are the working roads that run through the vineyards. For the energetic a hillier but much prettier route up a wooded valley through Arcenat (where they grow blackcurrants) provides the most agreeable route into this rich and much-visited town, whose centre nevertheless remains untouched within its ring road and ramparts.

From Beaune you move into the Haute Côte de Beaune and some of the prettiest vineyards with some of the most delicious white wines. I ended my day at Meursault.

I was woken by the cawing of rooks: and the world was golden, with yellow light streaming through my window in the Hotel des Arts. Then they switched off the street lamps and the sun went out: the world became grey and cold, with snow clinging to the tall roofs of the houses opposite. Nor was my accommodation luxurious, with a shower into which the human form of a certain size could be insinuated only with difficulty, and a crack in the corner through which water was working itself into the fabric of the building on a seek-and-destroy mission. Nor did the doors wholly meet, so that more water sprayed over the lavatory, a patent *broyeur* whose like could be heard all over the house making gastro-mechanical noises, to which my creaking furniture was an accompaniment. But I would not have changed that one-star hotel for a whole constellation of comforts: for not only was it friendly, but it had also cooked me an excellent meal the night before with *jambon persillé* that tasted of ham, wine jelly and parsley; *boeuf Bourgignon* cooked in the local wine; good local cheese and pears in wine with real blackcurrants, as a piece of real stalk witnessed. It all seemed to me a proper traditional French sense of priorities – one to which I was happy to subscribe. On top of that was the golden memory of the dearest half-bottle I have ever bought in my life – at 160F, 20F more than the cost of my room. The '89 Latour Labille Meursault had turned out to be a complex and thrilling experience down to the last ravishing drops, a wine to remember and by which to judge others. So I remembered it, and was content.

I left the Hotel des Arts in the direction of the rooks, who had taken over the best horse chestnuts in the garden of a pretty château called 'B' – for that letter was cut into the stone above the windows. *Boulanger, viticulteur* was written up before the long outbuilding opposite with its patterned Burgundian roof in gold, green, dark-blue and red. It seemed that every other house was a *viticulteur* with *vins fins*, *grands vins* and *premiers crus*. I passed one street called *rue de la Goutte d'Or* and thought it well-named.

There was hardly a soul on the road that cold morning as I rode out of Meursault, except a solitary north African riding high above the big wheels of his vine tractor. Snow lay among the vines, on the roofs, piled in the gutters, the water of the stream unfrozen but frigid. It was a wet cold, for the thaw had begun: my wheels slipped on the slush, rustled through it almost as through leaves with a sound like crisps where they crushed a lump of still-frozen snow.

All over the vineyards were isolated outbreaks of activity – a solitary pruner here, a discussion there, a van parked far from the road – but there were so many thousands of rows of vines that everything else was insignificant. Like cloves in a giant pomander, vine stocks stretched uphill to where the rocks began, down to the distant whisper of the motorway, ahead as far as I could see: with here and there thin columns of

Not far to Santenay, but a long time to the wine harvest: winter at la Rochepot.

smoke rising. I passed a young man pruning and discovered the source: *a chaudron*, a portable incinerator made out of an old oil drum cut in half lengthways with the top put back on hinges as a pair of doors. Add a wheel and handles like a wheelbarrow and you can burn your prunings as you go, even in the rain, and warm your fingers occasionally at the same time. Mine were tingling, even inside thick gloves. Yet cold was not a problem, the vigneron said, the wet was the worst.

I came to Puligny-Montrachet – not the town which was still some way ahead, but its vines, which had a sign of their own. Here a fat pruner with a *chaudron* was attending a little yellow cultivator that puttered along the rows guided by the stems of the vines themselves.

Going past Chassagne-Montrachet with its small château roofed in dark blue with gold lozenges, I was reminded of those sunnier days by a heap of something like red peat lying by the roadside. It was dark and full of strands; the residue of the wine vats.

Nor is the centre of Santenay to be missed for its terribly French town square with its fountain, *mairie*, tricolours, massacred plane trees and a wonderful First World War memorial with a lady in flowing robes pointing heavenwards from the rock on which she is standing, that leaves you with the impression that the heroic soldier standing on the ground in front of her is a dwarf. Taking care to turn left over the railway as you go out of town, you can follow the canal to Cheilly-lès-Mararges and turn up the valley of the Cosanne, a small and tranquil river.

At Sampigny-lès-Mararges, I left the church bells behind me ringing out in celebration of lunch, passing into a country that was fields and old orchards, as well as Hautes Côtes de Beaune. By the time I had climbed to Nolay, with its wonderfully beamed covered market in the square and quaint half-timbered houses, I was at the start of an ascent that would take me to Autun and the wild pastoral of Morvan. If you want to see the picture-book château of la Rochepot do it first thing in the morning because it is quite a climb up and on busy roads.

The main road to Autun is hilly as well as busy. The best gradients are those of a dead railway which may one day be made into a recreational path – at Epinac they have already smoothed it out for walking and cycling – but for most of its length it is still a track-bed of chunky gravel which you might attempt on a mountain bike, but which I did not try.

From Nolay there are no more vines, but pastures full of the white Charolais beef cattle Burgundy is famous for. For the first time you are among the round-topped hills of Burgundy, though not yet among its streams. At first you are too occupied with the hefty uphills to notice a lot, but when you come to the high road that runs flat you find yourself in a green country so smoothly sculpted that it is like a human body. The valleys squeezed between slopes of field and forest give the highlands an intimate, romantic quality that is echoed in the round towers and turrets of ancient buildings, in the casual antiquity of the farms and mills, and in the jumbled streets of the villages.

Balconies, arches, shutters, self-important gateways, great beams, round towers, square towers, walls that make crannies with each other are the best of old Burgundy. But most striking of all are the roofs, lordly slopes of warm, weathered tiles, which will sometimes be patterned in greens, golds and blues in respectful imitation of the great Flemish-style roof of the Hotel-Dieu in Beaune. The best trees of Burgundy are stately – oaks in field and hedgerow with room to spread themselves, and horse chestnuts which are a favourite tree around farms and churches – more than once I came upon a stone cross by the roadside with chestnuts around it, and whether it was the stone or the flowering tree which was the Burgundian's homage to something greater than good living was difficult to say. Good things and a good humoured enjoyment of life appear to rise naturally from the soil of traditional Burgundy, as quality grows up seemingly without effort from the roots of its vines: and with it all a certain fantasy that makes its way into the pinnacles of the châteaux and the vines and roses on the yellow stone walls.

People usually think of the châteaux of the Loire as fairy-tale palaces, but they are a story of the rich, the great, the powerful – great chunks of privilege you are expected to admire. Burgundy, on the other hand, is full of little pieces of fairy-tale, casual history – museum pieces which nobody thought to clear away just because they happen to be old: a dovecote or a fortified tower in a working farm, and an extraordinary collection of old water systems which made me realize for the first time how much we lost when we put water into pipes. No one wants to carry buckets again, but the effort and care which people had to devote to water then made it valued indeed and a whole communal life flourished around it, like green plants by a spring. Something of this special relationship is still to be seen in Burgundy, where they happen to have left in place wells and water pumps of every description and whole collections of riverside wash houses.

Epinac's charms are other, being a small but long-established coal-mining and industrial town with some interesting industrial archaeology in the shape of the Tour Malakoff, a very advanced air extraction system for the mine, which worked from 1755 until 1966. Most of the mines and industry are further south at Le Creusot and Montceau-les-Mines, and this area continues unspoilt. Sully has a vast château which at the time of the Revolution was under threat of confiscation on the death of the Marquise, but was preserved for the family by the servants pickling the corpse of the old lady in alcohol and putting her back in black whenever anyone came to check. (This is of course unusual among the aristocracy, who if they are to be pickled generally prefer it to be during their lifetimes.)

I continued by a roundabout way to St-Forgeot – where the old coal tips were sprouting resilient new life – since it meant smaller roads and a grand entrance into Autun by the one Roman arch through which the road still passes.

Overleaf: Nolay, last stop on the Côte d'Or – the old halles.

SOUSCRIPTION PUBLIQUE
Avec le Concours
du
SOUVENIR·FRANÇAIS
1900

Autun was formerly Augustodunum, named after Augustus, who carried on from Caesar's victory over the Gauls by razing their capital Bibracte and building this new one, most of which of course is now underground as part of the layer cake of history, though what is left of the theatre is still large as well as impressive, with its semicircles of stone seats now looking out on to a football pitch. Autun is a little city devoted to its past and culture. The twelfth-century Romanesque cathedral of St-Lazaire is the magnificent high point of a town filled with antiquity and treasures, from jumbled medieval houses over whose garden gates you may see views of green hills beyond, to the classical square in the centre big enough to fight a battle on – and, indeed, its name is now the Champ de Mars and the college at one end, the Lycée Bonaparte is in memory of a former pupil.

Having work to do, I put up at la Tête Noir for a few days, a comfortable, slightly crumbly old hotel with a new patron who, when he has finished his twelve-hour day, goes home and reads recipes in search of dishes to enliven further the excellent cooking. Here in February, when there was hardly anyone but me travelling, the cheeseboard flowed with perishable delights and the great Burgundian pudding of soft cheese with cream and sugar was topped with delicious orange biscuits. Nor must one forget the main courses; the *salade fraîcheur* was a perfectly balanced assembly of lettuce, segments of (real) pink grapefruit, basil, mushrooms and avocado, with the dressing just right. It being that time of the year when you see people with carrier bags wandering the fields plucking at something invisible at ground level, *Pissenlit paysanne* was on the menu – dandelion salad with bacon bits, as was *oeufs à la meurette*, eggs poached in red wine and parsleyed ham pressed in a white wine jelly. The whole was completed with a celestial *marc de Borgogne*.

I took to crossing the road to the Café-Bar St Louis of an evening for an aperitif, where I met the man from the bike shop opposite and a selection of the cycling youth of Autun. They were far out of my class; not only in athleticism, for one of their bikes was worth over £2000. They were also agreeable to a foreigner who was obviously eccentric, but probably not actually dangerous.

At Autun you are at the gates of Morvan, which is a special place for the beauty of its landscape, its traditions and its spiritual importance, not simply to Burgundy, but to France as a whole. The cycling route only crosses the southern end of it, because – in the eternal trade-off between interest and gradient – Morvan is extremely and continually hilly, wonderful for the fit and energetic cyclist, but not to be undertaken lightly. However, the cycling route is not so fearsome, beginning in flat country below Autun and climbing at various gradients (but none absolutely ferocious) for almost 24 km (15 miles) to Mont Beuvray, after which life is easier – apart from climbing up to the little that remains visible of Bibracte, the capital of the most powerful of the Gaulish tribes, the Eduens. Chain your bike at the bottom and be prepared for a walk of over a mile which is often very, very steep. (Mont Beuvray has a one-way system, and the downward road which you hit earlier is more gradual.)

Is it worth it? Well, the hill certainly gives you a respect for the Celts, and so does the extent of what was once a town and is now mostly an overgrown archaeological site, with a few examples of original construction methods and excavation sites in clearings in the beech-forest. A stone marker and the usual orientation table rather spoil the stunning view south from the bare top at almost 800 m (2624 ft), while a tiny classical-style chapel dedicated to St Martin rather adds to the magic of the place. All around are the twisted traces of ancient hedges, beeches that were once bent down and woven basket-fashion in the Morvan tradition of hedging, now grown out into strange shapes.

Mostly what you climb for is an atmosphere and a memory. When Rome threatened, it was here that the Celtic tribes assembled to make Vercingetorix their leader. And after Caesar had won, he took up winter quarters here and began writing his 'Gallic Wars'. Years later came the Celtic climb-down to the new Roman capital: Bibracte crumbled, became overgrown and was forgotten so completely that scholars thought that it had been Autun. Today, the site has become a Celtic hot-spot, the most important Celtic archaeological site in Europe. Scholars from far and wide come to dig away at a heritage, most of which is still undisturbed, and in the new French enthusiasm for its Celtic roots, President Mitterrand's parting gift to his people was a declaration that the site was of national importance and the building of a Celtic museum at the bottom of the hill – one so prestigious that roads had to be moved to allow neighbouring communes to share in its glory. The idea was more or less the equivalent of building a tourist centre at Stonehenge – costing a mint, bringing thousands of visitors and their cars and threatening to destroy the magic it was supposed to celebrate. For that wooded mountainside is still something of a sacred place to the people of Morvan, Burgundians generally and present-day Celts.

After Mont Beuvray there are two choices, the easiest being to squander the height you have gained on what is mostly a long downhill ride to Moulins-Engilbert – a charming small town with some typically quirky Burgundian houses along the old walls. You then have a short 16 km (10 miles) up to Château-Chinon the following day – but at the end it is very much uphill. It is probably best, therefore, to turn off to Château-Chinon at le Puits. After the start, the road is mostly through woodland and you have a succession of lesser ups and downs to cope with, but 18 km (11 miles) sees you at your destination with no climb to tire you out at the end of a long day. If you find it too long, there are small places stay en route, at St-Léger-sous-Beuvray and les Buteaux.

Morvan has long been poor, with twelve people to the hectare when the national average is a hundred. Its population is one-fifth of the size it was in the last century. The people have a similar reputation to montagnards elsewhere – independent and dour in comparison with the happy-go-lucky lowlanders. They do not lightly cast away their traditions. I saw my first hint of that in Moulins-Engilbert, which is in lower Morvan, where there were wooden clogs in the window of the gardening shop. *Sabots*

Hand-picking for the best results: the Burgundy vendange.

were still much worn after the war, and people speak well of them and their warmth in winter. There are not many *sabotiers* today, but where you can get them they are still popular for gardening. I only saw *sabots* made of birch, which in the old days was the cheapest sort, with alder and elm mid-price and walnut the most expensive.

It is not only that Morvan itself has cared about preserving its culture, but it has been an inspiration to other parts of Burgundy, a Celtic breath to a smouldering fire. Often, as with any revival, outsiders have been involved, since they are the ones who have a fresh vision of what is at stake. I met one enthusiast, a folk-accordionist, who was a Dutchwoman. Els O'Sullivan described the revaluing of traditional things in the seventies and eighties as the recapturing of a way of living – not of life as it was, but of the solidarity. Of doing things together: 'Things have changed, but not changed.

Ostentatious roofs of the Côte d'Or, Aloxe-Corton.

I have a tape recorder now, but I still play in an oral tradition. I have no written music. People have to leave to get work, but the countryside has been stabilized in one way – by others coming in looking for a better quality of life – people buying cottages, weekenders, even tourists.'

I heard her play for a country dance. There was certainly no possibility of using sheet music, since the make-up of the band was always changing – accordions, a fiddle, bagpipe, hurdy-gurdy (the specially Burgundian instrument), even a little girl with a recorder, blowing lively tunes with great solemnity, staring straight ahead. None of it was going to topple the charts, but it was fun – and it belonged.

In the little village of Villapourçon I encountered the school master who lived and worked in a school attached to the *mairie*. Outside his back door a pair of clogs were waiting which he had made himself. He was an enthusiast and saw himself as a guardian of the traditions of the Morvan, in particular the traditional music and dance, and he belonged to the *Galvachers*, who were the first Morvan folk revivalist group in 1952, performing the hotch-potch of old European dances handed down to them – polkas, Scottish dances, bourrées – in their mountain way. 'Lots of stamping,' he said, 'Morvan has always been a forgotten country, so things have been preserved here. When the group started in the fifties, we found the airs and dances almost unchanged. We want to guard that. It's not chauvinism. Each region has its own tradition, and you have to watch the little details, to stay close to the truth, or you quickly become all the same'

The original *galvachers* were the cowboys of Morvan, ox-drovers who would harness their team on 1 May and travel hundreds of miles carting goods and selling their labour throughout the summer and autumn, often not returning till the Anost Fair on 1 December. In the same way, the wives often left home, sometimes for years, to become wet-nurses to the babies of the rich. Noelle Renault, whom I met at Château-Chinon where she teaches, has made herself the expert on a fascinating chapter of social history. For Morvan girls were much sought after, being thought particularly healthy and nourishing, and took their highly-esteemed Celtic milk into the best society. When the fashion was at its height in the nineteenth century, three-quarters of all young mothers in Morvan went off at least once, some two or three times, to be cherished by wealthy families, dressed in fine clothes with ribbons in the family livery and themselves nourished on a luxury diet, since – even at one remove – nothing was too good for the infant of noble stock, except his own mother feeding him. With a wage three times that of a coachman, the inducements to a poverty-stricken peasant girl were immense, though she also paid a price. There would often be the enthusiasms of the master of the house to reckon with (though Morvan girls were celebrated for their forthrightness in expressing themselves on any subject, and many a man hoping for a girl on his lap ended up with a flea in his ear).

Château-Chinon is the capital of central Morvan, an important crossroads and market town that gained some national importance, since it is the town from which President Mitterrand set out for the Elysée Palace in 1981, having been mayor since 1949 and a Morvan deputy for thirty-five years.

As with the nourrices, this important connection has brought many benefits to the area, the oddest of which is a museum of gifts received by Mitterrand during his presidency. The most local of his gifts it is not possible to represent, since it is a pond which he owns in the area and which jocular locals dye red from time to time, but in any case it has nothing on a metre-wide wooden wheel with 2000 spokes made by one William Robin, '*modeste charron saintongeaus*', and offered by a grateful family in admiration. Remarkable as it is, it is the sort of present that goes the rounds, and I can imagine the delight of whoever it was in the family who had the brilliant idea of sending it to him with whom the buck must stop. When I stayed in the Hotel du Vieux

Morvan I realized too late that I should have asked for Room 15, where Mitterrand apparently stayed for twenty-two years. From my experience of the hotel, all I can say is that I wouldn't have.

Morvan was misty when I awoke in Château-Chinon. At first I could see nothing but vagueness, then rounded hill-tops appeared and the mist condensed to lie like streams of cloud in the valleys. At last there was a hint of rose, and the sun was coming. I was sad to leave Morvan, which is like a model of a country in which the modeller has been over-enthusiastic with the contour. The landscape of Morvan is alive, with the cleft of every curve becoming a dell, for the place is full of woods, and tiny but resolute streams cutting the grass of the meadows on their way to something hardly bigger than they are, and animals. They are everywhere, crunching up the mud in the fields, bringing clods of it into the lanes. Chickens and ducks spilling out over the roads of the crumbling stone villages scamper to safety when you pass, unlike the dogs which want to get run over – especially by a bicycle pedalled by an interesting ankle. In winter you notice the birds, flocks of them everywhere – finches glinting gold, turtle doves, black crows. Hawks of every kind sit beside you as you go by, or flap lazily away. There are herons and, at dusk, owls. Heavy shadows fall in the evening when woodsmen's fires glow among the trees like solitary eyes. And in the morning small birds cover the roads, and scatter as you pass.

Corbigny is downhill from Château-Chinon, passing by the Reservoir de Pannesière-Chaumard. Once you are in Corbigny, you are in a different country. Unlike the high Morvan, where all the water is in the process of getting somewhere fast, this is a place where it has arrived at an age of discretion and is taking life more easily and substantially. Corbigny is on the River Yonne and the Canal du Nivernais, which travels north to Clamecy, Châtel-Censoir and ultimately Auxerre and the Canal de Bourgogne. It was the Yonne that carried the *flotteurs* and their wood off to Paris: barge traffic came later, and in its turn is fading. Like the *galvachers*, the *flotteurs* often brought back progressive ideas which turned the Nivernais to the left, where it remained and which, until the time of Mitterrand, did not endear the area to the French government. Both Corbigny and Clamecy are deeply French and somewhat tatty at the edges, though Clamecy has a fine old centre, a good deal of quaintness and the tourism to go with it, including pleasure boats from the canal. (Otherwise, little happens on the water but the traditional annual water-jousting, which is found in a number of places along the river, but is now on boats where it used to be on logs.) By contrast, though it too is old and has pretty parts, Corbigny is a workaday place, a market town for the villages around. The vast eighteenth-century college, so tumbledown that it is barred off from the public, is an indication that the place is not rich. But I found it most friendly in the bar-tabac of Madame Perotel in the Grande Rue, and ate well and simply in a little old-fashioned hotel in the centre run by two ageing ladies, one of whom served while the other made a sound like a dragon eating pebbles, cutting the bread in the kitchen.

The Canal du Nivernais has its towpath, which I have only seen at intervals but on which you should be able to backtrack, if you like, to the Etang de Vaux, a lake which is a holiday and boating centre. Northwards, you follow rabbits along the river valley. They are the signs for the Black Rabbit route, which was one of the first tourist routes to be planned along picturesque small roads and which takes you above the river along the D985 to Clamecy. Here you cross to the west bank, where a small road follows the canal through the other water-jousting villages of Coulanges-s-Yonne and Crain to the delightfully named Misery, where you may cross back and make your way through the industrial outskirts of Châtel-Censoir, with its medieval village crowning the hill above. (Misery is not the only interesting name in this part. Opposite it is Merry and further north still, I came upon a sign for the village of Anus, but did not go there.)

Now three parts of the journey are done, though you may cut the rest short by following the canal north to the railway station at Auxerre or explore the best of the cliffs up towards Mailly, where there are many strangely-named villages and a very pleasant canal-side restaurant, Au Rendez-vous de Pecheur, at the port of Mailly-le-Château, which does excellent mussels. Otherwise, the route turns back for a moment through Asnières-sous-Bois and then runs east by way of les-Bois-de-la-Madeleine towards Vézelay, inescapable on its hilltop, with its great basilica hallowed by pilgrimage, aspiration and art, and its old town, with revived vineyards tumbling down the slopes below (though the finished product is hardly the Burgundy to which you have become accustomed).

Apart from the Christian pedigree of Vézelay itself, the area around is pretty and interesting, with St-Père below, a delightful crumbly old town with a wonderful church. (If you are the sort of person who does not mind mixing with heads of state and the like, l'Espèrance, Marc Meneau's posh restaurant at Les Asquins, is said to be among the best in France, though I do not know how the heads of state feel about people in cycling gear. And there is a cheaper offshoot.) To the south, the village of Pierre-Perthuis is almost perfect in its way, set high above a river with a château and a romantic old bridge. There the cycling route leads round two sides of the triangle made by the meeting of the rivers Cure and Cousin, following the Cousin to Avallon by way of Pontaubert, after which the valley is especially charming.

There are several ways up to Avallon on its hilltop: the most exciting being an extraordinarily steep footpath; the longest and prettiest being to wind round the hill until a cobbled street leads you into the old town, picturesque with its tower and half-timbering, carved doorways and little turrets. I stayed in a hotel that had an elaborate vine painted over its front, so that when I put my head out of the window it appeared among the leaves like a bunch of grapes. And since the Hotel d'Avallon Vauban has

The Canal de Bourgogne, a popular destination for British holiday-makers.

no restaurant I ate up the road at a convivial family-run place, le Cheval Blanc, where meals start with *goujères*, choux pastry cooked with lumps of gruyère, a Burgundian speciality as far away from a cheese straw as British Ruby Red is from Côtes de Beaune. I was surprised to find in the town a bar, les Caves d'Irancy, boasting a real dartboard, like an English pub, and the patron bemoaning the difficulties of getting good quality darts in provincial France – how fortunate I was to come from a dart-playing culture. However, on my expressing interest in a game, he said that he and his friends played one evening a week when he closed up early, especially for it. It was not for the customers – that would not be safe.

Avallon is a peaceful town, a real place with the slight whiff of a backwater whose charm the sprawl along the *route nationale* does nothing to diminish. I would have been sad to leave it, but for the beauty of the Cousin valley, along which I continued after a breakneck descent from the town. If there was ever a dancing river, this is one – rocky with many mills, rough pasture on one side and alders. Part of the charm is the texture of the place: the tussocks in the grass; the water rippling like the fantasies of some excitable hairdresser; old stone walls and rocks whose surface is many-faceted, with some faces bare and others lichened. By the time you have added the trees and rough old mill-wheels with the water pouring smoothly through them, the valley is a riot of shapes and textures. Sheep, very fluffy in their meadow, add yet another. Then it is up away from the river on one of the few real hills in this stretch of the journey and through Magny into a rolling countryside of big fields and occasional woods. The character of the villages changes to something poorer, they abound with dusty barns and farm shelters in which tractors rub axles with machinery that was well-worn before the sound of an internal combustion engine was ever heard in the world. Even more than in the presence of old stones and great architecture, you feel that Burgundy is a journey into the past. On a winter's day with mud lying thick in the gateways and rooks cawing in the treetops, there was something of past centuries that had not got around to dying because no one had noticed its time was up. Only in the rather neat village of Sceaux was the communal washing place filled with soil and made pretty with flowers, the big iron wheel of its pump standing idle, and Montréal shortly afterwards was a place of old walls and old wells.

Montréal is a small place on a hill, extremely ancient, for it was here that Brunéhaut, Regent of Burgundy, lived in the seventh century. The town still has its gateways and the church at the summit is very fine, with vivid wood carving. As for glory in this day and age, a sign on the outskirts says that it is a member of the *Association de Montréals de France*. There are seven of them and this is the northernmost, the next being in Canada. Appropriately, it had snowed – there were leaves hopping like sparrows in the wind and children flocking like sparrows to the dusting of white in the angles of the stones to make tiny snowballs.

I stopped for coffee in the new café-restaurant – converted and beautifully panelled by the grandfather, retired from selling shoes. There was a lot of good oak in the area, he said, and stone. Fifty years ago there were seven quarries in the area with their own train that ran to the main line for Paris. Sometimes you find one lintel for all the windows on one floor – 4 m (13 ft) long – and a single slab for the window jambs that goes right through a wall over 0.6 m (2 ft) thick. But there was almost no business in the village now, except a couple of cattle farmers. Everyone was either retired, or a visitor from Paris, for Montréal is not far from the motorway and the valley of the Serein is pretty.

Following the river Serein, you can take an attractive detour north-west to pretty Noyers with its old castle. But I continued east through Epoisses which has a gem of a château and produces the excellent Epoisses cheese, of which there are two local producers working fairly traditionally. Then the country becomes hilly again (the route as marked is not only the quietest way, but also the least difficult), and at Semur-en-Auxois you find yourself in the presence of a remarkable cleavage. The castle there is built on the edge of a partially domesticated chasm, since there are terraced gardens down part of one side of the precipitous slope and an old mill and sluices by the green river at the bottom. Indeed, the large crack from top to bottom of one of the towers makes you wonder whether the chasm may be winning, but in Burgundy it is unwise to generalize about cracks, since they may well have been there for centuries.

As I came across the bridge I found myself wondering how any reasonably ordinary place could possibly be so picturesque, but it got even more so as I came to the centre with its cobbles and half-timbering. Even the sausages hung across the window of the Charcuterie de Notre-Dame were quaintly shaped and two snails guarding one doorway of the church spoke more of Burgundian good living than ascetic religion. I entered the tall nave as some music died away and the sound of the organ breathed its last, followed by brisk clicks and thuds as the organist put it to bed.

After Semur you have a choice of ways to take you towards Dijon: the winding route of the Canal de Bourgogne, which I ruled out as long as it travelled close to the motorway, and three of the valleys that split the Mountain of Auxois – one carrying a major road, one a lesser road plus the railway, and one nothing but its minor self. The valley of the Ozerain also has the advantage of passing the scene of Vercingetorix's last stand in 52 BC, in which he was besieged by Julius Caesar in the hilltop town of Alesia, now Alise-Ste-Reine. Whether or not you make the considerable climb should probably depend on how you feel about Celts and Gauls. Personally, I would save my energies for making a detour to the very grand château of Bussy-Rabutin to the north-east or, continuing the route, for the climb to Flavigny-s-Ozerain, a very attractive old town which is one of the few places where you have any prospect of staying at the end of the short day and where there is a sweet smell in the air. If you are there in the morning, you can be shown round where it comes from: otherwise, you will just have to buy the boxes, which are among the most delightful sweet boxes ever made and contain aniseed balls, which have been made there for a thousand years – first by monks, then nuns, then by several small factories and now by one family firm which is one of the few factories in the world to live in an abbey and to have a remarkable collection of antiquities dug up on the premises as a family hobby.

The valley that follows is among the most smiling and peaceful of the journey. Only at the end does the road begin to undulate more, then climb quite steeply to barer country than it has been for some while, turning off to Sombernon at the hamlet of la Chaleur, which when I came through it was deep in snow. From Sombernon you descend to the Canal de Bourgogne, which is still keeping company with the motorway at this point, but which has small roads going along it (though they cross from side to side, rather) as well as the towpath itself. With this, difficulties in navigation are at an end, since you can follow the canal straight into the centre of Dijon and so, once again, to the airport.

Left: Vercingetorix as a romantic Celtic hero.

Opposite: Dijon, ancient capital of Burgundy, famous for wine and mustard.

Burgundy 11 days 423.5–430.5 km (263¼–268¼ miles)

⊟ Accommodation   ✗ Places to eat   ◊ Detour   [A] Alternative route

Map ref: IGN Green Series 28, 29, 36, 37. If this is too much there is a single IGN Top 250.

To get there and back: Road, rail or air to Dijon.

Weather: very hot and dry in summer, quite cold in winter.

Food and drink: Burgundy is the centre of French cuisine: everything is good including the bread. Try Charollais beef steak and Bresse chickens, both have an excellent flavour and a fatless, rather hard texture; or for an entrée, pressed parsleyed ham, snails, or *oeufs à la pleurotte* (eggs poached in wine). Salads are mustardy as you might imagine. Desserts are legendary and include fresh cream cheese and cream, and there are some delicious cheeses, like Epoisses and Ami de Chambertin. Burgundy is also the king of French wines, both reds and whites. Haute Côtes (de Nuits, or de Beaune) are cheaper than Côtes. But you must splurge at least once. Aligote is the normal white, but try it with fruit liqueurs like blackcurrant (for *kir*), peach and many others. And don't forget the superb after dinner Marc de Bourgogne.

Useful addresses: Logis de France, the hotel group, organizes all-in cycle holidays – Information Union Régionale des Logis de Bourgogne, 68 rue Chevreul, BP 209, 21006 Dijon Cedex, 80 63 52 51.

Day 1
Dijon Airport – Nuits-St-Georges
(34 km/21 miles)

If you are travelling by train go straight to Nuits-St-Georges and avoid Dijon, and pick up the route on Day 2.

Dijon (Longvic) Airport – Longecourt-en-Plaine
(11 km/7 miles)

Longvic Airport
Small airport with tiny bar. Accommodation available at Longvic village. Turn right out of airport then left at T-junction. Cross the canal bridge, and turn left on towpath past **Ouges**, **Bretenière** and **Thorey-en-Plaine**.

Longecourt-en-Plaine
See château.

◊   Detour down canal to **St Jean-de-Losnes**, a major inland port with June barge blessing and fête.

⊟   Hotel-restaurant Rey, place de l'Eglise, 21110 Echigey, 80 29 74 00, nearby (4 km/2½ miles down the canal and left to **Echigey**), with restaurant recommended as good value.

Longecourt-en-Plaine – Vougeot
(17 km/10½ miles)

Leave the canalside and turn right into village. Bear right at town hall and turn left on main road D968. After approx. 25 m (no sign), turn right on D25. Cross railway and river through **Tarsul** and **Corcelles-lès-Cîteaux**.

◊   Detour to **Cîteaux**, the original Cistercian monastery, still functioning with Gregorian chants five times a day.

Bear right round the church, and cross main road on D25 to **Savouges**. Bear left to **Epernay-s-Gevrey**, past church on D25 and cross motorway.

Gilly-lès-Cîteaux
Côte d'Or vineyards.
⊟   Hotels: Hotel Château de Gilly-lès-Cîteau (HH), 21640 Vougeot, 80 62 89 98.
Cross railway and main road, and turn left at T-junction.

Vougeot
See Château du Clos de Vougeot the famous headquarters of Burgundy's Confrèrie de Tastevins, with old wine presses.
⊟   Hotels: Hotel Bertagna (M), 16 rue du Vieux-Château, 21640 Vougeot, 80 62 86 00.

Vougeot – Nuits-St-Georges
(6 km/3½ miles)

Vougeot
To avoid the main road, cross bridge towards Beaune, and go round château. At fork take central route through vineyards (one of many small roads). Go left to **Vosne-Romanée** through pretty village with some of the greatest vineyards. Go right at fork, left at **Clos de Reas** and on through vineyards. Turn right towards *centre ville*.

Nuits-St-Georges
Exclusive wine caves in far from exclusive village. See old church. For wine tastings, the Comtesse de Loisy does very exclusive B&B weekend courses, Domaine de Loisy, tel: 80 61 02 72. In fact everyone in town is an expert and you can do your tasting more cheaply in the bars.

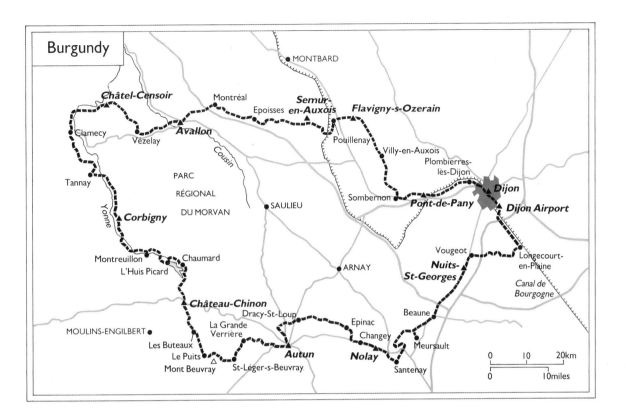

Burgundy

Hotels: Hotel des Cultivateurs (M), 12 rue Général-de-Gaulle, 21700 Nuit-St-Georges, 80 61 10 41, at end of pedestrian precinct, friendly; Hotel de la Côte d'Or (H), 37 rue Thurot, 80 61 06 10, Michelin-designated gourmet restaurant; Hostellerie la Gentilhommière (H), CD 25 la Serrée, 80 61 12 06.

Pizzeria, in pedestrian precinct, good value.

Day 2
Nuits-St-Georges – Nolay
(47 km/29 miles)

Nuits-St-Georges A – Beaune
(17 km/10½ miles)
Take tiny routes through vineyards (rather up and down, but nicer than the plains) to **Chaux** A². (*See church with patterned spire.*) Steepish ride up through **Villiers-la-Faye**, **Magny-lès-Villiers** and **Pernand-Vergelesses**. Turn left.

Aloxe-Corton
See château with good decorated roof.

Hotels: Hotel et Caves des Paulands (H), RN 74, 21420 Aloxe-Corton, 80 26 41 05; Hotel Ermitage de Corton

(HH), RN74 (route de Dijon) 21200 Chorey-lès-Beaune, 80 22 05 28, Michelin gourmet restaurant.
From here cross N74 through **Chorey** and **Gigny** and on to D20 through suburban outskirts of lovely old city. The ring road goes round the fortifications, cross it to the centre.

Beaune
Burgundy's rich wine capital. You can arrive here by train direct from Paris, as for Nuits-St-Georges. It is very pretty, but touristy. See the Hotel Dieu, museums and visit the wine *caves*.

Hotels: Auberge Bourguignonne, 4 place Madeleine (M), 21200 Beaune, 80 22 23 53; Hotel le Home (M), 138 route de Dijon, 80 22 16 43 (on main road into Beaune), looks nice, no food.

Bernard Morillon, 31 rue Mau Foux, 80 24 12 06; l'Ecusson, place Malmédy, 80 24 03 82 (both Michelin gourmet restaurants).

A Pretty, but very hilly, this alternative from **Nuits-St-Georges** goes over the top of the hills behind the vineyards. Take D25 through **Meuilley** to **Arcenant** into blackcurrant-producing country. Turn left on to D25f then on to D18 via **Fussey** to **Echevronne** and **Pernand-Vergelesses**. Go over the motorway and down into **Beaune**,

[A]² If you want absolutely flat cycling from **Chaux** take the lower road through vineyards back to the main road N74. Cross it on D20f to **Premeaux-Pissey**, **Comblanchien**. Follow the railway via **Corgoloin**, **Château de Langres**, and **Ladoix Serrigny** to **Chorey**. Go under motorway and into **Beaune**.

Beaune [A] – Meursault
(11 km/7 miles)

Haute Côte de Beaune, which starts here, is very attractive country. Go right out of ring road, N74 (follow signs to Chalons and Chagny). Still in town turn left on D18 through **Bligny-lès-Beaune**, then right to **Tailly**. Go right on D23, over main road.

Meursault
Pretty town, with the choicest of white Burgundies. See church and decorated roofs.

⊟ Hotels: Hotel des Arts (L), 4 place de l'Hotel de Ville, 21190 Meursault, 80 21 20 28, good food.

✕ Relais de la Diligence, à la Gare, 81 21 21 32, recommended by Michelin as good value.

[A] You can take a shorter route (17 km/10½ miles) along main road, D973, from **Beaune** to **Nolay** via **la Rochepot**. (See below.) It is pretty, but hilly and busy.

Meursault – Santenay
(10 km/6 miles)

Take D113b. These are choicest of white wines all the way to Santenay.

Puligny-Montrachet
⊟ Hotels: Hotel le Montrachet (H), place des Marroniers, 21190 Puligny-Montrachet, 80 21 30 06, with Michelin gourmet restaurant.
Continue through **Chassagne-Montrachet**.

Santenay

Santenay [A] – Nolay
(9 km/5½ miles)

Continue on D113a.

Cheilly-lès-Mararges
Place to eat here if needed.
Turn left on D133 and follow pretty valley north through **Sampigny-lès-Mararges**.

Paris-l'Hôpital
This is called the *Route Touristique Haute Côte de Beaune*. Go on to **Change**, then take D111e.

Nolay
Pretty little town with old *halles*.
⊟ Hotels: Hotel du Chevreuil (M), place de l'Hotel-de-Ville, 21340 Nolay, 80 21 71 89; Hotel du Parc (M), place de l'Hotel-de-Ville, 80 21 84 01; Hotel Ste Marie (M), 36 rue de la République, 80 21 73 19.

[↺] Detour 5 km (3 miles) back along main road to **la Rochepot**. Fine Burgundian château with decorated roofs and bridges.

⊟ Hotels: Le Relais du Château (L), 21340 la Rochepot, 80 21 71 32; Gîte d'étape: Mme Masson, 80 21 72 42.

[↺] For wine tastings, try Hubert Lamy, St Aubin, tel: 80 21 32 55. This area not quite so expensive as Meursault.

[A] This is a long, rather hilly route to the beautiful **Mont Uchon** which takes two days and re-joins the main route at **Autun**. From **Santenay** turn left over the railway to the Canal du Centre. Follow the canal towpath, or D974 where it fails, all the way to **Montchanin**. Just beyond the town, turn right on D102. Cross the main road D980, go between lakes, and right to **Charmoy**. Continue to D47 and turn left on it, then right on D279. There is a steep climb up then to **Mont Uchon** (681 m/2235 ft) – the 'Jewel of the Morvan'. Leave your bike in the parking lot beyond the small military area and walk to the viewpoint (spectacular views north towards Mont Beuvray). **Uchon** village is nearby. (See *church and open air theatre*.)

⊟ Hotels: Auberge la Croix Messier Jean (L), 71190 Uchon, 85 54 42 06, simple hotel-hostel-restaurant run by ex-world cycle champion, Josiane Bost Federspeild, who also does bicycle hire.
Go down via **Chapelle-s-Uchon** (very steep) on D275 to **Etang-s-Arroux**.

⊟ Hotels: Hostellerie du Gourmet (L), route de Toulon, 71190 Etang-s-Arroux, 85 82 20 88, food recommended by Michelin as good value.
Follow Arroux river valley to **Autun**.

Day 3
Nolay – Autun
(42 km/26 miles)

Nolay [A] – Changey
(5 km/3 miles)

Follow directions to Autun, cross main road D973 and go up on D33.

Cirey
Continue up and turn left on D33F towards Saisey, but turn left before you get there at unmarked crossroads and continue on.

Changey
⊟ Hotels: Hotel Oasis (M), 85 82 07 03. Chambres d'hôtes: Mme Comeaud, 85 82 07 55.

Changey – Epinac
(9 km/5½ miles)

You are now back alongside and level, with main road D973. Turn right at the tiny triangular green by a letter box with sign for chambres d'hôtes. Go through **la Forêt** and turn left at T-junction to **Réssillé**. Go left down hill.

Epinac

Old steel town now making precision instruments. Turn right at fork before curious **Tour Malakoff**.

⊟ Hotels: Motel du Pont Vert (L), route de la Piscine, 71360 Epinac, 85 82 02 99.

Epinac – Dracy-St-Loup
(17 km/10½ miles)

Go left through town centre, and right on D43, then left by old station towards Sully. Cross the river via humpbacked bridge, and turn right at crossroads on to D26.

Sully

See fine château, private estate of the MacMahons, the Dukes of Sully with Irish and Scottish connections (detour right in village).
Continue on D26.

St Léger-du-Bois

Cross the river and turn left on D26. Go left at fork on D151 following the river valley through **Champsigny** and **Muse**. Cross the railway.

Dracy-St-Loup

Dracy-St-Loup – Autun
(11 km/7 miles)

Cross the river and turn left on main road N81 towards Autun. At **Surmoulin** turn right on D116.

St-Forgeot

Once a mining centre, now with only coal tips and old Polish communities. Keep left, then go left towards Autun on main road D980. At **la Porte d'Autun**, keep on through the Roman arch and turn right at T-junction towards *centre ville*.

Autun

Wonderful old market town. See cathedral, Roman remains, *Hôtel de Ville*, museums, including wonderful *Musée Rolin*, summer spectacles in Roman theatre.

⊟ Hotels: Hotel le Petit Paris (L), 35 rue de Fauborg-St-Andoche, 71400 Autun, 85 52 11 92; Hotel Moderne et de la Tête Noire (M), 3 rue de l'Arquebuse, 85 52 25 39, our favourite Burgundy hotel, all faded glory, big rooms, good food; Hotel des Ursulines (H), 14 rue Rivault, 85 52 68 00.

✗ Chalet Bleu, 3 rue Jeannin, 85 86 27 30, central, recommended by Michelin as good value; Bar Chez Polo (near Hotel La Tête Noir), very friendly.

Ⓐ For mountain bikes with heavy tyres there is a disused railway line from Nolay which avoids the worst of the ups and downs and is shorter, but it is mostly rough stones. At Epinac it has been smoothed for cycling and walking and the whole route will be completed some day.

Day 4
Autun – Château Chinon
(50.5 km/31¾ miles)

Autun – la Grande Verriére
(14 km/9 miles)

This is the big one, but it goes up hill gently. Leave town on D978, cross over the railway and the river towards Nevers. At roundabout turn left on N81, and follow the river. Turn first right on to D3 following signs to Monthelon and Mont Beuvray. Go up past **Monthelon** (see château) continuing on D3.

La Grande Verrière

See château.

⊟ Hotels: Hotel de la Poste (L), 71990 la Grande Verrière, 85 82 52 41. Chambres d'hôtes: M. Blondeau, 85 82 58 21, a bit further up road by scarecrow figures, said to be friendly and do food. Gîtes d'étape: Gîte la Grande Verrière, Mme Guillon, 85 82 52 41, with food; Moulin du Pléjus, Mme Gonon, 85 82 58 37.

La Grande Verrière – St Léger-s-Beuvray
(6 km/3½ miles)

Continue on D3.

St Léger-s-Beuvray

Ancient mid-summer festival here, and on Mont Beuvray.

⊟ Hotels: Hotel du Mont Beuvray (L), 71990 St Léger-s-Beuvray, 85 82 52 23, full-up for lunch in winter, a good sign; Hotel du Morvan (L), 85 82 51 06.

St Léger-s-Beuvray – le Puits
(11 km/7 miles)

St Léger-s-Beuvray

Continue on D3 (moderately steep).

Le Reboul

Home to Europe's *Centre Celtique*, a museum of pre-Roman Europe and President Mitterrand's final gift to the nation, opening in 1994.

Ⓘ From here detour up steep hill to the most important pre-Roman site in Europe, Vercingetorix' Celtic capital, **Bibracte** (1.5 km/1 mile) – 796 m (2612 ft), with magnificent views. See excavations, strange rocks, little chapel and orientation table; and old grown-out plaited hedgerow beeches (post Vercingetorix).

From **le Reboul**, take the D18.

⊟ Gîte d'étape: at Gluxe-en-Glenne on D300 to right at l'Echenault.

Le Puits

⊟ Hotels: Auberge la Grande Halte, 58370 Villapourçon, 86 78 64 96.

Le Puits – Les Buteaux
(8.5 km/5¼ miles)

Le Puits
Go left on D27, towards Château-Chinon, and up round little **Lake Rangère**.

Les Buteaux
- Chambres d'hôtes: Fachin, M. Courault, 86 85 03 88.

Les Buteaux – Château-Chinon
(11 km/7 miles)

Continue on D27 through **Commune de la Comme.**

Château-Chinon
Capital of the Morvan, François Mitterrand was mayor and deputé here. See fascinating *Musée Septennat* with Mitterrand's official presents, and museum of Burgundian costumes. Also has viewpoint, a steep climb to 609 m (1998 ft).
- Hotels: Hotel du Lion d'Or (L), rue des Fosses, 58120 Château-Chinon, 86 85 13 56; Hostellerie l'Oustalet (L), route des Lormes, 86 85 15 17; Hotel de Centre (L), 86 85 08 36; Hotel de Folin, route Nevers (M), 86 85 00 80.

Day 5
Château-Chinon – Corbigny
(39–46 km/24–28½ miles)

Take either side round Reservoir de Pannesière-Chaumard: the east side is longer and follows the lake (swimming, boats, etc); the west side is more direct, with views down over the lake.

Château-Chinon Ⓐ – Chaumard
(14 km/9 miles)
Leave on D944 going down through town towards Lormes and Avallon. Continue on to **Montbois**. At the church turn right on D37 down through woods. Cross the river Yonne, passing Gaulish remains. Turn left on small road D12 through **Corancy** to **Lac de Pannesière**. Bear left along waterside. Cross left on the barrage.

Chaumard
- Hotels: La Vieille Auberge (L), 58120 Château-Chinon, 86 78 03 22. Chambres d'hôtes: M. Tessari, 85 82 58 21.

Chaumard – l'Huis Picard
(7 km/4½ miles)

Keep along the water's edge on D303 towards the barrage. Cross the bridge.

Vauminot
- Hotels: Hotel au Bon Accueil (L), 58800 Montreuillon, 86 84 71 76, lakeside, bicycles for hire.
Continue round lake, turn left over **barrage** and then right on D944.
- Hotels: Hotel-Restaurant aux Fins Chasseurs (L), 58120 Château-Chinon, 86 84 71 87, up steep hill.
Follow D944 and the river Yonne all the way to Corbigny.

L'Huis Picard

L'Huis Picard – Montreuillon
(8 km/5 miles)

Continue on D944 to **Chassy**. See mill and château. Turn left along the valley on D126.

Montreuillon
- Hotels: Hotel-Café des Sports (L), 58800 Montreuillon, 86 84 71 52; Hotel Cas Lauferon (L), 86 84 72 26.

Montreuillon – Corbigny
(17 km/10½ miles)

Continue past aqueduct, along river. Leave Park du Morvan past mill *'Le Patriarche'*, a fish farm worked by reformed drug addicts. Go down through **Mouron-s-Yonne**.

Marcilly
See château.
Turn right on *la Route Buissonière* (the black rabbit route) D985.

Corbigny
- Hotels: Hotel de l'Europe (L), grande rue, 58800 Corbigny, 86 20 09 87; Hotel la Buissonière (M), place St-Jean, 86 20 02 13.

Ⓐ As Eastern route through Château-Chinon up through woods to **Montbois** church. Stay on D944 to **la Mergerot**. Lake below right.
- Hotels: Hotel-restaurant-garage, le Relais, if desperate.
Continue on D944 to **L'Huis Picard**. Re-join the route, as described above.

Day 6

Corbigny – Châtel-Censoir

(44 km/27½ miles)

Corbigny Ⓐ – Tannay

(16 km/10 miles)

Continue on the black rabbit route D985 and follow it and the Canal Nivernais via **Courcelanges**, **Ruages**, **Monceaux-le-Compte** and **Cuzy**. The towpath is good in parts but not tarmacked here. You can continue all the way to Clamecy, but this route crosses the canal on D119.

Tannay

🛏 Hotels: Hotel le Relais Fleuri (L), 2 rue de Bèze, 58190 Tannay, 86 29 84 57.

Tannay – Clamecy

(13 km/8 miles)

Take D119 to main road D34. Turn right. Minor detour into **Asnois**, for château. Continue on D34.

Clamecy

Wonderfully decaying old town, delightfully Dickensian. Water jousts in summer.

🛏 Hotels: Hotel la Boule d'Or (L), 5 place Bethléem, 58500 Clamecy, 86 27 11 55, pizzeria; Hotel Anval (M), route de Brinon, 2 km (1 mile) out of town, 86 24 42 40; Hotel de la Poste (M), place Emile Zola, 86 27 01 55, rooms OK, food expensive and pretentious.

✕ Au bon Accueil, 3 route d'Auxerre, 86 27 91 67, good food, English speakers.

Clamecy – Châtel-Censoir

(15 km/9½ miles)

Clamecy

Follow the D144 north along the railway line, on west side of river/canal to **Surgy** and continue on same road.

Coulanges-s-Yonne

🛏 Hotels: Hotel du Lion d'Or (L), place de l'Hotel de Ville, 89480 Coulanges-s-Yonne, 86 81 71 72.

Turn right across river, (avoid **Misery**), then go left on D21 through **Lucy-s-Yonne**.

Châtel-Censoir

🛏 Hotels: Hotel Central (L), rue Coppeau, 89660 Châtel-Censoir, 86 81 01 98; Hotel de la Gare (L), 86 81 01 56.

Ⓐ There is a shorter route (48 km/30 miles) which is pretty but hilly, from Corbigny via Vézelay to Avallon. This combines two days, though you might like to break your route near Vézelay. From **Corbigny** take main toad D958 to **Bazoches** (17 km/10½ miles). See château and Vauban's tomb in church. Continue on D958 into the Parc National de Morvan (pass small road right to Avallon) and go on to **Pierre Perthuis**

(7 km/4½ miles). Tiny medieval village on river Cure. See château, ancient bridge at bottom, Roche Percée above. Return to D958 and follow Cure Valley. Turn off to **Fontaines Salées** (site of Gallo-Roman spa) right. Continue to **St-Père** (4 km/2½ miles) and **Vézelay** (see section below). Then continue on route as from **St-Père**.

Day 7

Châtel-Censoir – Avallon

(41 km/25½ miles)

Châtel-Censoir Ⓐ – Vézelay

(18 km/11 miles)

Take D100 and climb up by little river Chamoux to **Arvigny** and **Asnières-s-Bois**. Go left on D36 to **les-Bois-de-la-Madeleine** through woods and downhill with views of Vézelay. At main road D951, turn left and up.

Vézelay

Beautiful old hilltop town with wonderful Basilique Ste Madeleine. Many tourists.

🛏 Hotels: Relais du Morvan (L–M), place du Champs-de-Foire, 89450 Vézelay, 86 33 25 33; Hotel Poste et Lion d'Or (M–H), 86 33 30 92. Chambres d'hôtes: Mme Ginesty 86 33 25 74. (*Or see St-Père below*)

Vézelay – Avallon

(23 km/14½ miles)

Go down on D957 along vineyards slopes.

St-Père-s-Vézelay

Historic old village. See lovely church.

🛏 Hotels: Hotel la Renommée (M), route Principale, 89450 St-Père-s-Vézelay, 86 33 21 34, no food; Hotel l'Esperance (HH), 86 33 21 34, Marc Meneau is one of France's most famous chefs. (Cheaper establishment under same management opposite.) Chambres d'hôtes: Mme Demeule, 86 33 25 87.

🅓 Detour south D958 into Northern Morvan, to **Fontaines Salées**, and **Pierre-Perthuis**. (See above.)

Follow the river Cure north on D958 and turn right briefly on main road D951, then left to **la Buyere** and **Asquins**. Go right over the river, then left along river valley to **Givry**. Turn left at T-junction and go down through village, then left by bridge at the church and right again along a track by the river Cousin. Rejoin the main road N6 for a few yards. Cross the railway and turn left.

Valloux

✕ Restaurant Chenêts, 86 34 23 34.

Turn right under main road and go over river and turn left to **Vermoiron** and **Vault-de-Lugny**.

🛏 Hotels: Château de Vault-de-Lugny (HH), 89200 Vault-de-Lugny, 86 34 07 86, pretty with moat.

Carry on on this road.

Pontaubert

🛏 Hotels: Hotel-restaurant Les Fleurs (M), 69 route de Vézelay, 89200 Pontaubert, 86 34 13 81; Hotel au Soleil d'Or (M), 46 route de Vézelay, 86 34 15 74 (*and see below*).

Go left on main road D3. Cross the river and turn right along pretty river valley.

🛏 Hotels: Le Moulin des Templiers (M), vallée du Cousin, 89200 Avallon, 86 34 10 80, lovely old hotel but no food; Hotel Moulin des Ruats (H), vallée du Cousin, 86 34 07 14, not so pretty but posher than the above.

Continue along river towards Avallon with hilltop city above you. Take the bridge over end of valley road, and bear left then right at oblique 'T' with bridge road, D127. Turn right at roundabout below the city, bend round uphill, and continue round town (ignoring left turn for '*centre ville*'). Follow the cobbled street into the old town. Go left into Place de Charles de Gaulle and right into main square at top. There are quicker ways in but this is the easiest and the prettiest.

Avallon

Agreeable old fortified town.

🛏 Hotels: Hotel le Cheval Blanc (LL), 55 rue de Lyon, 89200 Avallon, 86 34 55 07, excellent food, reasonable prices; Hotel d'Avallon Vauban (M), 53 rue de Paris, 86 34 36 99, comfortable, no food; Hostellerie de la Poste (H), 13 place Vauban, 86 34 06 12, new young chef-proprietor.

❌ Pizzeria de la Tour, good food.

🅰 An easier, but longer, route to **Avallon** from Châtel-Censoir is to continue north on D100 along cliff-flanked canalside via **Merry-s-Yonne** and crossing over to **Mailly-le-Château**.

🛏 Hotels: Hotel le Castel (M), place de l'Eglise, 89660 Mailly-le-Château, 86 81 43 06.

❌ Restaurant-bar des Pecheurs, good simple lunch. Cross over D100 at **Mailly-la-Ville** and stay on D100 through **Bazarnes** 🅰 and the D139 where the Yonne joins the Cure. Cross the Yonne and the canal to join D39 to **Accolay**. Cross the Cure and turn right on main road N6 to **Vermenton**. Continue down to **Lucy-s-Cure** and cross the river to **Bessy-s-Cure**. Continue along the river via **Arcy-s-Cure**, as much as possible on west side, to join the route at **Givry**.

🅰 Go along the canal north to **Auxerre**. From **Barzarnes** follow river on D139. Cross river and canal to **Cravant** and turn left to **Vincelottes** along riverside on D362.

Opposite: Vézelay, an important stage on the pilgrimage route to Santiago de Compostella.

Right: Medieval Burgundy: Noyers-s-Serein.

🛏 Hotels: Hotel Auberge les Tilleuls (M), 12 quai de l'Yonne, 89290 Vincelottes, 86 42 22 13, with restaurant recommended by Michelin as good value. Continue along river via **Escolives-Ste-Camille** (See archeological site. Good wine at Irancy and Coulanges-la-Vineuse.) and **Vaux** to Auxerre, a lovely medieval city. See cathedral, abbey with oldest frescos in France. Lots of accommodation and restaurants. You can short-cut the journey here and take the train home.

Day 8
Avallon – Semur-en-Auxois
(44 km/27½ miles)

Avallon – Montréal
(15 km/9½ miles)

Go down to the river valley again. At **Cousin-le-Pont** go left on D427 to **Cousin-la-Roche** and **Mezuzien**. Continue along the route de Magny.

Magny

❌ Restaurant-bar.

Take D75 'Vers RN6', left of church. Bear left at triangular green and left again down the route de la Tuilerie. Cross main road N6 to **la Tuilerie**. Turn right at T-junction and right again by Alt Hotel on D51. Cross D146 going towards Charbonnière. Go over motorway on tiny road to **Sceaux** and continue.

Montréal
Pretty old town, one of many French Montréals.
☒ Les Deux Compères, 86 32 19 47, Irish pub, good
food.

Montréal – Epoisses
(13 km/8 miles)

Montréal
Turn right on D957 and go out through the lower town.
Fork right on tiny road D13, to **Treviselot** and **Trévilly**.
Turn left at T-junction. Go over river to **Courterolles**
and turn right on D11 towards Guillon. Fork left on
small road away from river and cross D44.

Toutry
Go right below church, fork left on D954 and go on.

Epoisses
Renowned for Epoisses cheese. See pretty château.
⊨ Hotels: Hotel Relais de la Pomme d'Or (L), rue des
Forges, 21460 Epoisses, 80 96 43 01, with courtyard.

Epoisses – Semur-en-Auxois
(16 km/10 miles)

Epoisses
Turn right in town down main street and fork left on
small road D36 towards Forléans. At **Changy** fork left on
D103a to **Foux**, and go over crossroads to **Torcy**. Turn
right at the cross down small road to **Ferme à Moulin à
Vent**, then right past pond to **Vic-de-Chassenay**. Go left
by fountain towards Semur in distance. Cross level
crossing and turn right on D954 at main road D980, see
viewpoint of city. Cross down and go over bridge to
castle and up.

Semur-en-Auxois
Lovely old fortified town. See château, church and old
bridge.
⊨ Hotels: Hotel des Gourmets (L), 4 rue Varenne, 21140
Semur-en-Auxois, 80 97 09 41, down at heel but nice-
looking restaurant; Hotel Cymaises (M), 7 rue du
Renaudot, 80 97 21 44, no food but very comfortable;
Hotel de la Côte d'Or (M), 3 place Gaveau, 80 97 03
13; Hotel du Lac (M), 80 97 11 11, at Lac de Pont, 3
km (2 miles) south; Hostellerie d'Aussois (H), route de
Saulieu, 80 97 28 28, swimming pool.
☒ Le Trombone, 13 rue Buffon, 80 97 07 87, good light
meals.

Semur-en-Auxois – Flavigny
(26 km/16 miles)

Semur-en-Auxois – Pouillenay
(16 km/10 miles)

Take main road D954 to **Villenotte**. Turn right on small
road D9a through **Juilly** and **Souhey**. Go right to
Magny-la-Ville, then right on D9a, left on D10c and
take the left fork on D10b to **Chassey**. Cross the canal
and turn left on D10 between the canal and the railway.
Cross the railway and turn right.

Pouillenay

⟁ Detour to great romanesque **Abbaye de Fontenay**
(21 km/13 miles) north along the Brenne river via
Venarey-les-Laumes (avoid the hotel there) and
Fain-lès-Montbard.
⊨ Hotels: Hotel Château de Malaisy (H), 21500 Fain-lès-
Montbard, 80 89 46 54.
Continue towards Montbard. Turn right at
Marmagne on D32 to the abbey. You can cut the
route short at Montbard where it is possible to take
the TGV.

⟁ Detour to fascinating **Château Bussy-Rabutin** (10
km/6 miles) where disgraced courtier displayed
portraits of his amours. Go north on main road via
Venarey, then on D954 through **Grésigny-Ste-
Reine** to château on the right. To stay in the area go
further on to **Darcey** (5 km/3 miles).
⊨ Hotels: Le Relais des Source (L), 21150 Darcey, 80 96
25 21, excellent breakfasts.

Pouillenay – Flavigny-s-Ozerain
(10 km/6 miles)

Take D9 and go left on main road D905 at **les Pres-
Hauts**. Turn right before railway crossing on to D103
following the valley of the Ozerain.

⟁ Detour up to **Alise-Ste-Reine** (4 km/2½ miles), an
old hilltop town, site of the ancient Gaullish city of
Alisia, and Vercingetorix' last stand against Caesar. It is
a very steep climb (407 m/1335 ft), excavation site not
much to see and there is a cloyingly romantic
nineteenth-century statue of Vercingetorix by Millet.
Views of Caesar's hill-camp opposite.

Continue on D103 along valley between the two camps.
Cross river and detour right on D9, steeply up hill.

Flavigny-s-Ozerain
Old hilltop town. See famous Flavigny aniseed sweet
factory in abbey.
⊨ Hotels: Hotel Auberge du Bon Coin (L), 21150
Flavigny-s-Ozerain, 80 96 21 53, good food and wine.

Day 10
Flavigny – Pont-de-Pany
(37 km/23½ miles)

Flavigny-s-Ozerain – Villy-en-Auxois
(15 km/9½ miles)

Back in the valley turn right again on D9, cross the river and continue through **Jailly-les-Moulins**.

Villy-en-Auxois

Villy-en-Auxois – Sombernon
(15 km/9½ miles)

Continue through **Chevannay** along valley (past **Avosnes** with its château to the right) and go on D9f to **St-Mesmin**. Meet the main road D9 at **la Chaleur**. Turn left.

Sombernon
- ⊨ Hotels: Hotel le Sombernon (L), rue Ferdinand Mercuzot, 21540 Sombernon, 80 33 41 23, at top of town as you come in; Hotel Belle Vue (L), rond-point Abreuvoir, 80 33 40 52, *'restaurant panoramique'*, at bottom of hill, looks scruffy but must have good views.

Sombernon – Pont-de-Pany
(7 km/4½ miles)

Take top road D9 past Hotel le Sombernon down to join main road D905 before motorway. (Without another big climb, there is no avoiding a short stretch alongside the motorway.) Go past sign which says *'sauf riverain'* (you can go on old roads either side of motorway), there is a smaller road initially on the left side of the motorway. Cross when smaller road goes on other side. Turn right.

Pont-de-Pany
On the river Ouche and the Canal de Bourgogne.
- ⊨ Hotels: Hotel-Restaurant le Pont de Pany (M), 21410 Pont de Pany, 80 23 60 59, looks good; Hotel Château la Chassagne (HH), Château de Pont, 80 40 47 50, swimming pool.

Day 11
Pont-de-Pany – Dijon
(20 km/12½ miles)

Pont-de-Pany – Plombierres-lès-Dijon
(15 km/9½ miles)

Take canal towpath. Cross under motorway and follow canal to **Fleurey-s-Ouche** and continue.

Velars-s-Ouche
- ✗ Auberge Goumande, à l'échangeur de l'A38, 21370 Velars-s-Ouche, 80 33 62 51, recommended by Michelin as good value.

Take the *Route Touristique* D10.

Plombierres-lès-Dijon
Suburban Dijon, but has port, old centre and fine railway viaducts.
- ⊨ Hotels la Combe-aux-Fées (M), 11 route de Dijon, 21370 Plombierre-lès-Dijon, 80 41 70 87.

Plombierres-lès-Dijon – Dijon
(5 km/3 miles)
Go back on canal towpath, and continue towards Dijon between canal and big boating lake. Go past the **Chartreuse de Champol**, through an attractive yacht harbour to the **Port du Canal**. Turn left into city centre.

Dijon
Capital of a state that united Flanders and Burgundy, centre of good food and wine, and mustard. See old city, palace of Dukes of Burgundy, cathedral, museums, etc.
- ⊨ Hotels: Hotels des Allées (M), 27 cours du Général-de-Gaulle, 21000 Dijon, 80 66 57 50, good value rooms (no restaurant but nearby restaurant le Sommatino has excellent pizzas); Hotel Wilson (H), place Wilson, 80 66 82 50, with Michelin designated gourmet Restaurant Thibert.
- ✗ Restaurant le Rallye, 39 rue Chabot-Charny, 80 61 11 55, recommended by Michelin as good value; Jean Pierre Billoux, Hotel la Cloche, 14 place Darcy, 80 30 11 10; Chapeau Rouge, 5 rue Michelet, 80 30 28 10, both Michelin gourmet restaurants.

For airport, take *Route de Longvic* south from Place Wilson. It is 4 km (2½ miles).

CHAPTER FIVE

Silk and Chestnut

Marvejols to Tarascon via the Gorges du Tarn,
the Cévennes and the Pont du Gard

An exciting ride through dramatic and different landscapes which crosses the southern edge of the Massif and ends in the Mediterranean plain. This is a rocky land where people have had to carve a frugal life from the soil. Those who remain are tough and independent, looking for new ways of making a living by combining tourism with their farming. Travelling north to south through three *départements* – Lozère, Gard and Hérault – it dips into the Gorges du Tarn and climbs to a bare limestone highland, the Causse Méjean, before continuing over Mont Aigoual, through woods of beech and conifer and alpine meadows. Continuing down through the chestnut terraces of the Cévennes and among the green oaks of the garrigue, it ends among the vineyards of the Languedoc on the edge of Provence – a countryside very different from the trip's beginning in the Lot valley on the fringes of the pastoral Auvergne.

I have two unforgettable images of that autumn. The first is of crimson leaves falling unwaveringly through the sunlight, one still morning after the first touch of frost. The second picture is of a street tree that continued to drop its leaves on a council sweeper as he tried desperately to clean them up. He swept, they dropped, he swept. He was doing it, he told me, in honour of William Wordsworth and the citizens of his birthplace, Cockermouth in Cumbria who were here for a twinning.

This was at the market town of Marvejols, in the valley of the Lot, where I began my journey. It is difficult not to love a town which sounds as if it has both 'marvel' and 'jolly' in its name: and when that town is anciently fortified with medieval gateways and a higgledy-piggle of houses and lanes within, it becomes impossible. So Cockermouth is fortunate to have been twinned with Marvejols.

Opposite the ticket office in Marvejols station is a picture of Cockermouth station (before they closed it), and in the station yard, opposite the Hotel de la Gare and the *abbattoir publique*, is a plaque: *'Cockermouth, patrie du poète W. Wordsworth'*.

Now there was to be another one in celebration of Marvejols and Cockermouth having been twinned for ten years.

The architect of the town-twinning, Phillippe Nogaret, was happy and nervous at the same time, like a hamster who has just discovered its first peanut and fears that it might somehow slip away at the last moment. For this was ten years of work to be summed up in a single, official gesture. No matter that the hundreds of visits and friendships were their own reward, Marvejols and Cockermouth had decided that they have to show their approval as communities. There was to be a week of junketings and visits for the coach party from Cockermouth.

For their part, the French had devised a ceremony of extraordinary complication. To enhance their own mayor, they had imported a senator who wore an expression of intense political seriousness throughout which, with his dark coat, gave him an air of professional mourning like an undertaker's assistant at a funeral, but one to which a brass band had been invited by mistake. In his speech, the French mayor turned to the park bench donated to Marvejols by Allandale District Council. It appeared to be an honour too great for the Marvejollies to bear: he said it would forever be for the citizens of Cockermouth to sit on. Politely, the English mayor insisted: no, it was for the French to sit on. The senator was too serious to say anything, but he cut a tricolour ribbon across the path leading to the bench, and continued cutting it into tiny pieces, which were distributed as mementoes.

I left Marvejols through a medieval gateway with cracks in it; for until they finish the Paris–Montpellier motorway this is a main route south, and the town has juggernauts pounding round it. I followed the lorries down the valley, but not for long, for I was hardly past the last house before my route took me off on to a smaller road to Mende and, immediately afterwards, on to yet a smaller one that crossed a bridge and wound uphill. I made a good start, not in terms of my speed, which was slow and steady, but in vegetation, for there was marjoram bearing the ageing flowers of summer and a wonderful mushroom, a hands-width across, white-gilled below, brilliant red above and looking fascinatingly poisonous. It was late September, with a hazy autumn sun and warm. This was the shady side of the hill – but it was hot enough with the exercise for me to be glad of the extra shade of the white oak and pine, which gave the breeze a resinous fragrance, that lined the hill above me.

It took me forty minutes to climb up to the village of Palhers after several stops, a number of smiles from passing cars.

Palhers is a pretty enough place with warm-coloured stone houses that were very likely younger than they seemed, since one barn that looked seventeenth-century bore the date, 1884, and a cross on its lintel. A patient dog, too patient even to bark, guarded a long house with grey shutters and a few last pears yellowing high in its orchard. But the treasure was in the orchard opposite: its trees even more decrepit, but its grass dotted with autumn crocus. They say that these *colchiques* take very badly to the ground being disturbed, so I suppose I was looking at turf from long ago. It was certainly green enough, with the colours of the crocus petals varying between light grey and a modest purple. It is a flimsy and spindly flower, but all the more beautiful for its fragility. Quite often there were tentative outbreaks of them in the fields that followed. Occasionally, too, there was yellow broom ridiculously in flower alongside the scarlet of rosehips.

At the top of the hill, the wind was up, and the sky clouding. The road undulated over the side of a long slope which began as a crag and eventually turned into a wide vale, green and peaceful. But one handmade sign by the verge said, *Touche pas à mon paysage!* (Hands off my landscape) and another, '*Autoroute = Fin de la Commune*'. Far away, in the round hills that bordered the vale, I saw the scar of a new cutting, and wondered where the autoroute would go from there. As my little road bent round the hill the wind increased, till some of the gusts were strong enough to stop me freewheeling on the downs. Above me, a big hawk was suffering the same problem – trying to ride the wind and getting blown backwards. Eventually it gave up its attempts as a bad job and disappeared into a clump of pines. I found my own refuge rounding the curve of the hill into calmer air. Below me the Lot hid within a green muffler of trees the centrepiece of a narrow valley that rose to a bare ridge of highland opposite – my next day's journey.

Space is cramped at the bottom of the valley, which is narrow here and has to fit in not only the Lot and a few meadows but the railway and the road down which I turned towards Mende. It was quite a busy road, and on my left the world ahead was threatening to get modern; but on the right there was a turreted château and in the pools of the river the sky reflected silver, with the shadows of the trees falling on the water like black lace. In comparison the tiny industrial estate of Chanac looked not only impertinent but impermanent, but I was soon able to recapture the past by climbing over an old bridge up to the real Chanac, a cluster of stone houses huddling below the tower of a ruined castle. Attracted to the Hotel des Voyageurs by the fact that it was also a newsagent – though Madame had all her copies of *Midi Libre* inside ('Otherwise,' she said, 'they blow away') – I was delighted to discover that she had tuned into my medievalist mood by hanging curtains of chain mail over the doorways to keep the flies out. As I came in, I surprised the chef having a quick one behind the gloomy bar: in his kitchen clothes it was rather like encountering a white deer in a dark forest, for he quickly wiped his mouth on the back of his hand and discreetly slipped away into the underbush towards the kitchen. I took it as a good sign, since I always prefer my chefs human. And so it proved, with a warm salad of *gésiers* (chicken gizzards) followed by duck breast with a green pepper sauce accompanied by courgettes in béchamel. A hefty cheeseboard and a crème caramel all came out of the 85F menu. I polished off a good bottle of Lirac and went to bed expecting to sleep well, though I had only spent a leisurely three hours on the road. However, I had reckoned without the *broyeurs*, which are a kind of waste disposal unit applied to lavatories and are popular in old buildings where the proprietors want to stuff in as many bathrooms as they can without tearing the place apart. Constant snarlings and grumblings came from all parts of the hotel, as if from discontented animals in their lairs. Something particularly mechanical and rumbly also lived behind my bedroom wall, causing a print of life in the Parisian demi-monde to live it up with a persistent rattle. Outside, the street was utterly still, with nothing moving but an occasional gleam of light on the leaves of the acacias in the garden opposite.

When I woke up the road was suspiciously dark and the leaves were gleaming with drizzle that turned to light rain as darker clouds spun in from the Mediterranean. During breakfast there was thunder and lightning, and when I put my head out of doors it was machine-gunned by raindrops so big that when they hit the road they exploded into rain-storms of their own. I pulled back my soaking-wet head, and spent the morning enquiring fruitlessly of the locals as to what might be the chances of a lone cyclist being struck by lightning. After lunch it was dry again, though grey, as I took the long climb out of the village up the side of a valley which had fields below, pines above, and me and a smell of mushrooms in between. There were still a few harebells out, damp but delicate.

Weary after my night with the *broyeurs*, I went slowly, alternating spells of pedalling with spells of walking. I was still quite close to the village when there was a noise which at first I took to be me wheezing, a happy, peaceful sort of sound, as if deep organ pipes were talking to one another. Then I recognized it: *sanglier*. They are everywhere in this part: shy creatures and not often to be seen, but they leave traces where they have rooted for fungi along the roadside or come down into an orchard after windfalls. I peered into the wood, but there was nothing, so I went on, more cheerfully.

The road climbed steadily through a country of scrubby grass, juniper and grey boulders, among which were fields of good brown earth that looked as if they had flowed into place among islands of pine trees. So pleased was I at the descent that followed, I missed the short cut via Grand Lac and turned left later by the grey village of la Capelle, which apart from its squat-spired church boasted a very little house, an extremely little house, a smallish house, an ordinary house and a couple of sheds.

At les Pelards there had been a marriage, for at the farm entrance an arch had been made of box branches and juniper bushes and dedicated to 'Matilde et Didier'. It was a picturesque old farm with strutting chickens, cocks crowing and a hunting dog baying at me from the yard. The road climbed towards a minor col and my pace slowed. There were more pines now, making it feel almost Scandinavian. I was well tired out by the time the road headed down a valley to Cabrunas, where I came round the corner at the Café-Restaurant du Panorama and suddenly became aware that there the world had lost its edge. Only a narrow grass verge separated me from

Overleaf: The perfect swimming river – the Gorges du Tarn.

nothingness. Far below, the river Tarn wound through its gorges like a curl of grey glass that turned green in the deeper pools. Roads and paths snaked like threads among the reddening bushes on the mountain opposite. It was a panorama indeed, complete with café tables and chairs. I wondered whether they have this sort of thing in hell from which to look down on the sinners in comfort.

The road ran along the edge of a precipice, and I was on the precipitous side. As I descended I found myself braking heavily, keeping in the middle of the road and – especially where the low wall had been broken by something or other, such as a falling cyclist – I felt the lack of a seat belt. Halfway down the slope, a small white car stood on its roof: I wondered why it bothered to stop there. At the first few drops of rain, I allowed myself to pick up speed down the hairpins to Ste Enimie. The rain became a downpour. Only, as I saw the town spread out like a toy village below, the church clock chimed to welcome me.

So I came into Ste Enimie in the dusk, as they were shutting up the shops. A church bell sounded like the clang of doom, the rain streamed, and the roads flowed. I was wet and tired, but Ste Enimie was indifferent, and the Hotel Bulatis was a forbidding building with scarcely another guest.

The town itself was tired, though it is a pretty place, with old houses huddling by the river, perching themselves on any flat patch on the hills above and the gorges towering over everything. But it had been a long, crowded season and most of the tourist establishments had decided that profitable days were over for this year and there was no sense hanging on for a few oddballs like me.

Next morning everyone was discussing the storm. I discussed fax machines struck by lightning with the hotel receptionist; the ruination of the wild mushroom crop with a chef who poked his nose out of a subterranean kitchen like a white mole, and Madame at the *boulangerie* handed me doom and gloom with the slice of pizza which I bought for lunch. There was a strong feeling that the season had been going on too long anyway, and if the weather was going to go on like this, well . . . .

Outside, the Tarn was still brown and impetuous. I followed it downstream past cafés, camp sites, signs for canoes and kayaks. The air was fresh, but the road was drying off already and I had it pretty much to myself. I thought it remarkable how little spoilt the gorges remained, considering the hordes that descend in July and August. I passed one tiny cottage built into the cliff like a fairy house, with a very fat man and his dog climbing up through its garden's precipitous terraces like a couple of oversized dwarfs. It had tiny windows, a leek patch, two gnarled trees hung with very green apples and no fewer than four home-made *'Propriété privé'* notices in curly writing. Here was a dwarf besieged by tourists, and it struck me that it summed up a good deal about the Tarn – a fairy-tale invaded. No less quaint was the picture-postcard village of St-Chély with its bridge, waterfall and stubby-towered church. Yellow kayaks upside down on its shore looked like strange seed pods, its picnic tables like brown mushrooms.

The traces of a harder existence than the tourist trade were everywhere, and weed-covered. Most of the old patches of cultivation clinging among the cliffs were overgrown, but I passed one vineyard hung with black, bloomy grapes full of cold, tart juice and with chewy skins. It came on to rain, so I sheltered under an overhanging rock, only to discover that the rain ran down through the porous stone, so that it was still dripping from the previous day. I went on, with nothing much else on the road, going through the occasional tunnel which was exciting instead of alarming. Above me, swallows flitted among the cliffs, like bats.

It was a journey full of memories, for I had cycled that road almost fifteen years before, when it was a little less rich and a little more real. I travelled it for the same reason, to come to the bottom of the hill of la Malène which rises up the side of the gorges like a Tibetan road-builder's nightmare. The hill directly up from Ste Enimie is longer and much busier; and the route along the Tarn and up the Gorges de la Jonte is long. La Malène was still a very pretty place with a château whose towers simply cannot manage to be straight all the way up and the road up the mountain curling as if in agony towards wisps of cloud. The romance was slightly impaired by a caravan of idiots blowing a hunting-horn and rock music at full blast from an empty and expensive *quat'quat'*, as the French call the four-wheel drives which are the curse of the quiet places of the Cévennes. In summer, I do not imagine that the firm hiring out boats with outboard motors greatly contributed to the tranquillity either.

From the hillside I could see more clearly the remains of real existence. One of the new canoe-hirers was revealed as a mill: below me was an overgrown cherry orchard, and a few hopeful olive trees. A slightly more sympathetic stretch of hillside had managed to develop some tiny, impoverished stone-walled fields. I was dawdling, picking marjoram for my pizza, passing twisted walnuts and curtains of Old Man's Beard. I was not surprised to see another cyclist spinning down towards me, shouting joyfully, *'C'est meilleur la descente!'* in sadistic camaraderie, but as I plodded on an hour or so later I was astonished to see a man in a pink shirt behind me. He had an old roadster, pumping at his pedals so fiercely that the bike gave a visible spurt with every stroke. It has to be a Dutchman, I thought, storming up like that on something so wildly unsuitable. For cycling, you need few muscles if you have patience, but for the hill of la Malène you need an awful lot of patience. Pink shirt spurted past me and continued pumping his way to the top, just before which he turned round and came back down again. Since he was less in a hurry, he stopped to chat: he was a German, he said – in German – and a pensioner. It was a little humiliating, but I can endure such things. I had the place to myself for it had come on to rain. La Malène was quite small below me, and between us were clouds. A sign warned me of a rock fall up ahead, which seemed an unnecessary complication. I thought that the pizza would be comforting, but something told me that I ought to be eating it in the dry because wet pizza is no fun. On the other hand sooner or later the rain would get through to it in the saddlebag.

I took to walking for stretches, then standing in the rain stock-still, looking like a red monk in a state of inconvenient meditation, the rain trickling down my cape and falling between my toes. Starting off again, my feet moved of themselves, as when one is drunk: it was helpful of them. Blinkered by my hood I had little else to look at without a special effort and the last part of the climb was distinguished mainly by smells – grass and herbs – and passing cars, particularly diesels. As I came to the top I found that I could still recognize where the last bend must be. I came round the corner and there it was as I remembered it, a steepish one followed by a little hump and beyond, the road ahead went down. Over the hump I saw first misty hills, pine-covered slopes, telegraph poles and at last the road itself. There was even a patch of shelter under a pine tree where I could eat a triumphal pizza, which was only a little bit wet and delicious with the marjoram. As I drank from my water bottle (something which I only do in extremis), I thought how odd it was to have to put water inside me when there was so much outside.

Peaceful among the clouds that floated among the hills of the causse, I felt quite happy, which is an extraordinary thing when you are soaking wet, going to get wetter, if possible, and you have a long ride ahead of you. My legs found it very strange to be going round and round instead of up and down and did not care for it very much. As I set off, the theme from *Gone with the Wind* came into my head and would not go away, however inappropriate.

Below: La Malène, facing the prospect of a long haul out of the gorges.

Opposite: The Gorges de la Jonte, less well-known than the Gorges du Tarn, but more picturesque.

Cut off as it is by gorges from most of the rest of France, the plateau of the Causse Méjean is not only an island but looks like one, with its rolling fells and huddled grey-stone farms, many of them in a picturesque state of decay since it is often easier to put up a modern agricultural building than repair the old one. There are fewer than 500 people on the causse and 20 000 sheep, bred either for meat or milk, much of which goes for Roquefort, whose mouldy caves are some 80 km (50 miles) away. It is difficult to get on to the Roquefort list, so other initiatives are being looked at including an experiment in breeding Prezwalski's Horse, and making new cheeses.

La Parade is a crossroads village boasting a church, garage and a small hotel-restaurant which is of the congenial old-fashioned kind where you do not have to fuss with different menus, for there is only one and it is set in front of you. The village has a story to it as well, for it was the scene of a massacre at the end of the Second World War when the Germans were tipped off that the local resistance had been running an airfield for British planes for years and slaughtered them to a man. That is half of the story: a monument commemorates it, a grey obelisk behind which, improbably, there was a gleam of sunlight as I passed. There is no monument to the rest of the tale: how the Germans then herded the local women and children into a building and were about to set fire to it until persuaded against the idea by the eloquence of the local *curé*.

It was late afternoon by the time I was past la Parade and on to the downhill stretch that followed. A wind had sprung up behind and the slipstream was cold against my wet hands and face. For the first time even my bare feet felt a chill and I allowed myself to think of the prospect of a hot bath. This part of the causse is very bare and dramatic, the colour of dry grass rolling unbroken into fells but for a few patches planted with dull, dark pines. I passed the turning for the show cave, the Aven Armand, and the long piece of level ground that followed took me to a sign for hairpins which for the first time that day, led downwards. As the wind grew stronger and the downhill steeper, the theme from *Gone with the Wind* became more appropriate. On my right opened the chasm of the Gorges de la Jonte, smaller than the Gorges du Tarn but hardly less beautiful. With clouds scuttering away on a level with me and the hills ahead darkening, there was a feeling of cycling through the air above the world. And there, glimpsed through the cleft of the gorge was Meyrueis in the distance, all rooftops and misty lights. I was stiff, aching and cold. The brakes and the road were wet and I had to hang on to my cape to stop it blowing. The town was miles away yet but it was downhill.

I arrived at Meyrueis at about six o'clock since there, too, they rang the church bells to welcome me, and walked into the Hotel Mont Aigoual with all the elegance of a duck with two sore feet. No one was about in reception, but in the kitchen I found a solid gentleman in chef's whites who took me to stable my bike in the garage where he kept his own, and discussed mushrooms all the way back, having just had the first ceps of the season brought in.

An hour or two of hot bath and a long beer later, I discussed them again, in an omelette, as a prelude to perfectly rosy lamb chops and a good bottle of Corbières. This chef-proprietor was an enthusiast for his work, an easy genial fellow who was the perfect complement to Madame, his wife, who was as quick as a bird, being one of those women of whom you can never be quite sure whether they are about to do something, or have done it already, and manage to look as if they have just stepped in off the Champs Elysées into the bargain. We chatted late, and I passed a more peaceful night than the previous one, when I had dreamt that my legs were going round at a tremendous pace, propelling me in all possible directions at once.

Meyrueis was once a frontier post between Gevaudan and the Languedoc. Today it is a stop on the tourist route between the Tarn and Mont Aigoual, as you can tell by the number of hotels. It is a pleasant place with an old tower and the river and the main street running together, used to being welcoming to strangers while keeping quite a lot of its own sense of community. I saw local life expressed rather gruesomely when a white van parked itself opposite the bar, and started bleeding into the road. The back doors were flung open by one of an attendant party of men in green and passers-by began to gather to stare at the body of a small fox that lay inside, so bedraggled it looked more like a rabbit, and a gigantic wild boar, all teeth and stomach. Cars paused for a look; small boys were asked whether they, too, would be hunters when they grew up (which they would) and little girls were encouraged to be feminine and shockable (which they would not, even a little one in ribbons who was handed the fox's brush, still bleeding). Whatever you feel about hunting – and it is not something I want to do myself – it is part of traditional culture here. On the causse, they trap thrushes with a bit of grain and a stone balanced on sticks: but the prize game is the *sanglier*, with tusky teeth that can kill a large dog and seriously wound its master, that is, if that gentleman did not happen to be armed with a rifle, which tips the scales somewhat decisively against the boar.

The hunters lugged the *sanglier* out into the road, as bristly and rubbery as if it were still alive and weighed it on an old balance. The burly, soft-faced young man who had shot it neatly behind the head said that 115 kilos (330 lb) was his best ever. He took no pleasure in killing, but oh, he did like hunting. Between 100 and 150 boars are killed every year around Meyrueis: so the contribution to the dedicated hunter's freezer can be substantial.

I left Meyrueis the next day part walking, part riding, for it is a long hill out of town, though not too steep, and there were blackberries along the verge. It began as a grey day, fresh, with a tinkle of sheep bells from the hillside opposite, a sound which stayed with me longer than the sight of the town, which was soon lost among the pines that crowded my side of the valley. As I climbed, clouds hung among them, peacefully and raindrops bright on acacia leaves pattered to the leaf below with the occasional breath of wind. It was not long before the pattering increased and the drops fell more frequently. Behind me the dry grass on the Causse Méjean blazed

Victim of twin Gallic passions for hunting and good food, a wild boar at Meyrueis.

yellow in sunlight. A quick squall sent me scrambling for my cape and I joined the chorus of pattering, since rain on a cycle cape sounds like rain on an umbrella, only more so, since you are actually inside it.

So, rather cold with two magpies squawking at me from the valley, I came to the place near Lanuéjols where you can look across mile upon mile of rolling highland and feel that the summit of everything is not far away.

My road curled round the hill through the Forest of Aigoual and I came to the Abime du Bramabiau, the unbelievably narrow ravine made by the modest stream of le Bonheur, which you pass flowing modestly through the meadows of Camprieu as if it had no thought of doing anything at all dramatic in the rest of its existence, and eased myself off the bike for a cup of coffee in the ticket office, which doubles as a snack bar. Not till I felt the warmth inside did I realize how cold I was. A scruffy dog came and shivered at the door, but no one would let it in. I knew how it felt.

The road wound up through the forest towards the Col de Faubel. There were puff-balls in the verge and – more often – rootings in the earth where *sanglier* had been after mushrooms. As it neared evening a weak sun shone, and animals came out: two small deer that in the mist and the shafts of light became a sepia print that faded into brushwoods and, wonder of wonders, the *sangliers* themselves, a family taking a stroll along the road – father all jaw, mother plump bottom and half a dozen little ones pit-patting at their heels. Apparently without a thought that I might be a hunter, they climbed the bank unhurriedly and disappeared, leaving me with the thought that they were more enjoyable living, than dead. I reached the top of the Col de Faubel and the minor ski resort of l'Esperou, where there are hotels, but not always snow. Guiltily, I passed the turn off to the summit of Mont Aigoual with its views to the Alps and the Pyrénées (when the air is clear). It is a hefty climb up to its weather station and museum. I understand the museum will give you a badge to say you did it, but I have none.

I had an hour of light left so I took the longest downhill stretch of all – 20–30 km (12½–18½ miles), depending how you go – to Pont d'Hérault. It was dusk now, and bitterly cold, but as I came round the hairpins a great hawk swooped along with me, coming close, swinging away and returning to cross my path further down, What it thought it was doing I don't know, but for me it was a kind of temporary, ridiculous and awe-inspiring dance.

The Cévennes are a series of mountains and valleys. From the crests you see them folding away into the distance, each valley with its separate life, each mountain community isolated. When monks began to open up the area at the start of the middle ages, introducing the sweet chestnut, they came to a beautiful wilderness. Painstakingly, over the centuries, people claimed tiny pieces of mountainside for back-breaking agriculture, heaping up soil on the slopes and bounding it with dry stone walls to which every sack, every bucket, would have to be borne on somebody's back thereafter. They tended their chestnuts and pastured their animals among them; they diverted the waters of springs and streams in complex systems of canals which were forever leaking and choking themselves with weeds, but from which you could drink without a qualm. They became hard-working, independent people, living mostly in what were not farms so much as small farming communities based on the family. Big landowners were few and irrelevant: but from a small-holding with water and a patch of pasture a family might spread its domain up the mountainside, enlarging its house as it went for sons and daughters, farm workers and labourers, until there was a whole interconnected hamlet built of local stone and chestnut beams – a rambling, up-and-down complex of rooms, barns and stables called a *mas*. There would be goats, sheep, a pig, vegetables and wheat from the terraces, fish from the river and a patch of poor vines. They lived by the seasons and were poor, self-sufficient and proud. And for centuries nothing broke this pattern of existence, except two things – religion and a greedy worm.

Religion brought an influx of Protestants seeking the liberty to live their own lives who caught the Cévenols up in a tide of persecution and religious wars that resulted in many abandoning their mountains for Switzerland, Germany or London. Today it is still a common question to ask if a stranger is Catholic or Protestant and villages are still divided along those lines. Another memorial is the fact that many a *mas* will have a small graveyard, for the Cévenols have the right to be buried in home ground rather than in the local Catholic cemetery.

The silkworm came in not many centuries after the chestnuts, but its great days were in the last two or three hundred years. It brought a precarious prosperity. A good year meant riches to a family, but all their labour and expense could be blown away by a puff of cold wind. The old *mas* and the severe, upright houses of the valleys would contain an enormous room called a *magnagnerie*, which you can always identify by traces of a fireplace in each corner. In a world without insulation, the worm had to be kept warm, being a delicate beast – and a capricious one – which could be put off its life cycle by a thunderstorm at the wrong moment.

Monsieur Costa, who has been responsible almost singlehandedly for a tiny but growing revival of Cévenol silk, showed me his empire at the small silk factory (called a *filature*) at Monoblet, above St-Hippolyte-du-Fort, which he shares with a couple of assistants, an apprentice and a loom-tuner with such a fine biblical beard that it struck me as a pity not to weave that, too.

Blindfold, your nose will tell you when you are in a silk factory, for the cocoons bobbing in hot water to loosen the thread are anything but fragrant. The factory works with a combination of older and newer equipment, humming, clicking and spinning to produce brightly-coloured thread and cloth. But some traditional ways they have not adopted.

'In the bosoms,' Monsieur Costa told me, 'women hung a bag of eggs, to hatch them. And in some villages, one woman went to bed for all the farmers.'

'All of them at once?'

'All the eggs of the village in bed with her for fifteen days to keep warm.'

I thought of the final moment when a slight wriggling sensation would tell the lady that she was about to be surrounded by worms; and decided I did not want the job.

Below Mont Liron live the brothers Liron: I suppose the mountain was there first, but it is tempting to think the opposite. As I write, they are the last in the valley to follow life as it has been led for centuries. They are *paysans*, a term which has nothing of the disdain in the English 'peasant'. Rather, they are wise men of the fields, who know more about plants and their growing than anyone: when to plant with the moon and when before or after. They are monks of the mountain, guarding a tradition that everyone respects, though few will follow it.

Their *mas* has the finest position of all – at the head of the valley that looks due south over ranks of neat terraces which are almost all that remain of a system of cultivation that once covered every available patch of ground. Their goat cheese was always the cheapest and best, but EC regulations do not take that into account – only the conditions under which it is made. The goats still go up the mountain to feed, but not for much longer.

The Lirons still have their *clède* for drying chestnuts – the old staple food of the Cévennes – but have recently abandoned its use with the labour keeping its fires going for weeks. The local sweet onions are still a viable crop, but hard work, carrying manure on their backs to the terraces below, humping the crop back up again. Worst of all, they are getting old. They have never had any transport with more than two wheels – not a tractor, not a car – and now time is catching up with them. They have already sold off some bits of the *mas* to foreigners who are there sometimes and when they sell the *mas*, probably for too little (as they sell their cheese), and retire to a little house in the plain, it will be the end of an era.

But the Cévennes have a way of continuing, and even bouncing back. There are many in whom at least something of the traditional knowledge of the Cévennes – if not its peasant way of life – carries on. Very few, for instance who are not infected with the local frenzy for mushrooms every autumn. Every chemist has a mushroom display in his window, for it is to him you take anything doubtful for identification, and at le Vigan there was a grand exhibition of two or three hundred varieties freshly picked in the forest. They have gendarmes on the gate and no wonder: you have never seen such passion since the Three Bears discovered Goldilocks. A pretty young blonde with a light in her eye normally reserved for the first excesses of true love scratched at stems in search of the smell of cinnamon, and plunged her nose into the mushrooms like a vampire who has not eaten for a century. There were whites, red, blues, purples, yellows, salmon-pinks and spots. *Ceps* brown as a teapot, self-contained as a piece of rustic pottery. Some labels carried a skull and crossbones, but generally the emphasis was not on what you could not eat, but what you could. That is the difference between the Continent and Britain.

All along the tables, noses wrinkled, and tentative nibbling took place (frowned on by the organizers for fear that some exhibits would disappear entirely). Arguments began, arms flew about in gesticulation, tiny children stood on tiptoe to hoist noses over tabletops and eyeball the fungi from below, as Alice did the Caterpillar.

All this goes on for two days, at the end of which the stalwarts of the event take themselves off and have mushroom feasts with particular friends in celebration of the booty of the forest. Booty it is, with not only the thrill of discovery, but a glorious sense of 'Mine, all mine!' overtakes even the most generous and social of people, who sneak out early with bags under their coats so that no one will know where they are going.

Jean-Yves Guillesson and his wife Lizzie live in a cottage so high on the mountain that the *sanglier* are always rooting up their garden, and I had my mushroom feast with them. They are of the generation who dropped out in the years after May '68: indeed, they met as students during the disturbances and fell in love on the barricades. As the Huguenots centuries before, many a young couple like them came to the Cévennes in search of remoteness and cheap land. They found both in what was almost a dead country – terraces untended, houses crumbling, roofs falling in. They never fell for the dream of three acres and a goat, but made their relationship with the Cévennes out of stones and nature. The little money they had, bought them what had been a goat shelter – little more than an arched stone shed against a rock. On this Jean-Yves built a granite house alone, wrestling stones out of the stream-bed, man-handling them down across the meadow, learning how to build walls with them, and cutting his own beams from the chestnut terraces.

Jean-Yves is a Breton with some idea of country ways: Lizzie, a middle-class English girl, found herself bringing up her son Tristan in an idyllic wilderness in hardship and poverty. To this day they have no electricity, but they make do with a tumbling brook, old trees, a waterfall called 'Wolf's Leap', because it was there that the last of the local wolves was killed long ago and a rapport with their surroundings that has made both father and son outstanding naturalists and bird-watchers.

We sat beside a fire of chestnut logs in their living-room and ate preserved *ceps*, followed by an omelette of *Trompettes de Mort* which are 'Horn of Plenty' in English. There was a British steak and horse-mushroom pie, and from Central Europe mushrooms with tomato, paprika and cream.

In the afternoon, Jean-Yves and I stood in the rocky corner by the brook where he will be buried one day. He has already chosen the gigantic slab and the four friends who will crowbar it into place – after many years working with stone, he knows exactly how it will fall. The spot is under beeches overlooking his meadow.

Mont Liron, and below the mas *of the brothers Liron.*

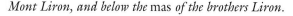

The Causse Méjean, more sheep than people: the milk goes to make Roquefort.

'You know,' he said to me, not at all elegiacally, for he is a quick, wiry leprechaun of a man who switches between seriousness and laughter as leaves between light and shade, 'In that meadow I have three times as many kinds of butterflies as in the whole of the British Isles.' It was an irrelevant point, but somehow it seemed to sum up everything.

From le Vigan, I rode south-east along the grey gorges of the river Hérault – they are friendly cliffs and there is good swimming here in summer – to Ganges, a small town of great charm with an excellent and lively market on Fridays. It should be in the *département* of Gard but it was exchanged for a seaside resort and given to the *département* of Hérault. It is not inappropriate because the little town has an air of the plains about it as if you are already close to the shores of the Mediterranean, which indeed is only an hour away by car. Even the building stone is different, for the granite and dark schist of the Cévennes gives way to a smooth pale limestone, which is eaten away into great gorges as you go south.

I went south-west into the *garrigue* and vines, past St-Hippolyte-du-Fort, and Durfort with the old towns and villages becoming increasingly Provençal in feeling. There were fields of what had been a fine crop of asparagus and orchards of bare peach trees. Some vines had turned yellow-gold, others red. Others had lost their leaves entirely leaving a few small bunches of fruit abandoned to the rain, with waterdrops hanging below them like more silver grapes. They were tart and delicious, though they needed inspecting for mould.

By the time I passed below the hilltop town of Vézénobres everything had softened into the less bracing existence of the plain. The Gardon river was wide and lazy. I crossed it first low down on a bridge almost level with the water like a raised ford, then on a bridge high above it. Here the landscape is wild and secretive, the river dark and deep, with caves that house the traces of some of the earliest men in Europe.

At last I came along small roads to within a few miles of the Pont du Gard, the most impressive Roman artefact in France, which you can only approach from the larger roads that bring in hundreds of thousands of tourists a year to admire it. Standing high above the river, an aqueduct and roadway combined, it is as perfect as the day it was built. For my last night I stayed in Collias at the Castellas hotel which is not the cheapest, but is among the most agreeable French hotels I know, with fine cooking, great charm and a touch of fantasy – they have the only hotel bathroom whose floor is covered in river pebbles that I have ever seen. There I rested in style after a long journey.

The Cévennes 8 days 261.5 km (163¼ miles)

⊟ Accommodation   ✖ Places to eat   ⟠ Detour   **A** Alternative route

Map Ref: IGN Brown Series 304 and Green Series 66 (or 65 if you finish at Montpellier).

To get there: Road or rail to Marvejols or air to Montpellier.

To get back: Road or rail from Tarascon or air from Montpellier.

Weather: Summers hot, winters chilly north of Mont Aigoual, mild in the south. Can have sudden violent storms.

Food and drink: No great regional cuisine, but good simple things. *Pelardons* are little disks of goats' cheese which come fresh, or old and dry. Try a salad with hot fried *pelardons*, or *gésiers* (giblets). There are some wonderful blue cheeses including Roquefort (Papillon or Société) and Blue de Causse. There is excellent local mountain-cured salami and ham (*jambon cru*). If you can find a *fête* with *mechouï* (barbecued lamb) it will be local lamb and delicious. There are also great *aïoli* feasts, where everything gets smothered in garlic mayonnaise. In winter there is game, especially wild boar. And if you want to know how people survived before 1950, try chestnut soup (if you can find it). The local wines are undistinguished. The local wines are undistinguished until you reach the plains. Finally you will find good reds like Côtes du Rhône, Costieres du Gard and Chateauneuf-du-Pape (see also Chapter 6). Try also Cartagene, a sweet fortified grape juice. Pastis is the summer drink.

Useful addresses: Ligue Languedoc-Roussillon, 31 rue de la Macreuse, 31430 Mauguio, tel: 67 29 34 95. NB: To book gîtes d'étapes contact the local tourist office as to what is available.

Day 1
Marvejols – Chanac
(15 km/9½ miles)

Marvejols **A**
Pretty old fortified town. Useful tourist office by north gate. Cycle hire from Hotel de la Gare (see below).

⊟ Hotels: Hotel de la Poste (L), 2 boulevard St Dominique, 48000 Marvejols, 66 32 00 99, cyclist owner; Hotel de la Gare et des Rochers (M), place Gare, 66 32 10 58, comfortable, nice views, but eat out.

✖ Le Griffon, light food, centre of town; le Moulin de Chaze, Palhers (see below),

⟠ Detour (9 km/5½ miles) to the **wolf park**, *les Loups de Gévaudan*, at **Ste-Lucie**. Go north on N9 7 km, then turn right on small road to pretty hilltop hamlet. One hundred and sixty wolves, including eighty saved by Brigitte Bardot.

⊟ Hotels: Hostellerie Ste Lucie (M), 48100 Marvejols, 66 32 35 91.

From **Marvejols** follow directions to **Chirac** on N9. Just outside town at **Pont-Presil**, go left by Peugeot Garage on N600 towards Mende. After approx. 100 m turn right over river on small road D31 and continue on other side.

Palhers
✖ Le Moulin de Chaze, 66 32 36 07, *restaurant gourmand*. Continue on same road, but leave river and start climbing. Descend to main road N88 at the river Lot.

⟠ See *Domaine Médiévale des Champs* (medieval farm and château) to right on N88 at **le Villard**.

Turn left along river, then first right across river on **Vieux Pont**.

Chanac
Old fortifications.

⊟ Hotels: Hotel Lou Cantou (L), 48230 Chanac, 66 48 20 10, seemed friendly; Hotel-restaurant Barbut-Gache (L), 66 48 20 14; Hotel Voyageurs (M), 66 48 20 16, reasonable. Fermes-auberges: Syndicat d'Initiative, 66 48 20 21.

A An alternative start is **Mende**. Follow the river Lot south-west along busy main road N88.

⟠ Turn right for brief detour to prehistoric remains on **Causse de la Changefege**.

Continue on main road, then first left at **Balsièges**. Cross river on D986 and climb past the Lion de Balsièges. Go left past unusual fortified farm **Tour de Choizal**. Continue to the **Gorges du Tarn** and **Ste-Enimie**.

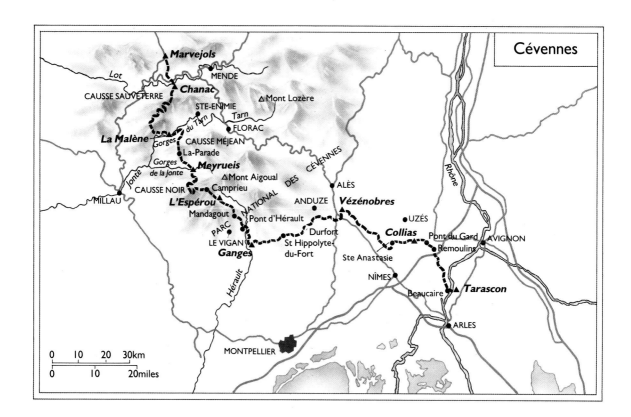

Cévennes

Day 2
Chanac – la Malène
(42 km/26 miles)

Go south on D32 climbing up to the Causse Sauveterre, a barren upland plateau with few habitations or roads, but many pre-historic remains. Once you are there it is easy cycling. Go past the **Baraq du Cros** with its unmanned shelter.

⟦↓⟧ Go left down GR60 for *dolmen* (prehistoric tombs).

At the **Baraq de Lutran** ⟦A⟧, the centre of the Causse, take the D998 left past **la Capelle** and **Laval-du-Tarn**. Descend down hairpin bends to the Gorges du Tarn, picture-book scenery, loads of tourists in summer with swimming and canoeing possible.

St-Enimie

Swimming, canoeing, etc.
⟦🛏⟧ Hotels: Hotel Burlatis (M), 48210 St-Enimie, 66 48 52 30; Auberge du Moulin (M), 66 48 53 08, pretty building, mediocre food.

Go west down the Tarn past the Cirque de St-Chély and the Château de la Caze.

La Malène

⟦🛏⟧ Hotels: Hotel Auberge de l'Embarcadere (L), 48210 la Malène, 66 48 51 03; Hotel Manoir de Montesquiou (H), 66 48 51 12, '*belle demeure quinzième siècle*'; Hotel Château de la Caze (HH), 66 48 51 01, 5.5 km (2½ miles) back east along Tarn on D907.

⟦↓⟧ You can make detours either up or down the Tarn along D907, but the road is quite busy in summer. Go west down the Tarn to **le Rozier** (20 km/12½ miles). A very pretty village at the juncture of the Gorges du Tarn and the Gorges de la Jonte.

⟦🛏⟧ Hotels: Hotel Doussière (L), 48150 le Rozier, 65 62 60 25; Grand Hotel des Voyageurs (M), 65 62 60 09.

⟦↓⟧ You can also detour south from here over Causse Noir to **Montpellier-le-Vieux**'s rocky chaos.

⟦A⟧ To go directly to **la Malène** (27.5 km/17 miles) at the **Baraq de Lutran** go over the crossroads with D998 for a quiet way into the Gorges du Tarn. Just after, at **le Domal**, turn left on D43.

Just before the descent, turn right towards the Pointe Sublime. Carry on to **St-Georges-de-Lévéjac**.

Hotels: Hotel-Restaurant Chez Malaval (L), 48500 St-Georges-de-Lévéjac, 66 48 81 07.

Turn left to Pointe Sublime (sublime but lots of tourists). Routes from here down to la Malène either east or west.

Day 3
La Malène – Meyrueis
(24 km/15 miles)

La Malène – la Parade
(12 km/7½ miles)

La Malène
Climb 4 km (2½ miles) on D43 up long series of hairpins to the **Causse Méjean**. As before, the Causse has few roads and the scenery is similar so choose your own route.

Caussignac
Prehistoric remains all around.

Hotels: Hotel Auberge de la Grive (L), 48210 St-Enimie, 66 48 52 21, simple friendly place open all year; Hotel les Aires de la Carline (M), 66 48 54 79, big, comfortable. Chambres d'hôtes: M Gal, **Le Bouffre**, between Drigas and Masdeval, 66 45 61 84, old working farm. Gîte d'étape, **Masdeval** (down D16 to right).

Continue on D986.

La Parade
In the middle of the Causse. There is a monument to the German massacre of *maquisards* (members of the Resistance), and a tiny exhibition of prehistoric things.

Hotels: Hotel-café (L), simple workman's lunch. Chambres d'hôtes: Mme Verhnet, **Viale** (D63 to west), 66 48 82 39.

La Parade – Meyrueis
(12 km/7½ miles)

Continue on D986 to crossroads with D63.

Detour right to *dolmen* **la Tombe du Geant**, the show cave of **Aven Amand**, and **Hyelzas**. (See museum of *caussenard* life and the vulture breeding experiment.)

Gîte d'étape.

Detour left on D63 to **Villaret** via **Drigas** for Przewalski horse farm (the horse of the prehistoric cave paintings).

Continue straight on and descend into the **Gorges de la Jonte**.

Mist and cloud make the Cévennes even more evocative than summer sun.

Meyrueis

There is a market on Wednesdays and Fridays. See the *Moulin de Capelan*.

- 🛏 Hotels: Hotel de la Jonte (L), les Douzes, 48150 Meyrueis, 66 62 61 62; Hotel Mont Aigoual (M), rue de la Barrière, 66 45 65 61, friendly; Hotel la Renaissance (M–H), rue de la Ville, 66 45 60 19; Hotel Château d'Ayres (HH), 1 km (½ mile) east on D57, 66 45 60 10.

- Ⓐ Two ways to avoid steep climb from **la Malène** to the Causse Méjean
  (1) Go down the Tarn to **le Rozier** (20 km/12½ miles), continue round the bend and come up the **Gorges de la Jonte** to **Meyrueis** (21.5 km/13½ miles). Moderately busy road.
  (2) Go up the Tarn on moderately busy road to **Florac** (26 km/16 miles) HQ of Parc National des Cevennes.

- 🛏 Hotels: Grand Hotel du Park (M), 47 avenue Jean Monestier, 48400 Florac, 66 45 03 05, good food. Take small road D906 following river Tarnon around the edge of the Causse and rising gently into pretty, very quiet country.

- ↻ Detour to **St Laurent-de-Trèves** for dinosaur footprints.

  Go on through **Salgas** and **Vebron** to **les Vanels** (15 km/9½ miles).

- 🛏 Hotels: Hotel Auberge du Tarnon (L), 48400 Florac, 66 44 00 05, pretty, simple place.
  Continue up over the **Col de la Perjuret** (1028 m/3374 ft) and either meet the route at **Meyrueis**, or turn left on D18 up to **Cabrillac** to meet the route on **Mont Aigoual**.

  To complete a circuit to **Marvejols**, go west along the **Gorges de la Jonte** to **le Rozier**. Continue down the river to **Boyne** and turn right on D32 up the Boyne river valley to the **Causse de Sauveterre**. Return to **Chanac** and **Marvejols**. Or, alternatively, go east up the river, over the **Col de Perjeret** to **Florac** (as above), then **Balsièges**, **Barjac**, **Chanac** and **Marvejols**.

Day 4
Meyrueis – l'Espérou

(27.5 km/17¼ miles *or* 42.5 km/26¼ miles with summit of Mont Aigoual)

Meyrueis – Camprieu

(20 km/12½ miles)

Take D986 all the way to l'Espérou. Climb slowly away from Meyrueis towards Mont Aigoual.

- ↻ Go right on D39, after 1 km (½ mile) to the **Causse Noir** and visit the **Dargilan** show caves.

Go past the **Château de Roquedols** and the **Parc National des Cévennes** information centre on the right for gîte d'étape, etc. Continue slowly up into the forest. Visit the Bramabiau show caves, where the river Bonheur disappears.

- ✖ Café/snacks at entrance to caves.

You come out of the forest into alpine meadows and sheep pasture.

- 🛏 Gîte d'étape: le Devois (to the left at crossroads). Carry on to the crossroads.

Camprieu

Good cycling all around here.

- 🛏 Gîte d'étape: 67 82 61 20
- ✖ Auberge du Bonheur (M), 30750 Camprieu, 67 82 60 65.

- ↻ Detour down D157 to pretty **Gorges Trévezel** and **Dourbie**. See various breeding experiments of *moufflon*, *chevreuil*, *cerf* (ask at the Parc's information centre).

Camprieu – l'Espérou

(7.5 km/4¾ miles)

Camprieu

Continue on D986, then go left at the fork on to D629.

- ↻ Detour to old abbey ruins in meadow on the other side of river Bonheur.

Continue to the **Col de la Sereyrède** (1299 m/4263 ft).

- ↻ Detour up to summit of **Mont Aigoual** (1567 m/5143 ft) (15 km/9½ miles round trip). See the observatory and observation table. Views on a clear day to Alps and Pyrénées. At night-time you can see the Mediterranean coast lit up.
- 🛏 Gîte d'étape.
- ✖ Simple café.

Turn right at crossroads D18 towards le Vigan and Valleraugue.

L'Espérou

Ever hopeful winter sport centre sometimes helped along by artificial snow.

- 🛏 Hotels: Hotel-restaurant du Touring (L), 30570 Valleraugue, 67 82 60 04; Grand Hotel du Parc (M), 67 82 60 05, cosy fire in winter. Gîte d'étape.

Day 5
L'Espérou – Ganges

(39 km/24½ miles)

L'Espérou Ⓐ – Mandagout

(19 km/12 miles)

At the crossroads at l'Espérou, go straight over and up on to D329, a quiet road between meadows. After a section of straight through dull pine forestry, enter beech forests then start to descend.

Col de Côte
1253 m/4112 ft high.
⌂ Gîte d'étape.
Descend on hairpins, staying with D329 all the way.

Mandagout
Area of Cévennes which is largely protestant with chapel and catholic church.
⌂ Hotels: Auberge la Bourie (L) 30120 le Vigan, 67 81 06 03.

Mandagout A – Pont d'Hérault
(9 km/5½ miles)
The route continues down on D329 to meet main road D999.

Le Rey
⌂ Hotels: Hotel Château du Rey (H), 30570 Pont d'Hérault, 67 82 40 06.

⌂ Detour right to **Le Vigan** on main road D999, which has a Saturday morning market. (See the Musée Cevenol and the old bridge.)
⌂ Hotels: Auberge Cocagne (L–M), place du Château, 30120 Avèze, 67 81 02 70, (on opposite side of river) friendly, attractive.

From **le Rey** turn right on main road D999.

Pont d'Hérault
⌂ Hotels: Hotel-restaurant Maurice (M), 30570 Pont d'Hérault, 67 82 40 02, good food.

A From **Mandagout** you can take pretty valley road D323 to **le Mazel** (7 km/4½ miles). See fine old *filature* (silk factory). Then turn right on D986 and follow the Herault river valley to **Pont d'Herault**.

Pont d'Hérault – Ganges
(11 km/7 miles)

It is possible to swim at various places along the river. Cross bridge on D999 and follow river Hérault.

St-Julien-de-la-Nef
⌂ Chambres d'hôtes: Château d'Isis, 67 73 56 22.
✕ La Cascade, 67 82 46 59.
Continue on D999.

Ganges
Relaxed old town, good Friday-morning market.
⌂ Hotels: Hotel aux Caves de l'Hérault (L), 14 rue Jeu de Ballon, 34190 Ganges, 67 73 81 09, so-so food, but pretty terrace; Hotel les Norias (M), 254 avenue des Deux Ponts, 35190 Cazilhac, 67 73 55 90, on the other side of the river Hérault, good food. Chambres d'hôtes: Mme Isnard, aux Trois Cedres, 67 73 50 77.

⌂ Detour to **St Laurent-le-Minier**, a pretty old mining village with good swimming. (See château.)

A Two alternative routes from l'Esperou: (1) From **l'Espérou** take D986 (dramatic descent but busier road) past **Source de l'Hérault** down into the Hérault valley to **La Penarie**.
⌂ Hotels: Auberge Cévenol (L), 30570 Valleraugue, 67 82 25 17, excellent, reasonably-priced food.
Carry on on same road to **Valleraugue**. Charming little town, possible to swim in river here.
⌂ Hotels: Hotel le Petit Luxembourg (M), rue de Luxembourg, 30570 Valleraugue, 67 82 20 44, small rooms, over priced; Hotel les Bruyeres (M), rue André Chamson, 67 82 20 06, food poor. Chambres d'hôtes: Simone Marie, 67 82 41 75, (to right off road, 4 km/2½ miles down the main road), good food, swimming pool. From Valleraugue carry on to **Ganges** on the D986, via Pont d'Hérault.

(2) The other alternative route from **l'Espérou**, is to go right on D48 down to **le Vigan** (see above) and from there to **Ganges.**

Day 6
Ganges – Vézénobres
(45 km/27½ miles)

Ganges – St-Hippolyte-du-Fort
(13 km/8 miles)

Go through the town past the *mairie* and turn left at roundabout on busy D999 towards Nîmes. Cross dry river and wind up hill out of town. Go through **Moules et Baucels**, passing *bas et pulls*, (Ganges is a centre of knitted goods), and independent wine producers right and left.
⌂ Chambres d'hôtes: Mas de Blancardy, to right past Moules et Baucels, 97 73 94 94, farm specializing in duck.
Continue straight on.

St-Hippolyte-du-Fort
See silk museum and wine co-operative.
⌂ Hotels: Auberge Cigaloise (M), route de Nîmes, 30170 St-Hippolyte-du-Fort, 66 77 64 59 on road to Nîmes; Hotel le Cheval Blanc (M), 66 77 21 03.

⌂ Detour on D999 to **Sauve**, an ancient city, with excellent Medieval Festival and Festival of French Music (both in summer).

St-Hippolyte-du-Fort – Durfort
(10 km/6 miles)

Go through town on D982.

Durfort
⌂ Chambres d'hôtes: Lino et Jeannette, 66 77 57 10, food.
✕ Restaurant le Real, route St-Hippolyte-du-Fort, 66 77 50 68, just the other side of town.

Durfort – Vézénobres

(22 km/13½ miles)

Continue on D982.

- ⌂ Hotels: Ranquet Hotel (HH), les demeures du Ranquet, 30140 Tornac, 66 77 51 63, 4 km (2½ miles) along D982.

Go straight on.

Tornac

Wine, monastery, ruined château on hill to the right. Continue to T-junction at busy D907.

La Madeleine

Pottery.

- ◊ Detour left to **Anduze** (4 km/2½ miles) and take the steam train to **St Jean du Gard**. See show cave at **Trabuc**, or the *Bambouseraie* (bamboo garden), and the Musée du Desert at **Mas Soubyran**, a Museum of Protestantism.
- ⌂ Hotels: Hotel la Porte des Cévennes (M), route de St-Jean-du-Gard, 30140 Anduze, 66 61 99 44. Gîte d'étape: 66 61 98 17.

Turn right on to D907 to **Attuech**. Fork left on D982. At the crossroads with D24 go straight on.

- ⌂ Hotels: Hotel des Arts (M), place du Château, 30350 Lézan, 66 83 00 60.

At junction with main road N110, turn left towards Alès **A**, then right onto small road to **Massanes**. Take D106 and cross river Gardon, then go under railway. Cross main road N106.

Vézénobres

Fine Medieval hilltop village with artists' colony. See château and orientation table.

- ⌂ Hotels: Hotel le Sarrasin, RN 106, 30360 Vézénobres, 66 83 66 83, on N106 to south.
- ✗ Restaurant les Trois Perdrix, 66 83 52 19.
- A It is possible to take a short cut home from **Alès**, on the N106, 11 km (7 miles) to the north, an old coal-mining area with a mining museum and railway.
- ⌂ Hotels: Hotel le Riche (M), 42, place Sémard, 30100 Alès, 66 86 00 33, restaurant recommended by Michelin as good value.

Day 7

Vézénobres – Collias

(39 km/24½ miles)

Vézénobres – Ste-Anastasie

(24 km/15 miles)

The next bit is a little complicated. From bottom of **Vézénobres** return to main road, then immediately take left turn on to small road, D120. Go over crossroads and take the first right, D191, skirting bottom of **Ners**. Turn

left on to D18. Go through **Cruviers-Lascour** and **Brignon** towards hilltop town of **Moussac**. Continue on D18 through fields to **St Chaptes**.

Ste Anastasie

See caves along riverside with evidence of earliest man where protestants hid during the Wars of Religion.

- ◊ Cross river to **Dions**. See château.

Ste-Anastasie A – Collias

(15 km/9½ miles)

Continue to **Vic** (pretty old village). Go on to crossroads with D979.

- ◊ Detour right to **Pont St Nicolas** and see medieval bridge and ruined monastery.
- ⌂ Hotels: Hotel la Chaumière (L), 30700 St-Anastasie, 66 22 16 06, other side of river.
- ◊ Detour north on D979 to **Uzès** (9 km/5½ miles), a lovely old town, home for 900 years to the Counts of Uzès. Good market.
- ⌂ Hotels: Hotel St Genies (M), route St-Ambrix, 30700 Uzès, 66 22 29 99, no restaurant; Hotel d'Entraigues (H), 8 rue de la Calade, 66 22 32 68, 'elegant gentleman's residence of 15 century'; Hotel Château de St Victor-des-Oules (HH), 66 22 76 10.

The main route goes across on D112 via **Sanilhac**.

Collias

Pretty old village which feels like Provence.

- ⌂ Hotels: Hotel le Gardon (L), 30210 Remoulins, 66 22 80 54, pretty, on riverside; Hostellerie le Castellas (H), 66 22 88 88, *'ancienne demeure gardoise'*, recommended, a delightful surprise in every way.
- A **Nîmes** (16 km/10 miles) is a good place to short-cut the journey. From Pont St Nicolas take a pretty route on D979 south to Nîmes and the railway. See the wonderful Roman remains and museums.
- ⌂ Hotels: Hotel l'Amphitheatre (M), 4 rue des Arènes, 30900 Nîmes, 66 67 07 79, no food; Hotel l'Orangerie (H), 755 rue Tour de l'Eveque, 66 84 50 57.

Day 8

Collias – Tarascon

(30 km/19 miles)

or Avignon

(32 km/20 miles)

Collias – Pont du Gard

(8 km/5 miles)

Follow directions Pont du Gard, turn left on D3 then right on D112, and right again on main road D981. Turn right.

Pont du Gard

Great river Gardon aqueduct, most impressive of Roman artefacts. Excellent swimming. Busy but plenty of space for everyone. Beware of thieves.

Pont du Gard — Remoulins

(3 km/2 miles)

Cross bridge on D981.

Remoulins

 Hotels: Hotel le Vieux Moulin (H), rive gauche, 30210 Remoulins, 66 37 14 35, views overlooking Pont du Gard.

Remoulins – Tarascon

(19 km/12 miles)

Remoulins

A maze of roads here. Take D19 to **Fournes**, and keeping as close as possible to the river, skirt Fournes on small road, D351, to **Montfrin** A. Cross the river and turn left on main road N986.

Beaucaire

See château and abbey.

⊨ Hotels: Hotel la Cauquière (M), 5 rue de l'Hotel de Ville, 30300 Beaucaire, 66 59 30 10; Hotel les Doctrinaires (H), quai Générale de Gaulle, 66 59 41 32, seventeenth-century college.

Tarascon

See château.

⊨ Hotel Echevins (M), 26 boulevard Itam, 13150 Tarascon, 90 91 01 70.

A For Avignon and the TGV take D126 from **Montfrin** to **Aramon**, then turn left to follow the Rhône to **Avignon** (21 km/13 miles). Historic fortified city, alternative pope's old capital. Good summer theatre festival. See Pope's Palace, etc.

⊨ Hotels: Hotel des Medievale (M), rue Petite Saunerie, 84000 Avignon, 90 86 11 06; Hotel le Prieuré (H), place Chapître, 90 25 18 20, with a Michelin gourmet restaurant, other side of river at **Villeneuve-les-Avignon**.

CHAPTER SIX

Wine Country

From Collioure to Montpellier via the Summit of the Pyrénées

This Mediterranean route goes through some wild country and other more cultivated areas, notably vineyards. It is long, but not as long – and much less hard – than it seems, with ups and downs but large stretches of flat terrain too. This is a country which offers good fresh food, cheap wine and plenty of sun, sea and mountains, but it is easy to adapt it to something shorter.

The ride begins on the coast near the Spanish border and travels inland across the vineyards of the Côtes du Roussillon before the Big Cheat, which takes you high into the Pyrénées on the single-track railway known as the Little Yellow Train, so that you can freewheel for many miles down through gorges before tackling the rugged area of Corbières with its Cathar castles. Reaching the flat lands at last, it follows the old Canal du Midi through the intensive cultivation of the Languedoc plains past towns which were established centuries before Caesar arrived, then picks its way through as little as possible of the modern suburban sprawl which surrounds much of the Mediterranean to end among flamingo lagoons and old fishing villages near Languedoc's civilized capital, Montpellier.

It was October and the grape harvest was going on all about me as I journeyed through Languedoc-Roussillon. Whenever the rain stopped for long enough the vineyards were alive with activity and a frenzy of little lorries filled with juicy fruit sped between field and co-operative press. *Vendangeurs* came down on the neat rows of vines like a flock of brightly coloured bullfinches, stripping the best bunches from stems exuberant with the end of summer.

It was the wettest autumn for decades (which in Languedoc-Roussillon is not quite as wet as it sounds) and things had to be done quickly. The grapes were picked hastily during dry moments for fear of moulds and rot, and in the desperate hope that the concentration of sugar achieved through so many hot summer days would not be diluted. Either way, a year's work could be lost. The press was going flat out, and the vignerons were working late into the night, up again at dawn.

I started my journey at Collioure, which has come a long way since it was a simple Catalan fishing village near the Spanish border, but which has never suffered the drastic over-development of much of the French coast. As pretty and colourful as it is with its mountains and rocky coast, it should have been thoroughly spoiled by now but remains charming. It has a small industry preserving anchovies, its own good table wine and the formidable Banyuls, which has the sun in every drop, but it is most famous as the haunt of artists – and artists there still are, of a lesser sort, and paintings in abundance in galleries and on easels on quaysides, though nothing can rival the hollow-backed sailing boats bright with yellow and red, the Catalan colours.

I wandered past the harbour and past the Hostellerie des Templiers, a former haunt within haunts of Picasso and Cézanne among others. It is a neat white and blue establishment with a glassed-in dining area at the front so that the cuisine may flourish undisturbed, which it deserves to do, and a bar which is filled with paintings given to its owner more as a token of esteem than an informal way of paying for dinner. A strange language emerged from the back of the bar where the patron and his friends were passing a peaceful afternoon: it was neither French, nor Spanish, but guttural Catalan.

I bought a *pâté-en-croûte* (a sort of Catalan version of the Cornish pasty) from a *charcuterie* shop where it lay in the window with its fellow pies all together in rows, dumpy and cocoon-shaped like golden babies, and wandered down to the beach to eat it while watching the cormorants on the fishing boats and feeling the sand between my toes. The waves lapped gently back and forth. It was a good beginning.

The route had chosen itself by default, as a consequence of the Pyrénées being simply huge – awesome to see, but awful to climb. *Le Petit Train Jaune* was an inspiration. It is not the only train of its colour in the French railway system, but its yellow paint is always taken as flaunting Catalan sympathies nonetheless; and though it is a favourite with tourists, it is also a necessity for many who live on the steep mountainside.

Catalonia crosses the borders of France and Spain, reaching from Barcelona in the south to Perpignan in the north and covering half the Pyrénées. Its language, Catalan, is the only one officially recognized by the EC which is not the language of a geographically distinct country. The Catalans are a lively, imaginative and energetic people – any area which can produce Dali, Casals and Gaudi has to be interesting. Long denied the political independence they felt – and some still feel – to be their due, they became thorns in the flesh of the ruling Spanish establishment, and during the Spanish Civil War bore the brunt of the conflict and the brunt of the suffering, eventually fleeing in thousands. Salvador Dali extolled Perpignan railway station as a road to freedom which carried his paintings to the outside world, but for many Catalans it was a gateway from one hell into another: either they stayed in Spain, and subjected themselves to the tender mercies of Franco and his Nazi allies, or they came to France and were put into internment camps.

There is no decent cycle route out of Collioure, but the stretch of main road is not long and you can soon escape from it to Argelès-sur-Mer (which is actually *sur terre*) and a succession of small roads through market gardens and peach orchards and a succession of small villages to go with them. Overlooking the charms of Perpignan railway station, I decided to give Perpignan a miss, for I had heard of the existence of a *Fiesta de la Bruixes* in a little place somewhere among the vineyards and if there were really Catalan witches, I wanted to know more. Travelling over the coastal plain that skirts the Pyrénées, you have two constant presences – the mountains themselves, snowcapped and dominated by the craggy cone of Mont Canigou (2785 m/9140 ft); and the vines which lead from the backdoors of one hilltop village to the doorsteps of the next. In due course I came to Tresserre, which has fewer than five hundred inhabitants and no fewer than nine wineries, each with a big doorway leading on to the narrow street as if the town was full of garages. An exciting smell of sweetness and fermentation wafted from them.

Enquiring about witches, I was directed to the local school, and found the festival to be the creation of the schoolmaster, a pleasant young man as far removed

Opposite: Collioure: an old Catalan fishing village that became an artists' colony.
Below: Snow-capped peaks above vineyards on the Côtes du Roussillon.

from black magic as a boiled egg. He had started it as a Hallowe'en project with his pupils and it had grown to a weekend festival which attracted five thousand people and brought in street performers and musicians from all over Catalonia. Even now they were busy with the preparations – the T-shirts, the programme, the schedule. I was told I should come back for it. But first, did I realize that one of the nine *caves* in the village was outstanding? I did not, but I went in search of this altogether different kind of witchcraft.

Many Côtes du Roussillon grapes go off to the *cave co-opérative* for pressing and vinification, and I always looked upon them as producing good-to-middling rather than great wines, in the tradition of the south, which in the past was the fountain of *vin ordinaire*. But some *vignerons* are starting to do things differently and my encounter with the Vacquer family brought a realization that not only were some *caves co-opératives* making some wines of rather high quality, but that there were some wines from individual producers which were exceptional!

Bernard Vacquer is dark and Mediterranean, and his wife Frédérique, is blonde and comes from Burgundy, where the two met at wine college. She is now a wine-maker in her own right in Roussillon – I tasted her Rivesaltes, a dessert wine of the region that deserves to rank with all but the most unaffordable ports as an after-dinner drink. (Sweet wines are something of a speciality of the area: Muscat is very common for miles around and very pleasant with puddings, but Rivesaltes is outstanding.) Bernard's reds and whites were in the tradition of his father Fernand, and like Fernand's wines bore only the year and the name Vacquer. They have an *appellation controlée*, but do not use it, since they work to a higher standard, refusing to bottle at all in a year which they find unsatisfactory and selling the wine off to some other *cave* which is only too happy to have it. A beaming cherub of a man, always anxious to give the credit to others rather than himself, Fernand Vacquer turned towards high quality at a time when a large majority of southern *vignerons* were still stuck in their old ways.

Out in the fields the grape-pickers had been at work since dawn. Their homes were far away over the Pyrénées – some had come from as far away as Andalucia. Every year they come for work and a combined holiday – old, young, men, women, whole families. Their fathers did it before them and their children will carry it on when they die. In the old days it was customary to drink your pay before you got it and go home on the train empty-handed. Now there is more money, but less fun. *Vignerons* have to pay official rates which means no more living-in and the great booze-up at the end of the *vendange* is generally a thing of the past.

From Tresserre the road switchbacks through the vineyards to Thuir. After that there is a substantial section of main road and before long it begins to go up and gets rather determined about it – but it is the only road up the valley and often busy. *Le Petit Train Jaune* starts from a tiny fortified village in the Conflent valley, Villefranche-de-Conflent, which has a direct rail link from Perpignan. For the less hardy it is probably best to seek closer acquaintance with Salvador Dali's favourite railway station or take the train from one of the stations in between, like Millas or Bouleternère.

Taurinya is a tiny village not too far from Villefranche, which is exceptionally picturesque – and it knows it – with a rocky river running below massive walls and a fort high above that. If you get off the Perpignan train one stop to the south at the more utilitarian, but nevertheless agreeable, town of Prades, you can cycle to Villefranche past the monastery of St Michel de Cuxa, through Taurinya and up over what would generally be called a mountain but in the Pyrénées rates as a foothill, especially when you look up to the snowy crag of Canigou. There are two things which make the effort worthwhile – one being the countryside, the other being the warmth of Chez Marie-Thérèse, with its creeper-hung garden which specializes in traditional Catalan cooking.

'Good solid food for mountain people,' said Marie-Thérèse: a woman with lively eyes behind her spectacles, a natural gift for hospitality and a body that was becoming generous to go with it.

As a special favour I was a guest at a family feast, where her son provided the music. Unaccustomed as I was to Catalan eating, the meal required courage. It has always seemed to me that the pig's trotter is more at home on the pig than on the plate, no matter how well cooked, and though these were quite beautiful – white and gelatinous with a sprinkling of green parsley and a sauce vinaigrette – I could not manage more than three. The Catalan meat balls were big enough to serve as ammunition for a small cannon, snug among their white beans and tomato and onion sauce. There was duck, salads of potatoes, anchovies, eggs and olives, *créme Catalan* – a caramel custard burned with the back of a red-hot spoon – and snails cooked in the local manner which was alarming. Roasting a creature alive on a barbecue was something new to me which I would not care to try for myself. Let alone baste them beforehand with a flaming torch made out of bacon fat and brown paper which dripped boiling grease on them every time they tried to raise their heads. I wish they had not been the best snails I have ever eaten.

The little yellow train left early in the morning from Villefranche-de-Conflent. It being the time of day when most passengers were coming down the mountain, I and my bike were almost the only passengers. In summer they take the roof off, but there was an autumnal chill that morning which grew ever more penetrating and windier as we went upwards. The line twisted and turned with the river valleys, crossing them on improbable viaducts to curl more easily up the other side. We passed through halts where the train had probably not stopped for forty years and only the station houses were left. Below, the river rushed and tumbled: above, the snowpeaks were an uncompromising white against an intense, clear blue. The mountainsides were lazily magnificent with their tumbled rocks and grasses tired and pale after the long summer, leaves crackling into autumn, edging into yellows, browns and reds.

At last hilltops began to appear among the peaks with pastures on them, and I came to a tiny station with a yellow bench to match the train and a self-important station clock. I got off in the middle of nowhere among alpine meadows.

I was at the edge of the Cerdagne, a vast plain that lies among these mountain tops, stretching over the Spanish border. Here you may easily cycle into Spain, cross through the middle and be back in France within half-an-hour, since a piece of Spain was broken off centuries ago by the Treaty of the Pyrénées, which fixed the Franco-Spanish border: and it remains a political island to this day. The town of Llivia is centred on a hill some 5 km (3 miles) from the Spanish border proper, with inhabitants who reply '*Buenos dias*' to your '*Bonjour*', and Spanish police, post office, wine and cooking. Below the old town with its narrow streets, solid apartment blocks and holiday homes was shuttered up. Too late for summer, too early for winter sports, there was little open but the grocer, the chemist and a tapas stall where I had a plateful of Spanish olives and anchovies before pottering back into France, thinking to myself that the concept of the political island has a good deal of potential.

The Pyrénées have not only the most days of sunshine in France but the best quality: and it was here in the post-war years that a remarkable scientist, Felix Trombe, inspired, cajoled and politicked the French government into financing a series of experiments in the use of solar energy. (It was only appropriate, since Trombe was a powerhouse in himself, with a creative mind, great determination and an extraordinary range of enthusiasm for everything from music to potholing.)

Trombe's first experiments used army surplus searchlights, and he went on to build his first solar furnace as a saucer of mirrors on the battlements of Mont-Louis, an old fortified town a few kilometres down the mountain. Disused for some years, the laboratory had opened as a museum and tourist attraction a few months before I passed through, only to have part of its mirror array collapse when one bolt rusted through.

The intermediate solar furnace at Odeillo, not far from where I got off the train, is a strange sight in the meadows of sheep and cows. It looks like an office block-cum-warehouse with a gigantic concave mirror for its north wall and a chorus line of reflectors occupying the whole hillside above, subtly swinging in time with the sun. Below are the sad remnants of more modest experiments: solar houses that make the best possible use of the energy that is free for all, but which have not succeeded in convincing anyone but the enthusiasts and environmentalists that they are worth what it costs to build them. Professor Trombe deserves a better monument: as it is, his name is enshrined in the Trombe Wall, which captures heat during the day and lets it out again in the evening.

The fortified town of Villefranche-de-Conflent, terminus of le Petit Train Jaune.

These high meadows at the edge of the valley are a Mecca for outdoor activities – skiing in winter, hiking and mountain-biking in summer. There is precious little else to support the inhabitants but tourism and some farming and Font-Romeu above Odeillo has become a major tourist centre. Downhill towards Mont-Louis the country is much more traditional and when you turn north to Matemale and its lake it is wilder too. After a not very stressful climb to the Col de la Quillane, there is little but downhill for a good 32 km (20 miles) or more. At first it is a wide landscape of short grass, mountain and pines, but as you descend further along the course of the river Aude, which is only a baby stream to start with, you come into a series of valleys of rocks and beech woods which – when I came down – were a glory of red, green and gold. The road bends down the side of the mountain, revealing one woody vista after another, passing below grey crags and through gorges so narrow they eventually become almost a tunnel. It is immensely exhilarating, though after a while the speed, the wind and judderings become almost mesmerizing and you will want to stop for a picnic.

I was not far down the first grand slope when I met the cow. She was an alpine creature with a mournful expression and a bell round her neck that tolled like Doomsday. She was also a solid animal and on no account to be hurried. Coming at her fast round a corner, I was hard put to stop in time. But even having been almost run over she refused to abandon her position in the middle of the road, insisting on ambling ahead. It was only a small road with a steep drop on one side, and since we were both of a certain girth there was a shortage of passing space. I waved my arms – her rump was impassive: I mooed at her – she took no notice. Her only acknowledgement of my presence was that if I attempt to pass on one side, she would lurch in the same direction. For a moment it was like a dance of my bike with her hindquarters. Then I was past her and picking up speed once more. Looking back, she was still ambling down the road from side to side ruminating on my progress, grass dangling from either side of her mouth, unaffected by the loss of half of her cloud of flies which had fixed upon me as a livelier prospect for the next few kilometres.

I met other cows but no other person until, rather surprisingly, in the middle of the wildest and most deserted mountainside, I came upon a shop. It was like a Wild West company store and well-stocked with local produce: wine, honey, cheese and sausages. I went in to buy myself a picnic. Two policemen were busy being furious about Italians who were coming by the coach-load, they said, to steal their Pyrénéan *ceps*, the highly prized forest mushrooms which in Italy are called *porcini*. I was so distracted by the force of their conversation that I forgot my picnic, and the trio in the shop were so busy being cross about the *cep* thieves that they noticed neither my coming, nor my going. So it was that I had no lunch.

The Aude is the prettiest of valleys, rugged with a rushing river continually accumulating rivulets and tributaries and getting bigger all the time. The occasional fragment of a ruined castle towered above me, but otherwise there was little sign of human habitation. The valley became ever narrower as I descended and the short autumn day was drawing in, for I had started too late and dawdled too much. So it was getting dark when I arrived in Escouloubre-les-Bains, a ghostly old spa with elegant but faded buildings, built lankily in the narrow valley. An old woman in black, bent like a witch from a fairy story as she unpegged her laundry slowly from the washing-line, was the only person I saw.

There was one hotel open; a long, severe barrack of a place with a ragged old notice on the wall attesting to its membership of a French cycling association. It was not very welcoming but my arrival eventually brought out a girl who was unexpectedly young and pretty for that lonely place – a spa where springs flowed, the river flowed, but where the flow of those who would take the waters had long since dried up. My room was bare-boarded and spartan, and the supper frugal.

I escaped early next day and was into the Gorges de St Georges long before the sun, which is late in a place where the cliffs are tall and precipitous. Narrower than it was possible to imagine, the gorge towered high above me squeezing out the light, its green sides covered in fronds and running with water. Then suddenly I burst into the open and the valley began to broaden. Down the Aude I came to Axat, which is a smallish town, but larger than anything I had seen in some time, with more than one hotel. Carcassonne lies ahead, but I was looking for less visited places, so turned east along the main road to St Paul-de-Fenouillet, returning to wine country. It was coming up to Toussain, All Saints' Day, and all along the main road chrysanthemums were for sale to those who wished to remember their dead, adding their subtle pinks and golds to the colour of the vineyards.

This is border country – just inside the Pyrénées Orientales, almost in Aude, sandwiched between Catalonia and Occitania, the land where they said *'oc'* for 'yes' instead of *'oui'*, and where troubadour poets invented the idea of courtly love. Here Cathar saints tried to create an equal society, an idea which did not appeal greatly to either the Roman Catholic church or the French king, who was after the Cathar land anyway. And the Cathars were labelled as heretics and murdered for not much more than being egalitarian, religious and a little odd sometimes. Though Catharism accordingly died out, it may not be too fanciful to hear whispers of the old ideas in the area's continuing tendency towards left-wing politics and echoes of old Languedoc in the country's continuing love of music. St Paul-de-Fenouillet has a fine church, and a religious community which is not far off the old Cathar ideals: men and women together, married couples and single people, sharing everything, working together as a community, singing together. This is a country that – like the troubadours – sings passionately. The village choirs are social as well as working units. Annual competitions between villages are taken very seriously, so much so that one village even paid

Overleaf: Early morning mist in vineyards below the Pyrénées.

for the return of one of their sons who had become a famous singer abroad. That year they won.

The road through the valley vineyards is comparatively gentle: above is a rugged landscape of vineyards and scrub-covered mountains dotted with impressive castles. The Corbières are nothing like the Pyrénées, but they wind up and down, and the first part is mostly up. This route has now been labelled the *route des Cathars*, and its castles the *Châteaux des Cathars*. But the Cathars were pacifists, their only interest in castles being for protection, which they received from the many southern knights sympathetic to them – some knights even going as far as taking up the faith themselves, hanging up their swords and disposing of their possessions to join their serfs in the villages. In the end, however, no protection could avail against the vindictiveness of Simon de Montfort, the most cruel and obsessed of the northern crusaders. Defeating the Count of Toulouse in Carcassone, he burned the last *perfectus*, as Cathar priests were called, in 1344 in Villerouge-Termenès.

There are few gorges more dramatic than Galamus, since the road runs not at the top or the bottom but along the middle, above the tiny hermitage of St Antoine where a modern-day semi-hermit, Christine Ollie, offers physical and spiritual sustenance to weary travellers. Always narrow and winding, it is sometimes almost like a tunnel below the jutting rock face until it emerges in a wild landscape of *maquis* through which it climbs to a valley whose vineyards are overlooked by the castle of Peyrepertuse itself, obstinate against the skyline like a row of broken teeth and Quéribus, a dramatic tower more like a rock than the rocks it stands on.

I stayed in the welcoming hotel at the hilltop village of Cucugnan, where the chef-patron greeted me with the news that he had wild boar on the menu that night.

'What? Him?' I said, pointing to the hairy hunting-trophy snarling on the wall behind him.

'*Son cousin,*' replied the chef, not batting an eyelid.

The mayor of Cucugnan met me with black hands, having just covered himself with oil mending his tractor. As well as being a vigneron like everyone hereabouts, he was also a great engineering do-it-yourselfer, who took me upstairs at his house in the lift he had built himself. He is also a great Cathar enthusiast, a passion dating back to his childhood relationship with an ageing archaeologist who came to the valley to study the castle of Quéribus, then privately owned. Still fascinated by the castle and its history when he became mayor many years later, he decided that the community should acquire the castle, which had changed hands and was being used as a private club, with stories of strange goings-on and the fabric of the building being altered. After years of legal battles he succeeded in restoring control of his favourite castle to the community, and it is now being renovated. He can see the castle from his window and as we said goodbye I could see that his attention was divided. His eyes pulled, as if by an invisible thread, to gaze on Quéribus.

The road that followed is remote, climbing through a mixture of rough country and vineyards with just a little general cultivation around a few small villages with even fewer facilities, though the Restaurant Saint-Roche below another castle at Padern has good home-cooking by a motherly woman known simply as Mère Ginette. Through Maisons and Villerouge-Termenès, the small road makes its way up and down through hill country to a point at which you see the plain of Languedoc extending to the horizon. Carrying on through the town of Lezignan-Corbières, which is slightly startling after so many hamlets and villages, you reach the river Auge again and the Canal du Midi, whose towpath is an agreeable route to the coast, with possible detours to visit nearby towns, or to cut off its more excessive windings as you feel inclined. The Canal du Midi is a stupendous bit of seventeenth-century engineering skill, cutting a water route from the Atlantic to the Mediterranean. It used to carry goods, now it carries holiday-makers.

Where the Pyrénées and the Corbières are mostly wild countryside and beautiful, it is more difficult to find pretty routes on the plains, much of which is either covered in scrubby vines doing their bit to fill the great European wine lake, or some other kind of intensive agriculture – this being the biggest fruit and vegetable growing area of France. But the Canal du Midi offers good cycling. Always shaded by trees, sometimes you are raised above the plain, sometimes level with it and sometimes set down between its banks. You may join it where you please, but joining it at Roubia is as good an idea as any.

There is a detour particularly worth making as you near Béziers. This is very much Roman France and I have always been fascinated by the Via Domitia, sections of which are said to be still visible. This was the main Roman road running east–west like the modern motorway. I wasted a good hour hunting among the vineyards before I decided to call it a day, but when I climbed the Oppidum of Enserune I saw it clearly from the top. Enserune is a town-site from the sixth century BC, one of the most important in Europe. Archaeologists have uncovered links with pre-Roman civilizations like ancient Greece, trade which included wine, olive oil and pottery. It is impressively big, and so steep I had to walk most of the way. But once up there the view was worth it, like looking at a huge map with the country spread out below. You can see where you have come from and where you are going. There is an orientation table to explain what you can see below and not only could I make out the Via Domitia but also an extraordinary circular pattern that I am sure was made by a UFO. (A scholarly blurb insisted it was the work of engineer-monks, but I like to be romantic about these things.) So, unlike the fragments of the Domitian Way, Enserune is worth the detour – especially if you also visit the nearby town of Nissan-lez-Enserune, which is a typical small town of the sunny plains and with a most friendly atmosphere. Personally, I had much rather stay there than Béziers, where I have never happened to find good food, a good hotel or much of a welcome. I assume that was my bad luck, for it is a largish and quite interesting town from the point at which you leave the canal and its stairway of nine locks to cross the old

The Canal du Midi, a shady path through the Languedoc.

Roman bridge into town. Like most towns hereabouts, it is situated on a hilltop and was founded in Roman times. Viewed from the bridge it is picturesque, and its centre is old and quaint, but now it is ringed with main roads and has extensive suburbs of council flats and supermarkets. Many of the social problems connected with poverty add to the feeling that the place has fallen on hard times.

From Béziers, I detoured via Serviran and Alignan-du-Vent to Pézenas, where I had another appointment. The town is much smaller and more friendly than Béziers, a gem of a place filled with lovely houses built during the seventeenth and eighteenth centuries for the rich southern *bourgeoisie*. It was an important centre for the wine trade and is still an important cultural centre. Among the things Pézenas values highly are wine, its association with Molière, and little pies. My appointment was with the pies.

The *petit pâté de Pézenas* is a small top-hat of a pie which Pézenans eat in enormous quantities and which is even making its way into a few villages beyond. Perhaps one day it may come home to England, because England is where it began. In a little-known fragment of eighteenth-century history, Clive of India betook himself and his chef off to Pézenas, where he settled into a mansion on the outskirts of the town. He was ill and aggrieved at his treatment by the English government, who had impeached him for helping himself to substantial benefits from the country under his control. As is still the wont of English folk abroad, his cook (who may have been an Indian and given to extravagant spicing) proceeded to make him the English food to which he was accustomed, which included a special pie.

Clive left Pézenas, but his pies lived on, going from strength to strength, to the point where today they have their own guild: *La Confrèrie de la Petit Pâté de Pézenas*, with a dozen main members soon to be increased by one. The *confrèrie* adopted me as a brother at the same time as Pézenas had its *vin nouveau* festival. Dressed in blue silk robes and floppy burghers' hats, they initiated me with the ancient oath and ceremony devised three or four years ago when the *confrèrie* was founded, in the search, I suspect, for publicity. There were four promises along the lines of eating

The old Roman bridge at Béziers.

quantities of *petit pâtés*, upholding the reputation of *petit pâtés* and spreading the word about *petit pâtés*, etc. It all took place in the ancient theatre with a bust of Molière watching proceedings from the stage. We thus combined under one roof, culture, wine and *petit pâtés* of which I ate rather too many in a spirit of testing, and drank rather too much in the aid of tasting. Confronted with a *petit pâté* for the first time – and on a public stage – I was astonished. It was quite obvious to an Englishman what the citizens of Pézenas were cherishing.

'Why,' I said: 'it's a mince pie.'

'Meence pie,' repeated my *confrères* and connoisseurs (very few of whom, if any, appeared to be bakers). '*Il dit que c'est un* meence pie.'

'*Mains pyee*', '*Mans payee*,' went round the circle. The object was a tall puff pastry filled with mincemeat and sugar. It may well represent the last vestige of the original English mince pie, since the meat is real meat titivated with dried fruit and spices in a way which is close to the medieval.

Next morning I bought a last little pie to take away with me. I said I was a new *confrère* and Madame told me to be on my guard against frauds. Her pies were artisan, but a factory had just started up mass producing them: '*C'est la guerre!*' she growled and insisted on telling the *pâté* story once again. This time Lord Clive was the cook who had created these pies specially for the French king. Thus is history created. Was there a song to celebrate the event, I asked? 'No, but we do have our own Pézenas song – the Song of the Camel.'

'The camel?' I inquired doubtfully. 'Could you sing it for me perhaps?'

'Certainly not, it makes you dance!' the lady replied.

With the pleasant image of the good burghers of Pézenas leaping about to the Song of the Camel, I set off towards the coast light hearted – if a touch heavy in the stomach due to the large quantity of pies.

The plain was good cycling and its colours autumnal – vines turning yellow, red, maroon; buff-coloured villages lit gold by the sun, and outside the *caves co-operatives* mountains of rusty must still fermented fragrantly after their pressing.

Passing the hilltop town of Castelnau de Guers, I spied what looked remarkably like four *petits pâtés* on its church tower. It was probably my imagination but the country was more attractive as I took little roads through vineyards with evocative names: Listel, Pomérols, Picpoul, home of so many refreshing white wines, down to the sea.

The homing spirit upon me, I whizzed through the pretty fishing village of Frontignan where they make Noilly Prat vermouth; through Mèze and Bouziges with their oyster nets stretched across the Etang de Thau, and views stretching over the water to the volcanic outcrop of the fishing town of Sète. I dipped into Balaruc-les-Bains where ordinary folk come to take the waters: mud by day, dancing by night, with a little casino for added fizz.

Seagulls wheeled over the fish-market in Sète which was called appropriately *la*

Criée. Sète also has its little pie, the *teille*, an octopus-filled deep-fried pie which came with the Italian families who dominate the fishing here. I sat in a bar opposite a *teille* stall on the quayside, watching the activity. A fat Italian mama was sweeping up outside, chatting with marketeers, passers-by, and her equally well-distributed family, who were busy preparing hot fat for the evening fry-up. I watched the fish buyers shifting their purchases to the waiting lorries in small fork lift trucks. A man was shovelling crushed ice out of the back of his van while a group of children made it into snowballs. Other folk were packing trays of mixed fish into the boots of their cars for *bouillabaisse* that evening. I would have liked to stay.

Failing to find a way out of Sète along the canal, I was forced on to the main road through a heavy industrial wasteland. At least it had a cycle track. Around me were the internal organs, the guts and workings of France. I preferred them to the suburban sprawl and commercial centres around the resorts. The Mediterranean coast has undergone a great transformation in the last fifty years – like much of the French coastline, mostly for the worse. East and west, far and wide along the south once spread marshes and lagoons crowded with birds. Patches of this survive – in the Camargue, at Gruissan, near Narbonne. Through the casually attractive old town of Villeneuve-lès-Maguelone I came to open water where there were no big roads, but a floating bridge powered by an outboard motor that swings across the canal channel to take pedestrians over to la Cathédrale de Maguelone and the sandspit between the sea and the brackish waters. A thin sun shone on the shallow water of the lagoon. Birds flocked there: pink flamingos, ducks, egrets. The nose of the *passerelle* clunked to against its gangway in front of a strange, lonely gate which seemed to lead to nowhere.

'What's beyond?' I asked the ferryman.

'Nothing,' he replied. '*La Cathédrale* of course. The sea. Beyond that, Africa.'

I turned left at the sea, and so came along the sandspit and into Montpellier.

Languedoc – Roussillon 11 days, 474–479 km (299–302 miles)

⊟ Accommodation   ✕ Places to eat   ◊ Detour   🄰 Alternative route

Map Ref: IGN Green Series 72, 65

To get there: Road or rail to Collioure, air to Perpignan.

To get back: Road, rail or air from Montpellier.

Weather: The Pyrénées are sunny with snow in winter. Languedoc has a Mediterranean climate; hot in summer, mild in winter. Normally it does not rain much, but when it does, it pours.

Food and drink: Catalan cooking, snails and heavy peasant dishes. Cakes including marzipan and quince cheese (jelly), *bungettes* (crispy crêpes), and doughnut-like *rusquelles*. Puddings include Crème Catalan burnt with a red-hot poker. Heavy sweet wines, Muscat, Banyuls, Rivesaltes, etc. Marc de Banyuls can be excellent. The red full-bodied wines of the Côtes du Roussillon villages, Corbières, and Minervois are good, some are excellent. Languedoc has an abundance of wonderful cheap fruit and vegetables. The coast and lagoons supply excellent fish and shellfish. Most wine is still very ordinary but some *vignerons* are making wonderful wines, and there are some good fresh white wines: Pomérols, Picpoul de Pinet, Listel etc.

Useful addresses: Ligue Languedoc-Roussillon, 31 rue de la Macreuse, 34130 Mauguio, tel: 67 29 34 95.

Day 1
Collioure – Thuir
(41 km/26 miles)

Collioure – Argelès-s-Mer
(8 km/5 miles)

Collioure
An old Catalan and Templar fishing village, haunt of artists, with the ancient castle of the kings of Mallorca, fortifications, museums and local wine and anchovy-preserving industries.

⊟ Hotels: Hotel les Templiers (L), 12 Quai de l'Amirauté, 66190 Collioure, 68 98 31 10, where famous artists used to stay.

✕ Nouvelle Vague, 7 rue Voltaire, 68 82 23 88, has been recommended.

Take main road north, N114, out of town following the coast. It is pretty busy but there is no option – except a footpath below, if you dare risk it (the French do). Leave the main road as soon as you can and turn right.

Argelès-s-Mer
Wonderful centre for watching migrating birds.

⊟ Hotels: Hotel l'Hostalet (L), 32 rue de la République, 66700 Argelès-s-Mer, 68 81 06 62.

◊ You can go north via city of **Elne**, with its magnificent cathedral, to **Perpignan**. It has the old palace of the Mallorcan kings, a cathedral, museums, and is a centre of Catalan culture with music and dance (the sardane), bull-fighting, and gypsies. It is the centre for craft jewellery, especially religious, made from garnets (*grenat*) and gold.

⊟ Hotels: Hotel Park (H), 18 boulevard Jean Bourrat, 68 35 14 14, 66000 Perpignan, with gourmet restaurant.

Argelès-s-Mer – Tresserre
(19 km/12 miles)

Argelès-s-Mer
From Argelès take D618 to **St-André** and **St-Génis-des-Fortaines**, the aim being to skirt the foothills of the Pyrénées. These are the Côtes du Roussillon.

◊ For accommodation go west on D618 towards **le Boulu**.

⊟ Hotels: Hotel le Canigou (L), rue J.B.A. Bousquet, 66160 le Boulu, 68 83 15 29; Hotel Le Domitien (M), route d'Espagne, B.P. 101, 68 83 45 90; Hotel Neolous (M), route de Céret, 68 83 38 50, big, modern; le Relais des Chartreuses (H), 106 avenue d'en Carbonner, 68 83 15 88.

◊ Detour to **Céret** (19 km/12 miles) from le Boulu. Go left on N9 through **Bains-du-Boulu** to **St-Martin-de-Fenellar**, then right on D618 to **Mareillas-las-Ulas** and **Céret**, the centre of surrealist art with important collections of modern art. There is a local industry in espadrilles, and a sardane festival in summer.

⊟ Hotels: Hotel des Arcades, (M), 1 place Pablo Picasso, 66400 Céret, very friendly.

✕ Les Feuillants, 1 boulevard La Fayette, 68 87 37 88, Michelin gourmet restaurant.

From St-Génis turn right on D2, crossing the Tech river and continue to **Brouilla**. Turn left on D40 to **Banyuls-**

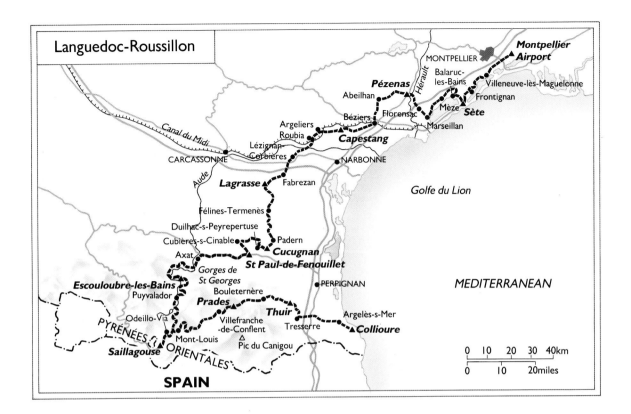

s-**Aspères**. Go under the main road and over the motorway.

Tresserre
The centre of the Côtes du Roussillon vineyards with a wonderful Hallowe'en festival – the *Fête des Sorcières*. The Vacquer *cave* offers expert *dégustation* for prospective purchasers.

⊟ Hotels: Village Catalan (H), by RN9/A9, 66300 Tresserre, 68 21 66 66, no food.

Tresserre – Thuir
(14 km/9 miles)

Continue on D40 to **Passa** with its old priory. Turn left to **Fourques**, then right on D615 through **Terrats** and **Llupia**.

Thuir
Byrrh *caves* produce famous fortified wine. See the biggest barrel in the world.

◊ Go up valley to the west on D48 to fortified village of Castelnou, one of the designated prettiest villages of France, dominated by its castle. Turn right to return (direction Millas) and re-join the route on the D615 just before it meets the D58.

A top stop for le Petit Train Jaune, Odeillo.

Day 2

Thuir – Prades

(30 km/19 miles)

Thuir – Bouleternère

(14 km/9 miles)

From Thuir take the main road D615 to **Corbère-les-Cabanes**, then first left on D16 (after turn off to Corbère).

Bouleternère [A]
See the castle.

[🚲] Minor detour east to **Illes-s-Tet** for accommodation and beautiful rock formations, *les Orgues*.

Bouleternère – Prades

(16 km/10 miles)

From Bouleternère continue to main road N116 and turn left onto it. Follow the Conflent valley along the river Tet (dammed here into a lake). Go on to **Vinça** (fine church) and **Marquixanes**. Turn right on little road D35.

Eus
[✕] Le Grangousier, 68 96 28 32, good food.
Carry on on D35.

Prades
Centre of Catalan nationalism and Pablo Casals' hometown. There is a Casals Music Festival in summer.

[🛏] Hotels: Hotel Hexagone (M), round-point de Molitig, la plaine St Martin, 66500 Prades, 68 05 31 31, modern and friendly.

[A] From Bouleternère you can take a train up the valley to **Villefranche-de-Conflent** to pick up the Little Yellow Train. This would avoid the main road section between Boulternère and Marquixanes.

Day 3

Prades – Saillagouse, via Little Yellow Train

(61 km/38 miles – *mostly by train*)

Prades – Villefranche-de-Conflent

(5 km/3 miles)

[🚲] Detour 12 km (7½ miles) on D27 via the wonderful monastery of **St Michel de Cuxa** which still has monks, to **Taurinya**, with Mont Canigou, the sacred Catalan mountain above.

[✕] Auberge de Marie-Therese, 68 96 26 16.
Return via **Coneilla-du-Conflent** with its *grottes* (caves), **Vernet-les-Bains** if you feel up to it, and **Villefranche-de-Conflent**. This is hard cycling but avoids the main road section.

From Prades take the main road N116.

Villefranche-de-Conflent
A tiny gem of a fortified 'city of rose marble', with old church and Vaubin's Fort Liberia, 1000 steps above. There are working marble quarries and were once gold quarries. This has the railway station for the Little Yellow Train to the Pyrénées.

[🛏] Hotels: Hotel le Vauban (L), 5 place de l'Eglise, 66500 Villefranche-de-Conflent, 68 96 18 03; Auberge du Cedre (M), Domaine Ste Eulalie, 68 96 37 37.

Villefranche-de-Conflent – Odeillo-Via

(45 km/28 miles)

Take the Little Yellow Train up the Conflent Valley through **Serdinya**, **Ollette-Conaveilles-les-Bains**, **Thuès** and **Fontpédrouse** (nearby at **St-Thomas-les-Bains** 15F will give you a health-giving hot sulphurous bath).

[🚲] Get off at **Mont-Louis-la-Cabanasse** if you want to stay in the Pyrénées for a while. Information about bicycle hire and circuits from Hotel Clos Cerdan, RN 116, 66210 Mont-Louis, 68 04 23 29.

Get off at Font-Romeu-Odeillo-Via. (The train goes on via Saillagouse to Bourg-Madame and la Tour-de-Carol-Enveitg on the Spanish border.) These alpine meadows are la Cerdagne.

Odeillo-Via – Saillagouse

(11 km/7 miles)

From the station take D29.

Odeillo
See the Fort Solaire solar research centre (there is a little hermitage at Font-Romeu).
Take D618 towards Villeneuve-des-Escaldes, then little road left, D33E (to the right Targassonne has accommodation and an impressive rocky chaos). Go through **Estevar** to experience a little bit of Spain at **Llivia**. See what's said to be the oldest pharmacy. Return to France at Estevar and turn right on D33 through **Ro**.

Saillagouse
[🛏] Hotels: Planes Hotel et Planotel (M), place des Comtes de Cerdagne, 66800 Saillagouse, 68 04 72 08, nice comfy hotel with big bathrooms and good views.

Day 4

Saillagouse – Escouloubre-les-Bains

(46 km/29 miles)

Saillagouse – Mont-Louis

(12 km/7½ miles)

- ⌂ Detour to **Llo** in its beautiful site.
- ⊟ Hotels: Auberge Atalaya (H), 66800 Llo, 68 04 70 04, *'joli auberge rustique'*.
  For the very hardy go on to **Eyne**.
- ⊟ Hotels: Auberge d'Eyne (H), route des Pistes, 66800 Eyne, 68 04 71 12.
  Return on D33 via **St-Pierre-dels-Forcats**. Turn right on main road N116 to re-join the route for the next day at Mont-Louis.

From Saillagouse, take the main road N116.

Mont-Louis

See Vauban's eighteenth-century fortifications and early version of Fort Solaire.

- ⊟ Hotels: Hotel Corrieu (L), Llagonne, 66210 Mont-Louis, 68 04 22 04; Hotel Lou Roubaillou (L), rue des Ecoles Laoques, 68 04 23 26, Catalan cuisine; Hotel le Clos Cerdan (M), 116 route Nationale, 68 04 23 29.

Mont-Louis – Puyvalador

(19 km/12 miles)

Take D118 over the Col de la Quillane (1714 m/5625 ft high), past a lake to the left, near the source of the Aude river. Pass **Matemales** Ⓐ where the *Maison du Capir* does mountain bike hire (VTT) with an excellent map (tel: 68 04 49 8). Pass **Formiquères** on the left and another lake on the right.

Puyvalador

- ⌂ You can take a minor detour west to **Fontrabiouse** with its *grottes* (caves).

- Ⓐ From Matemales go behind the lake and along the Aude. Take the GR (grande randonnée) path along the young river Aude to **Villeneuve**, **Real** and **Odeillo** to re-join the route at **Puyvalador**.

Puyvalador – Escouloubre-les-Bains

(15 km/9½ miles)

From Puyvalador pass the Pic du Carcanet, and continue to follow the Aude all the way down to the foothills of the Pyrénées.

Escouloubre-les-Bains

There is a very basic hotel here. (It takes time, but very little effort to continue to Axat, since it is almost all downhill.)

- ⊟ Hotels: Auberge de la Chapelle (LL), 11140 Axat, 68 20 41 14.

Day 5

Escouloubre-les-Bains – St-Paul-de-Fenouillet

(48 km/30 miles)

Escouloubre-les-Bains – Axat

(25 km/15½ miles)

Continue on down past **Carcanières-les-Bains** (see its château perched on rocks to the left) and **Usson-les-Bains**.

- ⌂ Visit the Grottes de l'Aguzou which give the adventurous a whole day underground, by appointment (tel: 68 20 45 38).

Carry on to **Gesse** (see château). Go through the impressive Gorges de St-Georges, cross the railway twice.

Axat

- ⊟ Hotels: Hostellerie du Grand Duc (M), 11140 Axat, 68 20 55 02.

Hotels also at Quillan.

Axat – St-Paul-de-Fenouillet

(23 km/14½ miles)

From Axat take the main road D117 right and go past **Lapradelle** with the wonderful Puilaurens castle to the right.

Caudiès-de-Fenouillèdes

See old hermitage and St-Jaume's Gorges.

- ⊟ Chambres d'hôtes and gîte d'étape: Castel Fizel, 68 59 92 94.

Continue on D117 along edge of Corbière.

St-Paul-de-Fenouillet

Interesting old church. This is the Corbière, wild and pretty, but hilly.

- ⊟ Hotels: Hotel le Châtelet (L), 2 km (1 mile) on route de Caudiès, RN 117, 66220 St-Paul-de-Fenouillet, 68 59 01 20; Hotel le St Pierre (L), 17 avenue Jean Moulin, 68 59 14 55, Hotel le Relais des Corbières (M), 10 avenue Jean Moulin, 68 59 23 89.

Day 6
St-Paul-de-Fenouillet – Cucugnan
(30 km/18½ miles)

St-Paul-de-Fenouillet – Cubières-s-Cinable
(10 km/6 miles)

Leave St-Paul (directions Gorges de Galamus) on D10 turning to the left and start to climb. Continue on into the spectacular little Gorges de Galamus.

⊟ Gîte d'étape and 'repas champetres': Christine Ollie, l'Ermitage de St-Antoine, 68 59 20 49, a peaceful atmosphere, good food and interesting cave-chapels.

Carry on on D10.

Cubières-s-Cinable
This is the so-called Cathar country with old border castles on every rocky peak.

Cubières-s-Cinable – Duilhac-s-Peyrepertuse
(15 km/9½ miles)

From Cubières turn right on D14 to **Soulatgé**, past Peyrepertuse Castle to the right (too steep to cycle but you should make the effort to climb. If you want a guide, ring Jean-Louis Gomez, [tel: 68 34 97 36]). Go on through **Rouffiac-des-Corbières**, over the Col des Gres (406 m/1332 ft) and down.

Duilhac-s-Peyrepertuse
⊟ Hotels: Auberge du Vieux Moulin (M), 11350, Duilhac-s-Peyrepertuse, 68 45 02 17, good food served in an old barn.

Duilhac-s-Peyrepertuse – Cucugnan
(5 km/3 miles)

Continue on D14.

Cucugnan
Quéribus castle sits on hilltop to right – another steep climb. There are little vineyards all about here.

⊟ Hotels: Auberge du Vigneron (M), 2 rue Antoine Mir, 11350 Cucugnan, 68 45 03 00.

☒ Auberge de Cucugnan, 2 place de la Fontaine, 68 45 40 84, excellent food.

Day 7
Cucugnan – Lagrasse
(43 km/27 miles)

Cucugnan Ⓐ – Padern
(7 km/4½ miles)

From Cucugnan take the D14.

Padern
Also has its castle above

☒ Saint-Roche, 68 45 09 41, excellent plats du jour.

Ⓐ There is an alternative route via **Tuchan** and the **Château d'Aquilar**.

Ⓓ Take minor detour to **Tautavel** to see the 450 000-year-old man unearthed in cave just north at **Caune de l'Arago**. Tautavel now has an interesting new museum of prehistory.

From Tuchan go via **Villeneuve-les-Corbières** and **Durban-Corbières**.

☒ Le Moulin, 68 45 81 03, Michelin-recommended gourmet restaurant, an old mill in vineyards. Rejoin the route at Narbonne.

Padern – Félines-Termenès
(19 km/12 miles)

Take D123 to Maisons. Go up over the Col des Prat (444 m/1457 ft) through **Davejean**, then take D39 and D613.

Félines-Termenès

Félines-Termenès – Lagrasse
(17 km/10½ miles)

Continue on D613 to pretty village, **Villerouge-Termenès** (see castle where last Cathar *perfectus* was burnt alive). Continue to fork and go left on D23, then D3.

Lagrasse
See castle and Abbey, another of the 'prettiest villages of France'. There are gorges on the river Orbieu to the west.

⊟ Hotels: Auberge le St Hubert (L), 9 avenue de la Promenade, 11220 Lagrasse.

Day 8
Lagrasse – Capestang
(51 km/32 miles)

Lagrasse Ⓐ – Fabrezan
(11 km/7 miles)

Ⓓ Take a long detour on D3 to **Carcassonne**, the most impressive of fortified cities, heavily restored and touristy, where the Count of Toulouse held out for years against the King of France's pogrom against Cathars. See its double fortifications, cathedral, etc. It is now something of a centre of Occitan culture and nationalism, with a lively town outside the walls. Masses of tourists, plenty of accommodation and good food (cassoulet a speciality). Return along Canal du Midi via **Olonzac** to join our route at **Roubia**.

A To complete a circuit and get back to **Collioure** in four days, take D3 and D613 via **Ornaisons**. Accommodation is available here. Go on to **Narbonne**, (the oldest Roman town in Languedoc, with fine cathedral and archbishop's palace). Plenty of accommodation here too. The old River Aude course is now la Robine and there is a towpath all the way to the sea. Take it to **Gruissan** (pretty little fortified town with castle, lagoons, bird sanctuary, strange stilt houses and accommodation). Go round the **Montagnes de la Clape** on tiny roads made for cycling, through vineyards. See sailors cemetery. **Fleury-d'Aude** has accommodation. Return along coast road to **Collioure**, or follow la Robine back to Narbonne and take train.

Take D212 following the river Orbieu via **Ribaute**.

Fabrezan
See interesting church.

Fabrezan – Lézignan-Corbières
(9 km/5½ miles)
From Fabrezan take D611 and cross the motorway by the airport, then the railway.

Lézignan-Corbières
The hills are over. Lots of accommodation here.
🛏 Hotels: Hotel le Tassigny (M), place de Lattre Tassigny, 11200 Lézignan-Corbières, 68 27 11 51.

Lézignan-Corbières – Roubia
(5 km/3 miles)

🚲 You could follow the Aude River north of Narbonne to **Sallèles d'Aude** (with its treasure-trove of unearthed Roman pots), **Coursan** and **Salles-d'Aude**. Then explore the unspoilt Montagne de la Clape (see detour above from Lagrasse).
Take D67 and cross the river Aude.

Roubia

Roubia – Argeliers
(14 km/9 miles)

Just before Roubia you meet the Canal du Midi which links the Atlantic to the Mediterranean. Before the canal turn right on D124 and continue till the road parts company with the canal. Take the towpath and continue all the way to **Béziers** (you might persuade a boat to give you a lift since your pace and theirs will be about the same). Continue along towpath past **Ventenac-en-Minervois** to le **Somail**.
🛏 Hotels: Hotel Domaine Hotelier du Somail (M), 11590 Sallèles d'Aude, 68 46 36 36, swimming-pool.

🚲 If you have had enough of towpaths, there is a metalled road here right to **Ouveillan**, then D418/161, and left on D16 to **Capestang**.

Follow towpath.

A new confrère du Petit Pâté de Pézenas.

Argeliers
🛏 Chambres d'hôtes: Mme Aurelle, Domaine de Saugras, 67 55 08 71
❌ Le Chat qui Peche, pretty, by canal.

Argeliers – Capestang
(12 km/7½ miles)

Continue on towpath.

Capestang
An old hilltop town.
🛏 Hotels: Hotel Franche Compte (M), 34310 Capestang 67 93 31 21. Gîte d'étape: Lou Castel, 67 93 40 90, le château.

Day 9
Capestang — Pézenas
(41–46 km/26–29 miles)

Capestang A – Béziers
(20 km/12½ miles on canal, or 15 km/9½ miles on main road)

Continue on towpath to **Poilhes**.

[♢] At D162, detour left up to the sixth-century BC site, the **Oppidum d'Enserune**. Accommodation just south at **Nissan-lez-Enserune**.

[⊟] Hotels: Hotel la Rèsidence (M), 35 avenue de la Cave, 34440 Nissan-lez-Enserune, 67 37 00 63.

Go past **Colombiers** to the tier of locks called the *Escalier d'Ecluses*, or *les neuf ecluses*. Go over the old Roman bridge.

Béziers

Famous as the capital of French rugby. It was an old Roman staging post, but today is a focus for many Mediterranean social problems. It has an old part but plenty of poverty too. The city is ringed by industrial estates.

[⊟] Hotels: Hotel Splendid (L), 24 avenue du 22 Aout, 34500 Béziers, 67 28 23 82 no food; Hotel Imperator (M), 28 allées Paul Piguet, 67 49 02 25. Chambres d'hôtes: Mme Granier-Marechal, ancienne route de Bedarieux, 67 31 26 57, to north.

[✕] Le Framboisier, 12 rue Boeildieu, 67 49 90 00, Michelin-recommended as good value; Le Jardin, 37 avenue Jean Moulin, 67 36 41 31, Michelin gourmet restaurant.

[A] From Capestang take main road D11 through hilltop town of **Montady** to **Béziers**.

Béziers – Abeilhan

(15 km/9½ miles)

Go through Béziers following directions north (Bédarieux), on D909. Turn off on D15, cross the railway and turn first right back across the railway to **Lieuran-lès-Béziers**, **Saussine**.

Espondeilhan

[⊟] Hotels: Château de Cabrerolles (M), 34290 Espondeilhan, 67 39 21 79.

At the fork go left on D33 through **Coulobres**.

Abeilhan

Abeilhan – Pézenas

(11 km/7 miles)

Carry on to **Alignan-du-Vent**. On the other side of the village take the right fork D33 to **Font Douce**, through **St-Simon**.

Pézenas

An elegant old bourgeois town, centre of wine and culture, arts and crafts, with many fine *hotels particuliers*.

[⊟] Hotels: Grand Hotel Molière (M), place du 14 Juillet, 34120 Pézenas, 67 98 14 00; Château de Rieutort Paulhan (HH), St Pargoire, 34230 Paulhan, 67 25 00 61.

Pézenas – Sète

(48 km/30 miles)

Pézenas – Florensac

(12 km/7½ miles)

Leave town on D32, cross the motorway and Hérault river to the hilltop town of **Castelnau-de-Guers** (see château-*cave*). Take the D32E to **St-Apolis** through vineyards. Continue on D32E.

Florensac

[⊟] Hotels: Hotel Leonce (M), 2 place de la République, 34510 Florensac, 67 77 03 05, Michelin-designated gourmet restaurant. Chambres d'hôtes: Mme Valentin, 67 77 91 54; Mme Poisson, Domaine de Fonde Rey, Pomérols, 67 77 08 56.

[♢] Detour on D32 to **Agde**, the most ancient town in south-west France, on a volcanic outcrop with a cathedral built of black basalt. The Canal du Midi finishes here and there are excursions from les Bateaux du Soleil (tel: 67 94 08 79).

Florensac – Marseillan

(7 km/4½ miles)

Carry on along same road.

Marseillan

Pretty fishing village, home of Noilly Prat aperitif wine.

[⊟] Hotels: Chateau du Port (M-H), 9 quai Résistance, 34340 Marseillan, 67 77 65 65, no food. Table d'Emilie, 8 place Couverte, 67 77 63 59.

Marseillan – Mèze

(13 km/8 miles)

Go left to the main road D51, turn right onto it, then first right.

Mèze

Shellfish capital of Languedoc. Pretty village with fine views across the étang to Sète.

[⊟] Hotels: Hotel Du Port (L), 67 43 81 16; Hotel le Marseillais (L), 67 43 80 42; Hotel de Thau (M), rue de la Parée, 67 43 83 83. Gîtes d'étapes: Village Club Thalassa, 67 43 82 74, near the beach.

Mèze – Balaruc-les-Bains

(14 km/9 miles)

Follow lagoon round on the main road N113. Take the first right.

Bouzigues

Another pretty village with views across *étang* and oyster beds. Accommodation available.

Follow the coast back to the main road N113. Take the

first right D129 into **Balaruc-le-Vieux**, an old fortified
village.

　📫　Chambres d'hôtes: M Cutuli Issanka, 67 78 71 34.
Continue.

Balaruc-les-Bains
Baths of 45°C, used medicinally since Roman times,
popular with the rich in seventeenth and eighteenth
centuries, and popular now for ordinary folk. Mud baths,
dances and gambling. Lovely views across the *étang* to
Sète and a competitive market in accommodation.

Balaruc-les-Bains – Sète
(9 km/5½ miles)

Follow the coast round and take a right turn on D2E.

Sète
Important fish market, the *Criée*, boat jousts in summer
and good seafood. This was home of Georges Brassens.
Getting into Sète is a bit difficult for cyclists because of its
impenetrable industrial estates and main roads. Mont St-
Clair, another volcanic outcrop (like Agde) has a road all
round it.

　📫　Hotels: Hotel du Midi (L), 13 rue P. Semand, 34200
　　　Sète, 67 74 98 87; Hotel National (M), 2 rue Pons de
　　　l'Hérault, 67 74 67 85, comfy.

　Ⓐ　If you do not feel like battling the road problems, give
　　　Sète a miss. From Balaruc-les-Bains go straight to
　　　Frontignan, right and left through the industrial estate
　　　at **Balaruc-les-Usines** and then D129 to Frontignan.

Day 11
Sète – Montpellier
(35 km/23½ miles)

Sète – Frontignan
(7 km/4½ miles)

Follow the coast road.

Frontignan
More water jousts in summer.

　📫　Hotels: Hotel Vila (L), 17 avenue Célestin Arnaud, 3
　　　km (2 miles) north at la Peyrade on N112, 34110
　　　Frontignan, 67 48 77 42; Hotel le Mistral (M), 6 avenue
　　　Mistral, 67 48 14 12.

Frontignan – Villeneuve-lès-Maguelonne
(14 km/9 miles)

Before Frontignan turn right on the main road along the
coast road D30. Follow this road between the sea and the
lagoon (*étang*), then turn left to follow the inside of the
étang on the D114.

Vic-le-Gardiole Ⓐ
　📫　Chambres d'hôtes: M Creissac, Domaine des
　　　Moulièges, 67 78 16 54.
Stay on the *étang*-side of railway.

Villeneuve-lès-Maguelonne
A tiny market town (Wednesday) with a fine old church.

　📫　Hotel le Riche (M), 34750 Villeneuve-lès-Maguelonne,
　　　67 69 48 22.

　Ⓐ　You can continue from Vic-le-Gardiole along the sand
　　　spit to the cathedral without going into Villeneuve.

Villeneuve-lès-Maguelonne Ⓐ – Montpellier Airport
(14 km/9 miles)

Go towards the sea, (directions *Cathédrale*) along a sand
spit between the *étangs* through flocks of wonderful birds
– flamingos, egrets, etc. A floating swing bridge
(*passerelle*) takes you across to the remnant of a splendid
fortified eleventh-century cathedral. (It has summer
concerts and a lovely doorway studded with classical
oddments.) (Note: the *passerelle* does not function in
winter.) Turn left and cycle along the path on top of the
sea barrier, lagoons to one side, sea on the other.

Palavas
An unpretentious little fishing village and yacht harbour.
Accommodation available.
For the airport, go first right into **Palavas-les-Flots**. Keep
on the sea road D21E going towards **Carnon-Ouest** Ⓐ².
Follow *'autres directions'* over a bridge towards Carnon-
Ouest, to a dual carriageway (main roads and fly-overs *in
extremis*). Turn left before Carnon to meet main road
D21. Turn left just before it (directions Perols). From
Perols continue on small road parallel with the D21.
Turn right to **Lattes**, then left, cross main road D21
following directions Fréjorgues International Airport.

　Ⓐ　Getting into **Montpellier** (10 km/6 miles) from the
　　　coast is not easy with lots of big roads to negotiate.
　　　Take D116 via **Poulaud** (or take the train from just
　　　outside Villeneuve). Montpellier is an elegant city with
　　　an interesting old centre, and new neo-classical city
　　　(known affectionately as Ceauçescuville), botanical
　　　gardens, museums (including the fine *Musée Fabre*) and
　　　many fine *hotels particuliers*. One of Europe's oldest
　　　universities is here. It also has a wonderful Sunday
　　　morning flea market at **la Paillade** to the north, plenty
　　　of accommodation and good international food.

　📫　Hotels: Hotel Arceaux (M), 33 boulevard Arceaux,
　　　34000 Montpellier, 67 92 03 03, no food; Hotel
　　　Noailles (M-H), 2 rue Ecoles-Centrales, 67 60 49 80,
　　　'demeure du dix-septième siècle', no food.

　✗　Le Menestrel, place Préfecture, in the *'ancienne halle'*,
　　　67 60 62 51, said to be good value; Chandelier, 3 rue
　　　A. Leenhardt, 67 92 61 62; Jardin des Sens, 11 avenue
　　　St-Lazare, 67 79 63 38 – both gourmet restaurants.

　Ⓐ²　For a touch of the Carmargue (and if you have an extra
　　　day), **Aigues Mortes** is only 23 km (14½ miles) east
　　　along the canal. It is a wonderful old fortified city, the
　　　centre of the sea-salt industry, with bull-fights and
　　　games (but no killings). Accommodation and good
　　　restaurants available.

Essential Information

Tourism in France

Tourism is extremely important in France and the French know this. They operate a variety of information centres, so look out for any of the following signs: '**i**', **Info**, **Syndicat d'Initiative**, **Bureau de Tourisme**, **Office de Tourisme**.

Places too small for one of these, or where the office is closed for any reason, will have a *Mairie*, which is the *Hotel de Ville*, in other words the Town Hall. It usually has a secretary who is a local person and a gold mine of information. Tourist offices have lots of excellent literature, simple maps and all sorts of information about tourist sites which are all free, and it is a shame not to take advantage of it. There is usually someone who speaks English, and if you have trouble speaking French, they will be happy to help you in the way of booking accommodation, etc.

The French Government Tourist Office will send out literature on various parts of France. Call the hotline on 0891 244 123 (calls are charged at a premium rate). If you prefer, visit their office at 178 Piccadilly, London W1V 9DB.

If you would like more advice about cycling in France, or some different itineraries, contact the Fédération Française du Cyclotourisme (FFCT), 8 rue Jean Marie Jégo, 75013 Paris (tel: 45 80 30 21). Or the Maison de la Randonnée is very helpful. Their address is 2 rue Voltaire, 75011 Paris (tel: 43 71 13 09).

Many holiday companies also now organize

Industrial agriculture in the Norman plains.

cycling tours, so keep an eye out for advertisements in the national newspapers, particularly the Sunday editions.

Guide Books

On a bike, you do not want to load yourself down with guide books, even this one. It is better to read them before you go and make a note of anything you do not want to miss. It is true that places are much more interesting if you understand a bit about them and know what to look for when you get there.

There are numerous guides to France and its regions, some of which are extremely comprehensive. The best thing to do is to visit a good bookshop and ask for advice.

Maps

As a cyclist, you need two kinds of maps: one to show you where you are in general; the other, where you are in particular. The general one could be a tourist-office fold-out.

To find my way on the ground, I never cycle in France without the IGN (*Institut Géographique Nationale*) *Green Series* maps for the particular area. The *Série Verte* has seventy-two maps covering France (seventy-four if you include Corsica) at a scale of 1 cm to 1 km (1:100 000). For a two-week cycling holiday you will generally end up with between two and five of these, depending on how your route lies. This is not too much to carry. They have contour lines, many hamlets, most roads that you can call roads and some that you can't which is usually enough.

IGN maps are readily available in France from either a *librairie* or *maison de presse*. Outside France only very well supplied bookshops will stock the whole series, but any bookshop can order them for you. Alternatively, write to WLM Ltd, PO Box 17, Matlock, Derbyshire DE4 4XP.

You can cut out the parts of maps you need, but beware of taping the bits together or you may end up creating the cartographer's equivalent of Frankenstein's monster which is vast, refuses to fold properly, and wraps itself round your head on a wet and windy day.

Other maps are all excellent in different ways. Tourist maps mark important tourist sights in bold and the Michelin *Yellow Series* (1 cm:2 km) is useful because it marks the pretty roads in green.

In theory you need a transparent map case: handlebar bags often have them on the top. In practice, as you frequently need to take out the map, turn it over and open it out to another fold, the dream of cycling along with a quick glance down to see where you are going is not usually realized. So a back hip pocket is just as useful.

When map reading there is no substitute for looking and thinking. Maps are usually right, but if you only give them a casual glance you will not take in all the information they have to offer. Noticing a slight wiggle in a road, or a road that comes in at an angle can make all the difference between being somewhere or being lost. Of course, you also have to look carefully at what is around you as well as what is on the map. If you do get really lost and nothing makes sense, remember, look upon it as an adventure – it will probably end up being the most memorable moment of the trip.

> VERNON'S RULE OF GEOGRAPHICAL INFALLIBILITY
> If puzzled, always assume there is a chance that you might be going in quite the opposite direction.

Roads

Major roads are described as A (*Autoroute*) or N (*Nationale* – sometimes called RN for *Route Nationale*): as a cyclist you are not allowed on the former, and it is better to avoid the latter where possible. D roads (*Départementale* – sometimes called CD for *Chemin Départementale*) vary from the quite big and busy to the very small and deserted. The same D road will sometimes change its number without warning and for no apparent reason. Below this, road categorization is haphazard. You may find C (*Commune*) and V (*Village*) or, more generally, nothing. Do not worry about this. On smaller roads it is quite usual not to know which road you are on until you get there, since signposts often do not carry road numbers. Sometimes D roads acquire a whole series of letters after the same road number, so that you have the D113A, D113B, D113C and so on. All this means is that they are generally in the same area – and that whoever gave out the road numbers ran out of imagination at a critical moment or was late for lunch.

Canal towpaths are sometimes metalled, sometimes gravel, and sometimes disappear into grass. There is a national project to upgrade them which has got off to a good start in Alsace. They are well worth investigating, especially on canals that are fairly well-used, and in some hilly areas can offer the only remotely flat route.

The French Highway Code & Road Signs

Many road signs are international, but a number of organizations and some guide books provide lists of those you are most likely to see.

Generally France is extremely well signposted, but no country can possibly put up road signs to every tiny place and no French maps, except the very largest scale, show all hamlets or farms. (According to the area, the traditional French farm may be a small complex of dwellings rather than simply one house and outbuildings and therefore amount to something like a hamlet in itself.) Hamlets sometimes have their names on small signs, usually a dark colour like blue or brown. Towns and villages mark their boundaries with larger white signs on the significant roads: these also carry the road number in yellow, so at least when you get there you have some idea of which road you were on.

Various attempts are being made to improve road signs which include diagrammatic summaries of small roads in some places, and small thin white signs with names and an arrow to tiny places, individual farms, etc. There are generally signs to hotels and important places on main roads at the entrances to towns and again in the centre, eg. *Syndicat d'Initiative*, *Hotel de Ville*, *Gare* or *SNCF*. Wine areas have a stack of signposts to all the local *caves*.

A new idea devised by tourist boards gives a special focus to a route or circuit and can be anything of interest in the area, such as cider, wine, cheese, a particular river, a set of touristic towns or natural features. The green arrow 'bison' routes (marked *'bis'*) are especially chosen as being attractive and off big roads but, like all the others, they are chosen for motorists.

An inscrutability of the French highway code is *priorité á droité*, which means whenever you are travelling on a main road through a town or village, cars and lorries are encouraged to rush out from side roads without warning and knock you down. Watch for a white line across turnings on the road and if there is none, beware.

Railways and bicycles

At one time the SNFC, who are just as bloody-minded about bicycles as British Rail, attempted to set the record straight by having bicycles on hire at stations and this is still possible – sometimes. But many stations found this so much trouble that they have given up. So if you want to hire a bike, you should always check beforehand, if possible with the people at the station itself, or at the local tourist office. The great drawback with practically all hire bicycles is that they have to be delivered back to the same place, though you could try arranging with the hirers to send the bike back by train and sort out deposits and so on by post, though it's unlikely.

If you want to take your bike on the train, neither of you will travel in style. Be prepared to put up with the slowest, most infrequent trains with the shortest routes. If you have to change too much you could find it easier (and faster) to cycle.

At the end of your holiday, however, you can avoid the problem by disowning your bike and entrusting it to the care of SNCF Baggage. This will enable you to get a fast train home. But remember to book your ticket a couple of days in advance, or you may have to wait in order to see your bike off.

Equipment
The bicycle

An ordinary touring bicycle is really the best – one with a minimum of ten gears. If you are buying one, always go to a reputable dealer. And choose a good second-hand one rather than a cheap new one. Mountain bikes, called VTT (*vélo tout terrain*) in France, are great for rough land, but heavy for touring on roads. If you already have a bike, make sure it is thoroughly checked and adjusted before you leave.

Remember French bikes have different wheel sizes from English ones, so you may have difficulty with spares. A tyre is a pain to carry and while it is not unknown for covers to be damaged beyond repair in the course of a shortish trip, I prefer to take only two spare tubes.

Light holders and lights: Take both front and back lights of the same type in case you get caught at dusk. This gives you a built-in backup for the back light in emergencies. Put in new batteries before you go.

Panniers: You need a good support for panniers. Use light-weight single or double panniers behind and a lift-off handlebar bag in front for valuables.

Bike repair kit: pump; puncture kit and/or new inner tube. (See box for useful vocabulary in the case of a breakdown.)

bicycle	= *la bicyclette, le vélo* (*le VTT* = mountain bike)
pump	= *la pompe* (à bicyclette)
chain	= *la chaîne*
battery	= *la pile*
inner tube	= *la chambre à air à l'intérieur*
tyre	= *le pneu* (tyre pressure = *la pression de gonflage*)
headlamp	= *le phare*
padlock	= *l'antivol* (m)
panniers	= *les sacoches* (f)
pedal	= *la pédale*

What to Take

Clothing

I am not qualified to advise anyone about clothes, since nobody makes cycling gear in my size. I cycle in shirt and jeans (which are not as quick to dry as some other materials) or light trousers. But for those whose legs do not frighten the horses, shorts are best in reasonable weather. It is generally better to wear layers of light garments rather than one heavy one. An anorak that breathes is highly desirable, as is a cycling cape. In summer, with a small bag of washing powder, you do not need much clothing: something to cycle in and something to relax in at the end of the day. What you take in the way of socks, underwear and shirts, jumpers etc, is up to you.

Choose comfortable light-weight shoes or sandals. Shoes with ridges on the soles are a curse with toe-clips (and you should have toe-clips). So avoid them and be careful of any footwear which has projections that could catch and prevent you getting your foot out of the toe-clips. There is a certain logical elegance about coming to a stop and toppling helplessly to one side, but it could kill you.

In summer, always carry a bathing costume in case you encounter a swimmable river or lake, of which there are many more in France than in Britain.

Handkerchiefs are also useful as all-purpose cloths or bandages.

Toiletries, Medicines and First Aid Equipment

Remember that soap, and often shampoo, will usually be provided in hotels. Other than that, take whatever you feel is essential for your personal hygiene.

Some useful extras to consider are:

Athlete's foot powder or cream (useful for dealing with excessive friction and perspiration)
Suntan cream
Plasters

It's downhill all the way from the top of the Pyrénées.

St Chély: one of the most popular spots in the Gorges du Tarn.

Pain killers (expensive in France)
Paper tissues and/or toilet paper (they have a variety of uses)
A small bag of washing powder
Large safety pins (for attaching wet washing to bike for drying, as well as other emergencies!)
De-greaser (I usually carry a film canister of this to help me remove traces of my inevitable encounters with the bike chain)
Plastic bags for protecting paper items from the rain.

Water bottle

Always carry a water bottle. Fountains and taps in villages generally have a sign saying *Eau non potable* if the water is not drinkable. Springs are usually OK, small streams in mountain or hill country can often be perfectly drinkable, but it depends what is above you.

Miscellaneous

Camera and film
Small dictionary (if necessary)
Salt, pepper, corkscrew/bottle opener and knife for picnics

Passport, personal papers and money

You will need your passport as a means of identification. If you are visiting from a non-EC country, remember to check up on visa requirements.

Money

Internationally accepted credit or debit cards are invaluable. You can pay for most substantial items with them, so you never need to carry more currency than necessary. Don't keep all your money together in one place.

Security

In general the countryside in France is pretty safe, but obviously you should make sure your bicycle is secure whenever you leave it unattended. At hotels ask if you can put it somewhere safe, up in your room if necessary, but at least in the hotel yard. French hotels are usually cyclist-friendly and happy to help.

Large towns and much visited tourist sites are also much visited by professional thieves. But it is probably true to say that riding a bicycle does not give the impression that you are a member of the moneyed classes.

For bicycles, the solid metal hoop lock is effective, but not unless it is not locked round an immovable object because the bicycle can be picked up and put in a van. Since this type of lock is so heavy, I prefer a stout cable which will go round railings and other small bits of the landscape more easily.

It is probably worth fastening the panniers to the luggage rack with a piece of the very lightest chain and a cheap lock to prevent someone with nothing better to do from simply lifting them off. Keep your pump in a bag rather than on the bike (and never travel far without one). Take at least two keys for all the locks, and keep them in different places. Carry your handlebar bag with your valuables with you at all times.

Insurance

It is always wise to sort out some form of insurance before you leave home. Medical cover is provided under an EC agreement and you should fill in Form E111, which once completed will last you forever.

Casualties

For the non-serious sort, ask a chemist. He/she will tell you if you need a doctor. If it's more serious you will probably end up at *la clinique* which is very nice, but very expensive. That is when you will be glad you completed Form E111.

Accommodation

Hotels

General information and lists of every kind of accommodation are readily available from all tourist offices. There are very few hotels which choose to stay off the official lists (which does not mean if you find one it is to be scorned). Most hotels are part of a group which will have a set standard and all the groups have their own booklet with their associated hotels listed. (Logis de France is the biggest of them.) If you find a hotel you enjoy, look on the desk for a list of others belonging to the same group. Hoteliers are also usually pretty good judges of other hotels, so do ask their advice.

Private bathrooms and telephones are now the norm everywhere. Many hotels have been completely re-constructed, others have sub-divided their old rooms into bedroom and bathroom, or at least installed one of those ghastly plastic all-in-one shower/lavatory cubicles in a corner. It inevitably means the bedroom is smaller and it often means the bathroom is unusable with a lavatory squeezed in under the basin to cause the maximum discomfort. Many rooms now have a television, but not all.

The awarding of stars (ie two, three or four, etc) is a good guide as to the facilities a hotel offers, but not necessarily to the size of the rooms. Hotel prices, which are agreed by the local authority and displayed on the back of your room door or in the window outside the hotel, can vary considerably within a category. The price cannot be higher than it says, but it can be lower. Most hotels have a range of different kinds of room, so do ask for what you want – bigger, cheaper, with or without a view. Big hotels have an unpleasant habit of filling their farthest corners first: and you do not have to put up with that.

Out of season you may be able to negotiate some good deals on price. Remember the more expensive the hotel, usually the better the deal. You could end up in a château for the same price as you would normally pay for a modest hotel, especially if you book more than one room or for more than one night – but you need to do it well in advance. Remember in hotels that *pension* or *demi-pension* will always save you money. You may not have a choice of evening meal, but that can be quite a relief. (If you wish to telephone a hotel in France to book a room, see Telephones, p. 188.)

Beware the dead season of January to March when many hotels close down completely. In the high season, if you have not booked, you may be grateful of a bed at any price (even in August there are hoteliers who pack up and go on holiday themselves). If you do get to a hotel and find it is full, hoteliers are usually very nice and will help you to find another, but it is frustrating at the end of a hard day to find you have to cycle another few kilometres. So better to think ahead. I would recommend booking the following day's hotel at least on the previous night (and in popular tourist areas like Alsace, well in advance). Once again, your hotel will usually be happy to guide your choice, or make your booking for you (especially helpful if your French is shaky).

Chambres d'Hôtes

The most recent threat to the French hotel is the advent of the *chambre d'hôte*, modelled on our English B&B (but without bacon and eggs for breakfast which would be going beyond decent chauvinist limits). They have burst onto the scene fully-fledged and in a more splendid form than their English counterparts. At a stroke they remove many of the hotelier's tax headaches: no employees needed and he/she can keep their regular job. They also help pay for all the improvements the owners want to do to their home. And as many of them also provide meals, they can be creative in the kitchen without the pressures of running a big dining room. There is a whole range of *chambres d'hôtes* from rooms in simple houses to farms, old monasteries or even châteaux. For the guest it means a more informal welcome with homely touches, and usually better accommodation and a more interesting meal than you would get in an equivalent hotel. Prices average 200F for two with breakfast. Ask if they will do dinner for you and if not where you can eat nearby.

Gîtes d'Etapes

These are simple hostel-like places of various standards; some with private rooms, some with dormitories, most with four to a room. Prices vary between 15–50F a night plus a communal meal for 50–60F. You are not encouraged to hang around in the morning, or get back too early in the evening.

Fermes-auberges

These offer meals and sometimes accommodation with the emphasis on home-grown produce. You usually need to book, even for a meal.

Camping

France is excellent for camping, especially in the south, where the reliable weather means that you need to take less with you. Camping *sauvage* – strewing yourself anywhere over the landscape you happen to fancy – is now discouraged, especially where there is a lot of tourism, though it is still practised to some extent. (Of course, you can camp on private property with the permission of the owner.) Do everything you can to make your luggage as light as possible – try to make big rear panniers, a good saddlebag and a handlebar bag enough. The enjoyment of your holiday will be much influenced by how much weight you are carrying (and I do not speak lightly). Choose to camp because you want to rather than to save money.

French camp sites are as well-organized as French hotels with some that have every facility imaginable. At the other end of the scale there are those which offer little beyond their own fresh farm produce.

Food and drink

Restaurants have their own independent standards from accommodation and you may find a two-star hotel with a three-star restaurant. You are not obliged to eat in the hotel restaurant, but in little, out of the way places it may be an important part of their economy. Whatever you choose to do, it is polite to say if you are eating in or going out.

Gault Millau and the Bottin Gourmand put up their signs where they recommend the food. It can be a good sign. The little red *Michelin* is a good general guide to hotels and food.

Overleaf: The river Cousin near Avallon has one of the most beautiful river valleys.

Our best meals have always been simple, either real home cooking or excellent ingredients well cooked. Often we have found them at lunchtime in little restaurants with *plats du jour* (the dish of the day) and lots of tell-tale cars outside, or in a *ferme-auberge* which uses its own produce.

Picnics are a must sometimes, but often end up costing more money than a café meal, and you have to carry your uneaten left-overs off on your bike with you afterwards.

Remember lunch is still an important meal for the French. There is something to be said for conforming to the French standard: you will get better value for money and it will be a truly French experience. Sunday lunch is the best, try to have at least one. And remember the time. Everything closes up between 12.00 p.m. and 3.00 p.m. Picnics must be bought before mid-day. Lunch is taken before 1.30 p.m. and on Sunday that will be too late. For dinner in some small places you should aim to be sitting down by 8.00 p.m.

Wine

If in doubt ask the waiter what is local and good (check the price before you say yes). It is a shame to miss the special wines of the area. If you just want something ordinary you can ask about the house wine. Usually it will be a Côtes du Rhône or a Bordeaux, sometimes an un-specified mixture. It is usually tolerable, and quite good enough for lunch. *Plats du jours* often include a bottle on your table and you can drink as much as you like.

Tipping

Service is usually included in the price of the hotel or meal, but no one will ever say no to a tip, so it really is up to you. Perhaps it should be the reward for some special service or services.

Telephones

To telephone France from Britain, dial 010 33 followed by the number of the hotel, etc. (There

are no area codes, except for Paris.) Remember, too, that France is one hour ahead of GMT.

French telephone boxes (*cabines téléphoniques*) are usually found in the centres of villages, often near the Post Office (*la Poste*) or the Town Hall (*Hotel de Ville*, or *la Mairie*), or you can ring from a bar. They may take coins or cards, so you should have both. Cards can be bought from newsagents (*tabacs*). Coins are 50-centime, 1-, 2- or 5-franc pieces. Sometimes you need at least two 1-franc pieces to start a call. Change is given unless you put in a big coin. To telephone abroad from France dial 19. Add 44 for Britain, followed by the local code minus the zero at the beginning, then the number of the person you are calling.

Directory Enquiries

Dial 12 in France. Telephone books are kept at the Post Office. Note that 'Ste', which is the feminine version of 'St' comes after the masculine in alphabetical lists.

Ask your hotel to help if need be. They have France Telecom's computerized system Minitel.

Social conventions

Greeting people in France is straightforward. The brisk handshake, which people use constantly, the '*Bonjour Monsieur*' at every encounter, and the kisses of greeting between friends (generally three in the south, two in the north, but sometimes as many as four) are an essential part of setting up the social conditions under which people can relate to each other.

People are people, though, so don't get hung up on this business of manners. Do respond to the '*Bonjour/au revoir Messieurs-'dames*' (or just '*'sieurs-, 'dames*' to which it is often reduced) as you enter shops or other public places. Usually it is followed with a '*Bonne journée*' when you leave. '*Bonsoir*' can start after lunch, and '*Bonne nuit*' is usually for going to bed.

Index

*Page numbers in italics denote route details and
bold numbers illustrations.*

Picture Credits

Michael Busselle pages 46–7, 59, 66, 102–3, 107, 122, 123, 130–1, 135 and 186–7; **Joanna Crawley** page 51; **Jennifer Fry** pages 110 and 166; **Robert Harding** pages 78, 114 and 143; **Michael Hutchinson** page 175; **Image Bank** pages 22–3 (A. Choisnet), 70 (Stockphotos/ J. Ramsay), 71 (H. Wolf) and 91; **Barrie Smith** pages 26, 43, 55 and 147; **Tony Stone Images** pages 2–3 (M. Busselle), 19 (R. Passmore), 27 (P. Marston), 30 (P. Cade), 50, 67, 74–5 (R. Bellone), 87 (C. Waite), 106 (S. and N. Geary), 115 (P. Poulides), 155 (M. Busselle), 162–3 (F. Ivaldi) and 178 (T. Craddock); **Tom & Sally Vernon** pages 14, 18, 39, 42, 62, 79, 99, 134, 138, 142, 154, 159, 171, 182 and 183.